The Oxford Library of Practical Theology

EDITED BY THE

REV. W. C. E. NEWBOLT, M.A.
CANON AND CHANCELLOR OF S PAUL'S

AND THE

REV. DARWELL STONE, D.D.
PRINCIPAL OF PUSEY HOUSE, OXFORD

BY THE SAME AUTHOR.

THE ATONEMENT. Crown 8vo. 5s.
(*The Oxford Library.*)

THE HISTORY OF THE BOOK OF COMMON PRAYER.
Crown 8vo. 5s. (*The Oxford Library.*)

THE CHRISTIAN TRADITION. Crown 8vo. 5s.
(*The Oxford Library.*)

⁎ *This book contains an account of the origin of Episcopacy, the three Creeds, the Ancient Western Liturgies and other institutions of the Church. Special attention is also given to the early history of Sacramental Confession and to the principle of Authority in the Church of England.*

LECTURES ON RELIGION. Crown 8vo. 6s.

THE GOSPELS

BY THE REV.
LEIGHTON PULLAN

Fellow and Tutor of S. John Baptist's
College, Oxford

WIPF & STOCK · Eugene, Oregon

Wipf and Stock Publishers
199 W 8th Ave, Suite 3
Eugene, OR 97401

The Gospels
By Pullan, Leighton
Softcover ISBN-13: 978-1-7252-9647-3
Hardcover ISBN-13: 978-1-7252-9648-0
eBook ISBN-13: 978-1-7252-9649-7
Publication date 1/5/2021
Previously published by
Longmans, Green, and Co., 1912

This edition is a scanned facsimile of
the original edition published in 1912.

EDITORS' PREFACE

THE object of the Oxford Library of Practical Theology is to supply some carefully considered teaching on matters of Religion to that large body of devout laymen who desire instruction, but are not attracted by the learned treatises which appeal to the theologian. One of the needs of the time would seem to be, to translate the solid theological learning, of which there is no lack, into the vernacular of everyday practical religion; and while steering a course between what is called plain teaching on the one hand and erudition on the other, to supply some sound and readable instruction to those who require it, on the subjects included under the common title 'The Christian Religion,' that they may be ready always to give an answer to every man that asketh them a reason of the hope that is in them, with meekness and fear.

The Editors, while not holding themselves precluded from suggesting criticisms, have regarded their proper task as that of editing, and accordingly they have not interfered with the responsibility of each writer for his treatment of his own subject.

W. C. E. N.
D. S.

PREFACE

THIS book has been largely based upon some informal instruction which I have given to my pupils in Oxford But I have endeavoured to make every chapter intelligible to readers who are unacquainted with Greek, the welcome which has been extended to my *Books of the New Testament* having proved to me that there are many persons who, whether they can read Greek or not, want to know the true history of the Gospels. It has been necessary to omit all discussion of many interesting questions. But I trust that attention has been called to all that are most vital, and especially to those which bear upon the Person and the teaching of our Lord Jesus Christ.

Much has been gleaned from works written in different languages and by authors of very different religious convictions. But nothing in the realm of New Testament studies seems to me to be clearer than the superiority of recent Christian scholarship over non-Christian scholarship. And, as a general rule, there can be found a marked superiority of genuine English work over the work produced in other countries. In this connection I desire to emphasise my debt to Sir John Hawkins' *Horae Synopticae*, and to the articles by Mr. C. H. Turner in the *Journal of*

Theological Studies, vols. x. and xi. I am also much indebted to the *Studies in the Synoptic Problem*, edited by Dr. Sanday, which were published when this book was far advanced. Perhaps I ought to explain that I had made a comparison between the different Gospels and the different lives of S. Francis before I read the similar comparison drawn by the Rev. B. H. Streeter, and that I applied to Christians the Moslem name of 'people of a book' before Sir W. M. Ramsay used a similar Moslem phrase in his delightful little criticism of Dr. Moffatt's 'results.'

In the study of the Gospels according to S. Mark and S. Luke, I have derived much benefit from Professor Burkitt's writings, though I cannot accept some theories that he has propounded.

The limits of this book have made it impossible for me to deal at all fully with the theology of the Gospel according to S John. The question whether this is genuine theology, or mere theosophy, to a great extent depends for its answer upon the further question whether the author was, or was not, an eye-witness of Jesus Christ. And to this latter subject of inquiry I have given all the space at my disposal.

CONTENTS

CHAP		PAGE
I.	THE CANON OF THE GOSPELS	1
II.	CRITICISM OF THE GOSPELS	32
III.	THE SYNOPTIC PROBLEM	65
IV.	THE SAYINGS OF OUR LORD	102
V.	THE GOSPEL ACCORDING TO S. MARK	133
VI.	THE GOSPEL ACCORDING TO S. MATTHEW	169
VII.	THE GOSPEL ACCORDING TO S. LUKE	206
VIII.	THE FOURTH GOSPEL AND THE SYNOPTISTS	243
IX.	THE AUTHOR OF THE FOURTH GOSPEL	276
	INDEX	317

CHAPTER I

THE CANON OF THE GOSPELS

§ 1. *One Gospel in Four Gospels.*

CHRISTIANITY is a life. But like the adherents of the religions which are its caricatures, Christians are what the Moslems call 'people of the book.' It was so with the followers of Mani, who in the third century endeavoured to combine Christianity with the religions of Zoroaster and Buddha, and it was the same with most of the Gnostics who anticipated him in the Roman Empire of the second century. In the seventh century Muhammad, using traditions of the Jews and Christians, but unacquainted with their literature, gave to his adherents a book which they regard as wholly infallible. In recent times the Book of Mormon and the lucubrations of Mrs. Eddy, the foundress of 'Christian Science,' rival the baser forms of Gnostic literature. Each of these books emanated from a single mind and was composed in a single lifetime. The sacred volumes of the Manichees were numerous, but they were all the work of Mani, and Mrs. Eddy tolerated no rival prophetess. Now the New Testament is a collection of books by different authors, written at different though not widely separated periods, collected afterwards as sacred books of the New Covenant made between God and man by Jesus Christ. Not a single book which it contains makes the claim to have been written by Christ. From whatever point of view He is regarded, this fact is important. In founding a new religion which was the reversal of Judaism as well as its development, He came forward as a Prophet, and was understood to be a Prophet. Yet many, if not most, of the greatest prophets of Israel had written books, and Jesus Christ began His teaching at Nazareth by reading a passage from the Book of the prophet Isaiah, which He declared to be fulfilled in His own Person. But we are only once told of His writing, and then He wrote upon the dust.

Why did He write no book? The explanation, if it is to be discovered by us anywhere, must be discovered in His own conception of His own Person and His work. Did He desire that His followers should be preserved from the risk of exalting the letter of His teaching above the spirit, until the life of His Church was vigorous enough to be trusted? Did He, as is now widely held by non-Christians, think that He would return to earth so soon after His death that a written document would be unnecessary to His followers? If either of these explanations be true, it implies a marvellous conviction and confidence with regard to the future. And if the fourth evangelist is correct in saying that He taught that He would return to the world in the coming of the Holy Spirit, who proceeds from the Father, then there is some truth in both explanations. From certain of His best authenticated statements we learn that His message rang with an unfaltering confidence. 'It was said to them of old time . . . but I say unto you . . . verily, I say unto thee' (Matt. v. 21 f.). He claims the authority to revise and alter even what had been said by Moses, whom the Jews regarded as the greatest of the prophets. Naturally the people regarded Him as 'a great prophet' (Luke vii. 16). He claimed more than this, teaching that even His forerunner, John, was 'much more than a prophet' (Matt. xi. 9); and He declared, 'Heaven and earth shall pass away, but My words shall not pass away' (Mark xiii. 31). We can thus readily believe that while the first Christians of Jewish origin would and did appeal to the Old Testament, saying, 'it is written,' they would also appeal to His words, and say, 'He Himself said' (Acts xx. 35).

In a later chapter we shall consider more fully the first records of His sayings. At present let us recall the familiar truth that the words have come down to us in somewhat long and elaborate settings. The four Gospels all contain a large amount of narrative, and 'the Gospel,' when our oldest manuscripts were written, was not considered to be four, but rather fourfold. Sometimes they are in a manuscript by themselves, called 'the Gospel.' Often the four books are headed simply, 'according to Matthew,' 'according to Mark,' 'according to Luke,' 'according to John.' There was therefore, in the idea of the early Church, one Gospel, one story of the good news of the life and teaching of Jesus Christ committed to writing by four different writers bearing well-known names. It is, however, an interesting point that S. Augustine tells us that Faustus, his celebrated Manichean opponent, held that the Synoptic Gospels were written by unknown authors, who made use of some records of Christ's own preaching.[1] This is almost certainly correct in the case of the first Gospel, as we shall see later. Faustus accepted S. John's Gospel, and it is clear that the above theory was invented to account for the divergence between the Gospels on the one hand and his own paganised doctrines on the other. He did not hold it on intelligent critical grounds. Thus the modern Moslems, who are aware of

[1] *C. Faust.* xxxii. 2 (cf. 7).

the wide difference between the Christian Gospels and the teaching of Muhammad, refuse to admit that the Gospel has come down in its original form, and assert that the Christians have corrupted the text. This is merely because they know that Muhammad praised 'the Gospel,' and do not know that he had probably never read it.

The word 'Gospel,' then, meant the message of salvation. S. Paul, when he speaks of 'my Gospel,' means 'my explanation of the Gospel,' and when he says, 'I had been intrusted with the Gospel of the uncircumcision' (Gal. ii. 7), he means that he had been appointed by God to preach the good tidings of salvation to the Gentiles, with special emphasis on the points most necessary for their instruction. By a natural evolution, the word which meant the message came to be applied to the book containing it. The word almost certainly means a *written* Gospel in the ancient Christian manual called the *Didaché*, or *Teaching of the Twelve Apostles*, in Chapter xv. : 'Reprove one another, not in anger but in peace, as ye have it in the Gospel.' It probably bears the same meaning in the old Roman homily known incorrectly as the *Second Epistle of Clement*, the date of which is about A.D. 140. The plural 'Gospels' is first found in a writing of S. Justin Martyr[1] about A.D. 152. He calls them 'Memoirs of the Apostles,' and he refers to them collectively as 'the Gospel,' inasmuch as they were, in reference to their testimony to Jesus Christ, one book. The plural 'Gospels' also occurs in the *Epistle to Diognetus*, xi. 6. This is probably late in the second century. In the apostolic age we can trace no desire to form a fixed and final list of Gospels, 'the Canon,' as it came to be called. The Christians, like the ordinary Jews living outside Palestine, had the Greek version of the Old Testa-

[1] *Apol.* i. 66.

ment, including what we call the Apocrypha. If they desired edification, that was the Bible which they read. If they entered upon a controversy with the Jews, it was the Greek Bible which both parties quoted. If they desired to convert the heathen, they appealed to the Greek Bible to show how impressively the predictions of the prophets had been fulfilled in the life of Jesus. Widely as modern Greek and Italian are now understood in the south and the east of Europe and the immediately adjacent countries, by people of very different nationalities, Greek was then understood over a larger area than modern Greek and Italian together. The Greek Old Testament was of inestimable value over this wide area, and late in the second century Melito, bishop of Sardis in Asia Minor, and Irenaeus, bishop of Lyons in the south of France, issued for Christians doctrinal books drawn entirely from this Greek Old Testament. It is no exaggeration to say that some of the early Christians found a great deal more in the Old Testament than it really contains. Such discoveries were effected by means of allegory. They inherited from the Jews of Alexandria a love of allegorical interpretation which was equal to any emergency. Possibly at the present day we are a little too impatient of allegory. I believe that the more closely we read the sayings of our Lord, the plainer it will become to us that much is allegorical or symbolical, and that we do not explain His words away, but explain them better, when we cautiously and reverently adopt such a line of interpretation. And allegorical interpretations of non-allegorical passages of the Bible, while they become positively mischievous when they are used as a basis for dogma, may be wholly good when understood as poetical illustrations. Allegory, then, must not be despised. But it was really good for the Church that the mass of Churchmen instinctively felt that their own traditions, based on the teaching of the Lord, were superior to the ingenuities which discovered the incarnation and the Cross of Christ signified by the Greek letters which denoted the three hundred and eighteen servants of Abraham, or detected the Gnostic goddess Achamoth in the woman at the well of Samaria.

Let us return for a moment to the fact that there are four, and only four, canonical Gospels. To the modern Christian this rightly appears indisputable and obvious, just as the modern Englishman rightly thinks it obvious that the United Kingdom includes and ought to include England and Wales, Scotland and Ireland. They are four countries, and no more. Once, however, the lilies of France were on English shields and flags, and once there were other Gospels which challenged a place in the reverence of Christ's followers. Yet our analogy is very imperfect. For the French lilies shone for centuries on the English arms. But in less than one century after their publication the canon of only four Gospels was regarded as fixed. The other Gospels got but a short shrift. S. Irenaeus looks upon the sacred four as similar to the four winds and the four quarters of heaven. There were sects of believers on the fringe of orthodox Christianity, or beyond it, who fixed their predilection on one only. Thus there were Jewish Christians who till at least the close of the fourth century had one Gospel, which they called *the Gospel according to the Hebrews*, and which was used by Hegesippus, an intelligent and orthodox Palestinian Christian of about A.D. 150. Another Gospel, that *according to the Egyptians*, advocated a strange Orientalised perversion of Christianity, and was probably intended to form the one and only Gospel for some sect in Alexandria. It manifests that opposition to the idea of marriage which was not uncommon in some semi-Christian circles. It was used by the Egyptian Gnostics, by the author of the *Second Epistle of Clement*, and by Clement of Alexandria, though the latter does not assign it the same position as the other Gospels. Like the Gospel of Marcion, which we must notice later, each of these writings was probably intended to be the one and only Gospel of the coterie from which it issued. Even in more orthodox quarters the instinct in favour of one authoritative Gospel asserted itself. S. Justin Martyr had a clever Syrian pupil named Tatian, who appears to have succeeded his master as a teacher of a Christian catechetical school at Rome. He developed Gnostic leanings, and left Rome near A.D. 175, and went to the East. Besides writing a defence of Christianity which contains a piquant satire on contemporary heathenism, he composed a kind of Gospel which Eusebius describes as 'a sort of conglomeration of the Gospels which he named the Diatessaron'[1] (*i.e.* fourfold narrative). It was what we should call a harmony of the Gospels. It was first written in Greek, and probably at Rome; it was soon translated into Syriac, and was regarded as a precious heirloom by Tatian's Syriac-speaking compatriots in and around Edessa until the fifth century. Not till then was it finally replaced by the separate Gospels.

The above instances have been quoted to show that in such widely separated quarters as Palestine, Egypt, and the regions of what was then the far East, there existed this very natural tendency in favour of one Gospel rather than four. At the same time, it is conceivable that Christians might have desired to reckon another Gospel with the four. We have some slight evidence for such a desire in the esteem felt for the Gospel according to the Hebrews and that according to the Egyptians. But there were other Gospels which seem more obviously intended to be supple-

[1] Eus. *H. E.* iv, 29.

mentary. Such is the *Protevangelium of James*, a Gospel giving an account of our Lord's infancy, known to Origen about A.D. 220, and possibly to Justin Martyr seventy years earlier. Its interest largely lay in the fact that it appeared to supply a gap in men's knowledge of our Lord's life, a dangerous attraction for that vitiated taste which in later times relished such stories as those about S. Mary in the 'Golden Legend.' Another work of the second century is the so-called *Gospel according to Peter*, which at the end of that century was used by some Christians of Rhossus. Serapion, bishop of Antioch, accused it of Docetism, the heresy which denies the reality of our Lord's human nature and treats His body as a kind of phantom. Part of this Gospel, the account of Christ's Passion and Resurrection, has been discovered in Egypt, and justifies Serapion's opinion of its heterodoxy. It has been thought by some of the best critics that Justin Martyr made use of this book, and his *First Apology*, Chapter xxxv., renders the statement in John xix. 13 in a manner very similar to that found in this apocryphal Gospel. If Justin really used it, we should probably have to date it about A.D. 120 or 130. In any case it is a work of very great antiquity, and yet it failed to secure recognition in the Church. These additional Gospels might be quoted here and there, but we have no ground for thinking that any one of them seriously threatened either to oust or stand beside the four canonical Gospels that we possess. The *Diatessaron* of Tatian, which was assigned such a high position among the Syrians, owed its popularity to the fact that it was the first in the field. It came to them before they were in possession of a vernacular version of the separate Gospels.

The thing which emerges for our consideration is this: that the Church would probably have kept one Gospel and not four Gospels, or, like Tatian, would have made one Gospel out of four, unless she had been very deeply convinced, by A.D. 140 or 150 at latest, that all were authentic, that their record was true, and that they issued from some highly competent authority. The inclusion of S. John's Gospel aids this contention. It is so unlike the other Gospels in many particulars that it seems to challenge comparison with them. The fact that in spite of its difference it was added to the other three, is a proof that it was regarded as having some very strong testimony in its favour, and it is a proof which cannot be rejected when the problem of its origin is under discussion.

No doubt it may be said that, as mere broken fragments of the non-canonical Gospels have survived, we are not in a position to say that the Church judged wisely in excluding such Gospels from the canon. But we can certainly say that, so far as has hitherto been ascertained, the Church acted very wisely, and showed a sound critical judgment which the Christian may fitly believe to have been guided by God. Even the Gospel of Peter, one of the best of the alien Gospels, shows a decided inferiority to the first three canonical Gospels, whose account of the Passion it copies and travesties. Of the sayings rightly or wrongly attributed to our Lord, several have survived outside the New Testament, and it is possible that more will be discovered as the result of explorations in the East. But the greater part of those which we possess are such as can hardly commend themselves to any one familiar with the dignity and depth of the teaching recorded in the Gospels.

A considerable time before the close of the second century the four Gospels had in the more important centres of Christian life certainly vindicated their unique position. The *Muratorian Canon*, Clement of Alexandria, and S. Irenaeus show us this position with the utmost clearness. The four Gospels were regarded as teaching one Gospel, and with them were numbered certain other books, more especially the thirteen Epistles of S. Paul, the Acts of the Apostles, the First Epistle of S. Peter, the First Epistle of S. John, and in some quarters the Revelation, which is referred to by S. Justin Martyr as the work of 'John, one of the apostles of Christ.' S. Polycarp, the pupil of S. John, and Polycarp's contemporary Papias, both quoted S. John's First Epistle, and both used the First Epistle of S. Peter. It would be beside our purpose to say much about the formation of the whole 'canon,' or list of New Testament writings, and the reasons which hastened or retarded the inclusion of certain books in that list. We will here merely quote the statement in which S. Irenaeus, writing about A.D. 185, gives a short summary of the origin of the Gospels: 'Matthew published a written Gospel among the Hebrews in their own dialect, Peter and Paul preaching the Gospel at Rome and founding the Church. After their departure, Mark, the disciple and secretary of Peter, also transmitted to us in writing the things preached by Peter. Luke, the companion of Paul, deposited in a book the Gospel preached by him. Then John, the disciple of the Lord, who had laid his head upon His bosom, also published a Gospel when he was living at Ephesus in Asia.'[1]

This shows how S. Irenaeus—and his evidence is reinforced by the earlier evidence of Tatian and S. Justin Martyr—regarded the four Gospels as documents of the apostolic age. They preserved from destruction the teaching about Christ which two apostles had written and two had given orally. It is quite plainly proved by his other statements that they were valued as works to which the Church could appeal to prove what she taught. In opposition to the numerous forgeries of the second century put forward by teachers of novel heresy,

[1] Quoted in Eus. *H. E.* v. 8.

the Church appealed to what she believed to be the true credentials of Christianity. These were attributed to two apostles, S. Matthew and S. John, and two companions and ministers of apostles, S. Mark, the companion of S. Peter, and S. Luke, the companion of S. Paul. Thus the testimony of the great apostle of the Gentiles was included with the testimony of the original Twelve, especially of their leader, S. Peter. The Gospels stood in the eyes of the Church as a tower four-square, not only confronting Jew and Gentile, but also the Judaising Ebionite and the Hellenising Gnostic.

This fact is really of the greatest historical importance. In view of controversies which have been active during the last two generations, it is of deep interest to notice that in the second half of the second century the Church believed that S. Peter, S. John, and S. Paul taught one Gospel, one plan of salvation, and that the books written by them, or as a result of their influence, were in fundamental agreement. At even an earlier date than that of Justin, the scanty evidence afforded by Papias and Polycarp points to the same conviction that the apostles were united. Still earlier, the long Epistle of S. Clement of Rome to the Corinthians, an undoubtedly genuine work written about A.D. 96, shows no trace of any division between the adherents of S. Peter and S. Paul. The same holds good in the case of the Epistles of S. Ignatius, written about A.D. 110. Both Clement and Ignatius refer to the two great apostles, and both speak of Christian belief and duty in a way which can be far better harmonised with the theory that the apostles agreed than with the theory that they widely differed.

§ 2. *The Gospels and Marcion.*

The notion that there was a schism in the apostolic college with reference to the observance of the Law and the being of Jesus Christ was nevertheless not the invention of the modern sceptic. It was vigorously taught by Marcion, an acute, ascetic, and argumentative native of Pontus, who founded a large sect about A.D. 144, and was recognised as a most dangerous enemy of Christianity. He saw that there was a different tone in different parts of the New Testament. And he had a theory to account for it, a theory which won a large number of convinced and enthusiastic supporters. He taught that there is a God of Law, who by Law rules Matter. This is the God of Judaism, the religion of Matter, and the Author of the Old Testament. Distinct from the God of Law is the God of Grace. This is the God of Christianity, the religion of Spirit. Jesus, who was the Son of the God of Grace, had no real flesh and blood, but was only Spirit. The two Gods and their respective systems were in absolute opposition. Marcion held that only S. Paul had really understood the teaching of Jesus, and that the original apostles were in grievous Jewish error. And the only Gospel which he accepted was that according to S. Luke. Even this he mutilated, as he also mutilated the writings of S. Paul. For though he could find in them an opposition between Law and Grace, the utmost ingenuity could not discover in these writings either two Gods, or a Jesus who had only a phantom body, or the Marcionite doctrine that marriage is evil. Marcion held that S. Paul was the only apostle who understood the teaching of Christ. Modern rationalist criticism is apt to insist that S. Paul radically altered His teaching, more especially with regard to His Person and work. Marcion held that Jesus was not really human. Modern rationalism insists that He was not really divine. The contrast is in many ways instructive. So far as we are now able to understand the second century, it would seem that if the Church had yielded to Marcion or some form of

THE CANON OF THE GOSPELS 13

Gnosticism laxer than Marcionism, and said, 'No Law, no Old Testament, no free will, no humanity of Christ,' Christianity would have been very popular. But the Church refused point-blank. It may be quite true that few Churchmen of that period were very clever. Those whose writings have survived fall far below the writers of the New Testament. But they were wise enough to avoid the commonplace line of action. For centuries orthodox Christians were invited to be logical and told to give up either Law or Grace, either the Deity or the humanity of Christ, either the Unity or the Trinity, either man's freedom or God's predestination. As a rule, they refused. Even if they understood these things imperfectly, and they sometimes understood them as imperfectly as ourselves, they knew that there were two sides in all these questions, and they tried to hold both. This was a difficult and adventurous method. But the Church crossed the rugged plains of time better than the opposing sects with their artificial simplicity. For life itself is very complex, and religion, if it be true to life, may be less simple than Marcion imagined.

Not only did the Church canonise the best Gospels, but her conflict with Marcionism shows that she also was willing to run the risk of people saying that the witness of the apostles did not agree. In spite of their diversity, they taught the same Gospel. And it is no small tribute to the intelligence of the early Christians that modern scepticism has been as powerless to revive the whole of Marcion's criticism as modern superstition has been powerless to revive the whole of his theology. The men who lay most stress on the divergence between S. Paul and the Twelve, declare that the writings of the New Testament which do not bear the name of S. Paul or S. Luke show traces, occasionally the deepest traces, of S. Paul's influence. They find these deep traces in the Fourth Gospel, in the First Epistle of S. John, and the First Epistle of S. Peter. They find at least some traces in the first two Gospels. And indeed the coincidences are so marked that either we must say there is a Pauline touch in almost all the books ascribed to the apostolic age, or we must attribute much that they have in common with S. Paul to an influence and atmosphere that affected both. This is one of the most crucial problems of modern theology. It touches the Person of Jesus Christ. The Gospels tell of His earthly life, how He travelled, spoke, and healed. S. Paul adores an exalted, glorified Lord, and tells us of His present action upon the world which He has left. Yet S. Paul shows an insight into the character of Jesus and the nature of His love to mankind which forces us to think that he knew much of the Master's life on earth. And on their side the evangelists all regard Jesus as the wonderful and wonder-working Son of God, 'the Lord.' Through the colours of their portraits of Jesus there glows a glory which proves that their faith in Him was not different from the faith of him who said that Christ Jesus was 'in the form of God.' We have therefore reasonable grounds for strongly affirming that the Christian Church regarded the four Gospels as coming from a good source and as presenting a real unity in diversity. When Clement of Alexandria contrasts S. John's Gospel with the earlier Gospels as being distinctly 'spiritual,' he shows that he realises an important difference between them, but he does not think it necessary to abandon a 'Synoptic Christ' who 'acts,' for a 'Johannine Christ' who 'claims.' Calling the Fourth Gospel 'pneumatic,' he does not assume that the original apostles of Christ held a theory which denied that Christ was a divine Spirit and implied that He was only an 'adopted' Son of God. Just as the more radical critics of the present day have found it impossible to retain even one of the Synoptic Gospels as substantial history, after repudiating the Fourth Gospel, so it was with the heretics of the second century. As a rule, if they rejected one Gospel, they refused to accept any one of the other three in its entirety. They were guided less by criticism than by an *à priori* theory as to what Jesus must have been.

§ 3. *The Gospels and Docetism.*

The instinctive but at first undefined sense on the part of the Christians of the superiority of their own traditions was in time bound to demand a collection of canonical books. The collection was not made suddenly, nor must the collection of the sacred books be regarded as contemporaneous with the creation of the books. But the value of the written Gospels, and the need of an authoritative list, were appreciated during a great struggle of which a good many footprints have been left on the sands of time. We can see the coming signs of that struggle in the Epistles of S. Paul, and we can see it hotly progressing in the Epistles of S. Ignatius. It is the struggle with Docetism, the heresy which denied the reality of Christ's human nature. We have already noticed the Docetism of Marcion, but Marcion was only a clever and effective exponent of a mighty movement which has not yet spent its force.

> East is East and West is West,
> And never the twain shall meet.

Docetism is part of the ancient Oriental scorn of matter, the dislike of what can be apprehended by the senses. The modern European materialist scorns Christianity as not sufficiently sensual, as a religion of other-worldliness, and foolish in preaching the crucifixion of the passions. The Buddhist and the Hindu dislike it because it is too indulgent towards the senses, too much concerned with the amelioration of this present life, not severe enough in preaching the extinction of every kind of desire. This was the attitude of many thinkers in the eastern part of the Roman Empire. They were willing to welcome Jesus as their Messiah, or as a member of their pantheon, but it must be a Jesus who belonged to their own set. He must be one who never made, in the language of modern so-called 'Christian Science,' any 'concession to materialism.' He must Himself be so unlike ourselves as to have only a kind of spiritualistic humanity. Some thought that He did not eat, some that He was not really born but appeared, some that He did not die. And to this day Muhammadans believe that He did not die, but that some other form than that of Jesus took His place on the cross.

We must not suppose that these fantastic errors, which blanched every feature of the human life of Jesus, were wholly irreverent or novel. It is extremely likely that they began among men who had read of those appearances of 'angels' in the Old Testament which seem to be represented as appearances of God in a quasi-human but spiritual form. For instance, in Genesis xvi. we read of 'the angel of the Lord who appeared to Hagar,' and immediately afterwards we read of 'the Lord that spake unto her,' as though God spoke in the angel. Again, in Judges xiii. 'the angel of the Lord' appears to Manoah and his wife, but when he leaves them and ascends, Manoah says, 'We shall surely die, because we have seen God.' These theophanies described in the Old Testament probably suggested the idea that the appearance of Jesus Christ in this world was a similar but more prolonged theophany, that God was in some way present in Him, but that all that men could outwardly see of Jesus was unreal. Such was probably the beginning of this view of the Person of Christ, a beginning which

THE CANON OF THE GOSPELS

was essentially monotheistic. But the view found acceptance in circles which were essentially polytheistic, and in which the Old Testament was regarded as a mill-stone round the neck of true religion.

Against all Docetic views of our Lord the Gospels are a standing witness. Jesus in the Synoptic Gospels is born of a human mother, He grows as a human Child, increasing in favour with God and man, He feels, He touches, He is hungry, He eats, He dies. In fact, the early date of the Gospels and their substantial accuracy is very cogently supported by the fact that they represent Jesus as supernatural and yet thoroughly human. They show us no trace of that morbid, perhaps we may say priggish, view of human nature which has sometimes made temporary invasions even into the midst of the Christian Church. S. John's attitude is essentially the same as that of the Synoptists, with this difference, that he does know of Docetism as an existing menace. His first Epistle unquestionably was written in view of certain heretics who deny that Jesus Christ has come *in the flesh*, who disbelieve that the Son of God submitted to the water of baptism and shed blood in death. The evidence of the Gospel of S. John is not so decisive. It is possible that S. John intends to contradict the Docetic fable that Simon of Cyrene was crucified instead of Jesus when he writes 'Jesus went out, bearing the cross for Himself' (John xix. 17). But whether this is so or not, S. John describes the divine 'Word,' the Son of God, as becoming flesh, he represents Him as sitting weary by the well at Samaria, he says that 'Jesus wept' at the grave of Lazarus, and exclaimed 'I thirst' when tortured on the cross. All this absolutely excludes the theory that Jesus was a man in appearance only. And the deep consciousness which the Church had of the real humanity of Jesus led her to canonise the Gospels which testified to that humanity.

Fortunately we are able to see how the Church met Docetism shortly after the end of the apostolic age. We learn from S. Irenaeus how S. John at Ephesus opposed the Docetic teacher Cerinthus. The story is in itself quite probable, and shows in S. John a trace of the old ardour which caused him as a young disciple to desire to call down fire from heaven on the Samaritan village which rejected His Master. In the letters of S. Ignatius we see the next stage. Ignatius was bishop of Antioch in Syria, one of the very first centres of Christianity, and he was taken away from Antioch to be put to death at Rome in the time of the Emperor Trajan, between A.D. 110 and 117. Led as a prisoner by a small company of soldiers, he passed from town to town on the coasts of Asia, Macedonia, and Achaia. On arriving at Smyrna he was entertained by the Church there and its bishop, Polycarp, and was met by delegates of the neighbouring Churches. At Smyrna he wrote four letters to the Churches of Tralles, Magnesia, Ephesus, and Rome. From Smyrna he went to Troas, and there wrote the other three letters that are still extant. His style is rough, glowing, and picturesque. His great desire is to promote the unity and coherence of the 'Catholic Church,' and to enable the Church to withstand a disintegrating heresy. The heretics separated from the Church and its bishops, and abstained from the Eucharist, denying it to be the flesh of Christ; but the root of their offence was their denial of the reality of Christ's human body. Ignatius with intense earnestness declares that Christ is 'fleshly' as well as 'spiritual,' that Christ truly suffered, otherwise why should Ignatius be willing to suffer martyrdom? Christ was truly 'nailed up in the flesh for our sakes under Pontius Pilate and Herod the tetrarch,' and 'after His resurrection He both ate with them (the apostles) and drank with them.' So sure is Ignatius of the union of the humanity and divinity in

Christ that he does not hesitate to speak of 'the passion of my God' and 'the blood of God.' He speaks equally plainly of 'the virginity of Mary.' And it is worth noting that whereas some modern writers have maintained that the belief that Christ was born of a Virgin was the result of an unwholesome scorn for the dignity of human nature and a dislike of a truly human Christ, Ignatius, the first writer outside the New Testament who mentions the Virgin birth, upholds it as emphatically as the truth that Christ was really Man.

On what did Ignatius rely for his assertions? It is practically certain from his language that he used the Gospel according to S. Matthew; and though critics are less agreed upon this point, I cannot bring myself to think that he had not read S. John's. His theology has a strong Johannine flavour, and some of his phrases seem to be moulded by, or actually borrowed from, S. John. But the Gospel for S. Ignatius, as for S. Paul, was one, even though he knew it as written in different forms. He tells the Philadelphians that he takes refuge 'in the Gospel as the Flesh of Jesus,' a significant allusion to the genuineness of Christ's life and the record or records through which he had learnt Christ's life. And he tells the people of Smyrna to 'take heed to the prophets, but more particularly to the Gospel.' On the other hand, the heretics profess to be content with the Old Testament, probably interpreted according to fanciful allegorical methods. He tells the Philadelphians how the heretics would argue. 'If I find it not in the archives (*i.e.* the Old Testament), I believe it not in the Gospel,' and when he said, 'It is written,' they answered, 'That is the question.' Now the phrase 'it is written' was at first strictly reserved for quotations from the Old Testament. In the writings of Justin Martyr about A.D. 150 it is applied to quotations from the Gospels, and there are possible cases of this kind in Polycarp and the so-called Epistle of Barnabas. It is conceivable that this passage in Ignatius means that the heretics questioned whether this or that statement was 'written' in the Gospel, but other evidence makes this interpretation precarious.[1] We can at any rate say with confidence that Ignatius himself relies upon some written Gospel record or records, and he does so partly because this record is a guarantee that Jesus Christ was not a phantom, or a divine Messenger who merely assumed the unreal appearance of a man.

§ 4. *The Canon and Gnostic 'Tradition.'*

If we pass on from S. Ignatius to the times of Justin Martyr, we can see both a more copious use of the Gospels and additional reasons for the grouping of this material into one unalterable canon. The process was then nearly complete. Justin was born in Judaea at Flavia Neapolis, now Nablous, about A.D. 100. His father or grandfather was probably a member of the colony which the Emperor Vespasian established near Sichem. Justin belonged to a pagan family, and was well educated; he studied Plato, and travelled from one philosophic centre to another. He passed through a series of doubts and disillusions. He became attracted by Judaism, and finally by the high morality of the Christian religion. He became a Christian at Ephesus in the time of Hadrian, and then went to Rome, where he became the teacher of a school of Christian philosophy. He died a martyr in the time of the prefect Junius Rusticus, between A.D. 163 and 167. As a controversialist he endeavoured to keep Christianity from the corrupting influence of Marcion, and the speculations of the Gnostics, who were merely using Christianity as the decoration of new forms of

[1] See Mr. C. H. Turner, *Journal of Theol. Studies*, vol. x. p. 27.

paganism. He also tried to draw the Jews from the prophets to Christ, and his *Dialogue with the Jew Trypho* is one of the most important specimens of the anti-Jewish literary debates that issued from the ancient Church. And as an apologist he tried to show the heathen that Christianity is the highest expression of wisdom, and that Christians were not guilty of the disloyalty or the obscene immorality with which they were charged by the heathen. His work against Marcion and his *Compendium against all Heresies* have perished. But his two *Apologies*, and the *Dialogue* mentioned above, throw the most important light upon the use made of Scripture by a man who was familiar with the two centres of Christendom, Rome and Ephesus.

By the time that Justin wrote his books Christianity was confronted by an overwhelming danger. In addition to Marcionism, there had been inaugurated a number of Gnostic systems of various degrees of excellence, but all popular. Not only did able men, such as the famous Egyptians Basilides and Valentinus, find a ready market for their doctrines, but a countless number of lesser teachers offered a new 'knowledge' of their own in Egypt, Italy, and Syria. In Gnosticism the sublime and the ridiculous met together. Occasionally we find Gnostic maxims and meditations of a really devout and spiritual character, reminding us of S. John himself. At other times we come across a trick such as that of Marcos, who made the wine in the Eucharistic cup change from white to red, and here and there we read of the moral degradation into which the Gnostic quacks led their unfortunate dupes. In fact, the baser heretics of the second century were on the same plane as the spiritualistic mediums in modern London or the founders of so-called religious 'abodes of love.' Now the more ingenious Gnostics appealed to tradition. Against the apostolic succession of the ministers of the Church such as we find taught by S. Clement of Rome, they raised the false apostolic succession of secret traditions handed down to a select initiated few. Thus Basilides, who taught at Alexandria in the time of Hadrian, claimed to be a disciple of 'Glaucias,' the interpreter of S. Peter. And Valentinus, who taught in Alexandria, Cyprus, and Rome in the time of the Emperor Antoninus Pius, pretended to be a disciple of 'Theodas,' a friend of S. Paul. The Church, which had so greatly prized the 'deposit' of oral tradition when S. Paul wrote to Timothy and Titus, and later when Papias made his inquiries, saw for the first time that her tradition, which was the word of her Lord, was in danger of being 'made of none effect.' Tradition was being brought into disrepute, because its name was used to cover a multitude of fictions by which the one true God was hidden behind a cloud of semi-Oriental deities.

Christendom has witnessed many subsequent theories which have put tradition and history in false opposition to each other. Within recent years Mrs. Besant, the priestess of Theosophy, has appealed to secret traditions of the early Church to support what she calls 'Esoteric Christianity,' according to which Jesus was born one hundred years before the Christian era, and reared at Mount Serbal in Arabia in the principles of Theosophy. Another more respectable appeal to tradition at one time made by Roman Catholic writers was that described by the late Father Tyrrell as an appeal 'to the *Disciplina Arcani* and to all that Christ taught the Apostles during those forty days after His resurrection. This was not written down, but was confided to the rulers of the Church to be dispensed according as exigencies might demand. All apparent additions to the creed were, from the first, known explicitly to a favoured but undefined few, who transmitted them to the episcopate or to the Pope. How much more these know only the future can tell. This is hardly consistent with *quod ubique, quod ab omnibus,* though it saves the *quod semper.*[1] In fact, the *Disciplina Arcani*, or giving of secret instructions to Christian converts, though it existed in the fourth and fifth centuries, did not exist among the Catholics of the second century. And when S. Vincent of Lerins taught that articles of the Catholic faith must have been held everywhere by every one, or they would be uncatholic, he was simply expressing in a terse, quick fashion what S. Irenaeus and Tertullian meant when they asserted that the genuine tradition of the Church was an open and official tradition corroborated by Christians from all quarters.

The Church of the second century saw that it would be fatal to allow the flood of spurious oral tradition to swamp the teaching of the apostles. Hence during this period we find a growing importance attached to an already existing episcopate as guarding the genuine Christian tradition. We also find the creed emphasised and expanded. It was a summary of the truth about the God of the Christians, a God made known to man in a Jesus Christ who was really born and crucified, and really rose from the dead. But Catholic Christians were also compelled to put their books in order, and thus partly consciously and partly unconsciously they fixed the Canon of the Gospels.

Justin's two *Apologies* and his *Dialogue with Trypho* are perhaps all the more valuable because the former are addressed to pagans and the last is addressed to Jews. He quotes the Gospels as authorities for the life and teaching of our Lord, and his quotations are so frequent that we can construct a brief outline of

[1] George Tyrrell, *Christianity at the Cross-Roads*, pp. 19-20 (2nd impression, 1910).

Christ's life from the passages cited. His view of that life is substantially the same as that which we should gather from the four Gospels. He had before him some narratives distinct from the four—possibly a Harmony like the *Diatessaron* of his pupil Tatian, possibly the *Protevangelium of James* with its stories of the birth and childhood of both Jesus and Mary, and possibly the apocryphal *Gospel of Peter*. I cannot feel sure that he used this apocryphal Gospel, for he had a keen eye for heresy, and would almost certainly have detected its Docetic tendencies. But the evidence of Justin enables us to say that in his time the four Gospels just fall short of having attained to exclusive canonicity. And we cannot with fairness discount his evidence by saying that it is evidence for himself only and not for the Church in general. His acquaintance with a wide area of Christendom, his own position in Rome, and the fact that these writings are intended primarily for outside critics, all do something to guarantee the fact that Justin's references to the life of Christ are such as the Church of his day would have been prepared to corroborate in all important particulars.

Justin calls the records which he quotes *Memoirs of the Apostles* (eight times); *The Memoirs* (four times); *Memoirs composed by the Apostles of Christ and their Companions* (once); *Memoirs made by the Apostles, which are called Gospels* (once). That these Memoirs included our four Gospels is certain. In common with Matthew, Justin mentions that to Christ the name of Jesus is given: 'For He shall save His people from their sins.' Various quotations are given from the Sermon on the Mount, and the comment that John the Baptist was the true Elias is in exact harmony with Matt. xvii. 13. Like S. Luke, Justin says that the census at the time of our Lord's birth was taken under Cyrenius, that Jesus began His ministry when thirty years of age, and that He changed the names of the sons of Zebedee to Boanerges. It is still sometimes denied that Justin was acquainted with S. John's Gospel, but the grounds for this view are generally regarded as thoroughly insufficient, and it is in conflict with the striking coincidences between the expressions used by Justin and S. John, and by Justin's assumption that Jesus is the incarnate Word of God. It is easy to see how Justin after a preliminary training in Greek philosophy could accept the doctrine which is summarised in the prologue of the Fourth Gospel, and in presenting that doctrine to his pagan readers colour it unconsciously with a tinge of Greek speculation. But it is only paradox to assert that the author of the Fourth Gospel derived his doctrine of the Word from Justin. This would imply that a Greek Christian doctrine was gradually turned back into something that was more Jewish at the very time when the Church was becoming so Gentile that Jewish Christianity was left in a lonely backwater. Justin surely shows his knowledge of the prologue of the Fourth Gospel when he says that the Word 'became Man' and that 'through Him God created all things,' and tells his readers that he has learnt that Christ as the Word is the 'only-begotten' Son of God. Like S. John, he regards the lifting up of the brazen serpent as typical of the crucifixion; like S. John and unlike the Synoptists, he describes the Eucharist as the 'flesh' rather than the 'body' of Christ; and when he speaks of baptism he says, 'For Christ also said, Except ye be born again, ye shall in no wise enter into the kingdom of heaven.'[1]

At first it seems strange that he does not mention the writers of the Gospels by name. But the solution of this difficulty is very simple. The early Christian writers when addressing readers who were not Christians

[1] *Apol.* 1. 61.

did not as a rule make mention of the authors of the sacred books of the Church. Tatian and Tertullian, who not only knew our Gospels but regarded them as exclusively canonical, do not mention the names of the evangelists when they write for heathen readers.

§ 5. *The Canon and Public Worship.*

Justin also shows us another reason why the Canon of the Gospels became fixed, one which is connected with the essence of genuine Christian tradition. This is the practice of reading the Gospels in public worship. As we have already hinted, secrecy in the second century was not a note of the Church, but of heresy or heathenism. Thirty years later than S. Justin Martyr, S. Irenaeus reproached the Gnostics with not teaching openly, but gradually luring on their converts to a greater depravity of creed and conduct by revealing to them secrets only fit for the initiated. Justin sees no need of secrecy. He writes quite plainly about the sacraments for the instruction of his pagan readers. And he tells how the Christians worship, thus publishing the first account of the Roman Mass:—

'On the day called Sunday all those who live in the towns, or in the country, meet together; and *the memoirs of the apostles and the writings of the prophets are read, as long as time permits.* Then, when the reader has ended, the president addresses words of instruction, and exhortation to imitate these good things. Then we all stand up together and offer prayers. And when prayer is ended, bread is brought and wine and water, and the president offers up alike prayers and thanksgiving with all his energy, and the people give their assent, saying the *Amen*. And the distribution of the elements, over which thanksgiving

THE CANON OF THE GOSPELS

has been uttered, is made, so that each partakes; and to those who are absent they are sent by the hands of the deacons. And those who have the means, and are so disposed, give as much as they will, each according to his inclination; and the sum collected is placed in the hands of the president, who himself succours the orphans and widows, and those who, through sickness or any other cause, are in want, and the prisoners, and the foreigners who are staying in the place, and in short he provides for all who are in need.' The general structure of the service so described is that common to all the ancient liturgies. And the universal practice in all these liturgies was to read part of the New Testament, and more especially part of the Gospels, before receiving the 'food' which, as Justin says, 'is called among us Eucharist.' The order of Christian worship was based upon the worship of the synagogue. The latter included readings from the 'law and the prophets.' So we read in Acts xiii. 27 that when S. Paul and his companions went into the synagogue at Antioch in Pisidia, 'after the reading of the law and the prophets' the rulers of the synagogue invited them to exhort the people. At Rome in Justin's time the reading of the Gospels had taken the place of the reading of the law. The reading of the letter of an apostle such as S. Paul, or a great bishop such as S. Clement of Rome, dates back far earlier than the time when Justin wrote, and probably did much to determine what was of really apostolic origin or not. Regular worshippers would soon learn to detect the difference between Gnostic kickshaws and Gospel meat.

§ 6. *The Canon and Montanism.*

Before the death of Justin there arose in Phrygia

the sect founded by Montanus. It spread westward, and was known in the south of Gaul before S. Irenaeus became bishop of Lyons about A.D. 177. Montanism is a suggestive movement to students of the Canon of the New Testament and the Canon of the Gospels. It is an instance of that ascetic but undisciplined enthusiasm which has so often manifested itself in Christendom when it has been felt that

> The days are waxing evil,
> The times are waxing late.

It hurled itself against the pagan world and a Church which it suspected of compromising with that world. It began by proclaiming that Christ would speedily return and establish His kingdom upon earth—Phrygian earth; and not content with the truth that Christianity is a New Covenant, it practically represented itself as one newer. Montanus and his female companions, Priscilla, Maximilla, and Quintilla, were hailed by their followers as uttering a new prophecy, improving on the revelation given to the apostles. They were 'spiritual,' ushering in a reign of the Paraclete to prepare for the second advent, teaching both a restoration and a development of primitive Christianity. Montanism cannot be understood unless it is seen in relation to the Fourth Gospel and the Book of Revelation, for it shows the deep influence which those books had already exercised on Christendom. It assumed while it perverted such an indwelling of the Holy Spirit in the Christian as is taught in John x., xv.-xvii., and it also assumed that a literal interpretation should be put upon the millennium foretold in the Apocalypse. The relation of the Church to Montanism has sometimes been misunderstood. The Montanists opposed the hierarchy of the Church, but they seem to have claimed for their own prophets, even after the time of Montanus, quite as much authority as any Christian bishop claimed for himself. If in the time of Cromwell Milton could say

New presbyter is but old priest writ large,

we can find a parallel in the fact that Tertullian, when he became a Montanist, allowed to the Montanist prophets an authority which he denied to the 'blessed pope' of Rome. Montanism was not therefore a movement in favour of the belief that the ordinary layman ought to have a share in the government and the progress of the Church of Christ. It was a new school of prophets. But the Church did not oppose it on the ground that prophecy had not continued in the Church after the apostolic age. As Dr. Gore has said, 'the gift of prophecy continued as a recognised endowment of the Church into the second or third centuries.'[1] S. Polycarp, who died a martyr in A.D. 155, was regarded as a prophet, and we find a prophetess, Ammia, in Philadelphia at a rather earlier date. But the Church did not believe that every one who claimed to be a prophet had a right to the title. The *Didaché* and the *Shepherd of Hermas*, both earlier than the rise of Montanism, distinguish false from true prophets, testing them by their love of gain and their ambition. Similarly the Montanist prophets were criticised for accepting payment, and they were also criticised because their utterances were irrational and delivered in an ecstasy, and an ecstasy that was artificially produced. It is no satisfactory reply to this to say that S. Paul and S. Peter saw visions in a trance, and that S. John's Apocalypse is the prophecy of a 'seer.' For S. Paul's ecstasy or trance was not turned into material for public preaching: he does not even mention it until fourteen years afterwards (2 Cor. xii. 2-4). S. Peter in Acts x. 10 f. and S. John in the Apocalypse retain their own consciousness and do not behave like a

[1] *The Church and the Ministry*, p. 361, note I.

Greek diviner, or like Saul, or a modern clairvoyant. Yet we can see that Catholic Christians might find it hard to say why the Montanists were wrong, especially when they were men of austere moral life, absolutely unlike the loose Gnostic teachers on the extreme left wing of semi-Christian sectarianism. If the Montanist was virtuous, if he had no love of filthy lucre, and if his ecstasy was occasional and his claims moderate, how was he to be refuted?

So far as we can judge, the Catholics of the latter part of the second century were profoundly convinced that the Holy Spirit does not impart new truths to the Church, nor cause the production at a proper moment of truths wrapped up, as it were, and deposited with a select body of teachers. Rather they were conscious that the Holy Spirit only gives a clearer understanding of what has already been revealed to the whole Church. Consequently they relied on two principles of action. One was that the authority of the prophet, as in the time of the apostles, must be subject to the regulative authority of the whole body. Prophets were not to be recognised as genuine prophets if they set at naught the constitution of the Church, which had been framed by the apostles. The second principle was closely allied to the first. Christ and His apostles had delivered to the Church the whole truth, and accretions were unnecessary and untrue. What was expressly contained in the written words of the Lord and His apostles, or could be obviously and naturally inferred from these words, was to be believed. Tradition was not despised. A creed was in use, with its simple summary of the revelation of God made to us in Jesus Christ, and where particular errors were arrayed against the Church the creed was already expanded so as to repudiate those errors. But the tradition enshrined in the creed was inseparable from the Scriptures. The New Testament alongside the

THE CANON OF THE GOSPELS

Old became, with the creed, the authoritative standard for Christian teaching. The Church appealed always to a past deposit. The result was that when S. Irenaeus wrote against heresies about A.D. 185 the Canon of the Gospels was irrevocably fixed, and the *Muratorian Canon*, probably written in his time, suggestively says concerning the New Testament, 'gall should not be mixed with honey.'

CHAPTER II

CRITICISM OF THE GOSPELS

§ 1. *Some Fundamental Problems.*

ONE of the most hopeful signs of the times is that all over the world there is an increasing demand that the truth and nothing but the truth shall be ascertained and written down as history. We cannot hope to recover the whole truth. We must be content with the best that we can do, in spite of knowing that much has been lost and cannot be recovered. But in every department of history it is considered necessary to get evidence by every means in our power, and the results, both negative and positive, are well worth the trouble. It is a laudable instinct to be intolerant of any literary fraud, though even this instinct requires to be balanced by the presumption that a large class of ancient statements may be trusted. In the case of the Gospels it is quite right that we should inquire whether the names blazoned by the writers of ancient manuscripts at the head of each Gospel are really correct, and whether the pedigrees assigned to the Gospels in ancient Christian books are also correct. For instance, it is right to ask whether the author of the second Gospel was really S. Mark, and whether S. Mark was, as the oldest record says, an interpreter of S. Peter. But the true historian, while narrowly searching the evidence, will be ready to think these

CRITICISM OF THE GOSPELS

traditions correct unless he has strong ground for believing them to be false. He wishes to weed, not to destroy, and he knows that during the last few years tradition has had many revenges.

Not only has the science of history advanced, but natural science has also greatly advanced. One consequence of this is a perplexity concerning the nature and possibility of miracles and, in some quarters, a denial of their possibility. The New Testament is a region of miracle. It is full of phenomena described as 'signs' or 'works' or 'acts of power.' In particular, S. Paul lives and moves in the midst of such phenomena. His testimony to them is absolutely genuine, and all the more impressive because it is ordinarily given in a manner quite foreign to that known as 'apologetic.' He is convinced that miracles have happened, do happen, and are worked by himself as well as others (2 Cor. xii. 12). The evangelists also evidently believe in the miracles worked by Christ. According to their record, He believed in His own power to work such wonders. He connected them with a special divine power within Himself (Luke xi. 20; John v. 19; x. 38). Whatever account we may give of these activities, it is clear that those who came into contact with Him believed that they were real, and were a proof that God was with Him in a special sense. Christ says, 'If I by the spirit of God cast out devils, then is the kingdom of God come upon you' (Matt. xii. 28); 'Woe unto thee, Chorazin! woe unto thee, Bethsaida! for if the mighty works had been done in Tyre and Sidon which were done in you, they would have repented long ago in sackcloth and ashes. . . . And thou, Capernaum, shalt thou be exalted unto heaven? thou shalt go down unto Hades: for if the mighty works had been done in Sodom which were done in thee, it would have remained until this day' (Matt. xi. 21, 23). The word translated 'mighty works' in our Bible is the equivalent of 'miracles.' Just as we find in all the Gospels a peculiar tone of authority in our Lord's sayings, so we find in His actions a peculiar power over spiritual, mental, and material phenomena. If we are prepared to be guided by the evidence we shall see that these sayings and these actions combined to impress upon the disciples of Jesus Christ the certainty that He was the Son of God. And if we reject the evidence, we can give no reasonable account of the origin of the Gospels at all.

If teachers of natural science are willing to believe that the universe is not self-sufficient, and that room should be left for the theory that it is guided by external laws and permeated by a divine Spirit, there seems no reason why the controversy about the miracles of the Gospel should not one day be set at rest. The crucial miracle, as the first Christians clearly perceived, is the resurrection of Jesus Christ. Most of the heavy artillery of modern rationalism is directed against it. Appeal is made to S. Paul, who is said never to use a phrase which implies that the grave of Christ was left empty on the third day, and all the evidence borne by the apostles to the resurrection is taken to show no more than the fact that they believed that the soul of the Crucified was alive at the right hand of God, and had somehow appeared to them. If this theory were true, we should find it very difficult to explain either the conduct or the language of S. Paul and the other apostles. If they thought that the resurrection of Christ meant no more than the survival of His soul in glory, they would obviously have believed that He 'rose' the instant that He died on the cross after commending His spirit to His Father. On the contrary, the belief that He rose 'the third day,' and not before, is perhaps the most deeply rooted and widely attested fact in all Christian belief. And that

He then rose and left His grave empty is taught in all the Gospels.

Critics who hold the above attenuated theory of the resurrection hold a corresponding view of other miracles. Few would now say that no uncommon manifestations attended the ministry of Jesus. But they would confine these manifestations to a beneficent power over nervous diseases such as is believed, rightly or wrongly, to be occasionally exercised by modern healers. That is not the view of the evangelists. In addition to the cure of serious nervous and physical disorders, they mention the cure of such ailments as leprosy and dropsy; and give instances of Christ's power over organic matter, as shown in the multiplication of loaves and fishes, and in the raising of the dead. The last kind of miracle is found in all four Gospels, the stilling of the storm in the three Synoptic Gospels, walking on the water in three Gospels, and the miraculous feeding of the multitude in all four. Miracles are woven into the whole texture of the record, so that nearly the whole fabric falls to pieces without them. In the case of many of the so-called ecclesiastical miracles of later times, the miracles can be extracted from the surrounding life of the saint. The alleged miracles which attended the discovery of the relics of the supposed S. 'Philomena' in Rome in 1802 leave us as ignorant as before with regard to the martyr's character and history. S. Philip Neri and S. Teresa would remain great if all their miracles were omitted. Of many ecclesiastical miracles we may say that they are so trivial that they are more in a line with the portents admired by ignorant peasants than with the stories in the Gospels. But in dealing with the life of Christ we find that as a rule the miracles cannot be separated from His teaching and history. Thus His teaching that 'the Son of Man hath power on earth to forgive sins' cannot be dissociated from His healing of the palsied man, and the beginning of the opposition of the Pharisees and Herodians to Jesus is best explained, as in S. Mark, by His healing a man with a withered hand.

Therefore even if we explain certain diseases and cures otherwise than in the language natural to the evangelists, the problems to be considered are (i) whether we still regard the passing popularity of Christ and the opposition to Him as only to be fully explained on the ground of His having performed miracles; (ii) whether He claimed the power to work miracles, and claimed it sincerely; (iii) whether such a power is in harmony with that special manifestation and interposition of the divine Presence in the world which we find in His own personality.

Thus we ask with regard to the Gospels not only, Were they written by the men whose names they bear? but, Did the acts recorded in connection with His ministry happen as they are said to have happened? Is the teaching of the Master correctly reported? Was He what the evangelists represent Him to be?

Here we find ourselves at once brought face to face with the difference between the first three Gospels and the fourth. The first three evangelists give the story of our Lord's ministry in one way, the fourth in another. There is no escape from the conclusion, even if we desired to escape it, that on the whole the first three are delivering a story which they have received, while the fourth evangelist is giving us a story as it has shaped itself in his own mind. But we must beware of exaggeration. S. Paul constructed a great theology, yet he speaks of delivering what he had received; he laid the Gospel which he preached before the original apostles for their approval; he never poses as an inventor. And we must not hastily conclude that the Fourth Gospel is a romance or a speculation, or that the central ideas are the product of the author's imagination. If he coined the gold afresh,

CRITICISM OF THE GOSPELS

he did not make the gold. The more closely we study the image and superscription, the more we are likely to recognise the Son of Man whom the other evangelists have drawn. They too differ among themselves. We cannot fairly say that we gather in every detail precisely the same impression of the Person of Christ from the first three evangelists. We have every reason to be glad that we do not. There are half-educated people who quarrel with a portrait because it is not precisely the same as a photograph. They do not know how the true artist seizes and interprets that which does not merely belong to a fleeting moment of a life but to its essential character. In this way the evangelists interpret Jesus Christ. It is a very poor apology for the fourth evangelist to say that he tells us of the Christ of experience and not the Christ of history. There can be no Christ of experience other than the Christ of history, who walked through the fields of Galilee and the streets of Jerusalem nineteen hundred years ago. And we ask why the fourth evangelist (whether S. John or another) identifies Jesus with 'the Word' or eternal counterpart of God, whether this identification contradicts the other Gospels, and whether it has a real spiritual value or not.

A kindred problem arises if we pass from considering the portrait of Jesus Christ in the Fourth Gospel to His discourses. All who have read anything about biblical criticism are familiar with the saying that, if He spoke as He is said to have spoken by the earlier evangelists, He cannot have spoken as He is said to have spoken by the author of the Fourth Gospel. That is the kind of dictum which should be strictly cross-questioned. It looks so persuasive at first sight that it is allowed to pass. There is such an obvious difference between the Sermon on the Mount in Matthew and the discourse on the Bread of Life in John. And further, the same kind of expressions and the same kind of ideas run through the discourses in John and the writer's own reflections, and even through his own prologue and the Epistles which bear his name. And we are forced to ask, Did our Lord speak just as the Sermon on the Mount reads, and did He, on the other hand, assimilate His manner so completely to the thought of a Hellenised Jew as the Fourth Gospel suggests? We should probably go far astray if we gave an unqualified 'Yes' to either or both of these questions. For a careful examination of the Sermon on the Mount makes it clear to us that it has been arranged in a scheme fitted for the instruction of members of the early Christian Church, and it is more than doubtful whether it was ever all uttered at once. And an examination of different records of the same sayings as recorded by the earlier evangelists shows us that the treasure of Christ's words was far too great for any one vessel to contain. He told them not to skilled reporters with modern appliances for recording sounds, but to simple, earnest men. He was not always perfectly understood by His disciples. Clear and pure as was the medium of their souls, it did not permit the whole truth to flow through and onward. There is another thing which every careful reader of the Gospels will at once admit. It is that the sayings of the Lord, though very simple, are so deep that no one will venture to declare that he fully understands them. They will always bring some new message to those who wait. They must pass into the life as well as the mind of the reader. The varying explanations which are still given of certain of Christ's sayings and parables ought to make us very slow to speak about their interpretation as if His meaning always lay on the surface of His words. It is not so. The Christian who in the early stages of his biblical studies was perplexed by the arguments of S. Paul may, many years later, find himself asking if he has ever really understood some of the sayings of the Lord in the first two Gospels. And before we decide that the discourses in the Fourth Gospel are philosophical compositions of the second century, we should ask if we have sufficient reasons for denying that these discourses can truthfully represent certain aspects of a doctrine which has always been too wide for any single mind to comprehend.

The topography of the Fourth Gospel, the chronology of Christ's ministry, and the sequence of the events recorded are all matters of controversy. The divergences which they present, when compared with the statements of the earlier Gospels, will be dealt with when we consider S. John's Gospel more minutely. At present it will be enough to say that whereas S. John's Gospel makes our Lord's ministry extend over nearly three years, and makes Jerusalem and its neighbourhood the principal scene of that ministry, the earlier Gospels give very little indication that the time was longer than one year, and describe the ministry chiefly in connection with Galilee. The extreme wing of adverse critics call the Fourth Gospel historically worthless. Others, like Renan, hold that it includes some sound historical traditions, and that in some particulars it is the most accurate of the Gospels. Those, again, who regard this Gospel as the work of an eye-witness and friend of Jesus Christ find in it many details which complete and occasionally correct the earlier narratives.

We have dwelt for a short time upon some characteristics of the Fourth Gospel, because the criticism of all the Gospels, even of some of the apocryphal Gospels, has been so closely dependent upon the criticism of that according to S. John. There have been more doubts with regard to its authorship than in the case of the others, many more than in the case of Mark and Luke, and more serious than in the case of Matthew. For while it is widely held that S. Matthew did not write in its present form the Gospel which bears his name, such a theory is quite compatible with the view that he did write a large part of the matter which it contains. But the theory that S. John wrote part of the Fourth Gospel, and that his work was incorporated into a larger work by a later writer, though it has been suggested, has been almost universally rejected. Moreover, the course of His ministry is depicted differently, and the miracles, though less numerous than those recorded by the Synoptists, are of special magnitude. And lastly, while our Lord is represented as living in perfect filial submission to the will of the divine Father, His equality in nature with the Father is more unquestionably taught by this evangelist than by the Synoptists. Critics have therefore felt for more than one hundred years that if the Fourth Gospel disagrees with the others, either its testimony or theirs must be preferred; whereas if they fundamentally agree, two testimonies are better than one, and the supernatural origin of Christianity gains strong support. The inquiry therefore lies close to the very heart of our creed.

§ 2. *Rise of Modern Antichristian Criticism.*

The older rationalism and semi-Christian theology of Germany wavered in its view of S. John's Gospel. Reimarus and Paulus, who were the apostles of German unbelief in the second half of the eighteenth century, endeavoured to reduce the Gospel to common-sense and Christ to the founder of a valuable ethical system. He showed His reasonableness by His substantial agreement with the contemporaries of our King George III. The marvels of the New Testament could be explained on merely natural grounds. Our Lord's miracles of healing were explained as effected by a knowledge of potent remedies, and the instances of raising the dead only involved cases of apparent death. He did not think it necessary—here we see Renan anticipated—to correct the mistaken opinions of those who attributed His actions to supernatural power. He swam with the tide. Just as He did not raise others from the dead, He did not Himself rise from the dead. When He was buried the cool sepulchre and the spices began to revive Him, and then a storm and an earthquake restored Him to His senses. He did not rise: He merely for a time recovered.

German Protestantism was thrown into a whirlpool by these and similar theories, and the result was a fresh investigation of the Gospels. Crude as these investigations may seem to-day, they gave a stimulus to scientific research. England, where the Deists had taught the advanced rationalism which had been imported into Germany by Toland (1670-1722), had the doubtful honour of publishing one of the first and coarsest of critical books. This was Evanson's *Dissonance of the Four commonly received Gospels*, A.D. 1792. He placed Luke first, Matthew he thought was probably copied from Luke, and Mark from the earlier two. He also denied the genuineness of the Fourth Gospel. The Tübingen school, so famous fifty years later, followed Evanson in his view of Mark, though as early as A.D. 1786 G. Chr. Storr had maintained the view, now almost universal, that Mark is the earliest Gospel. While Evanson was one of those who started the hypothesis of *borrowing*, Lessing and Eichhorn started the hypothesis of a *source* older than our present Gospels. Eichhorn held that all the Synoptists borrowed from an Aramaic Gospel now lost, but afterwards adopted the view that there was a translation of this Gospel into Greek which was used in variously corrupted forms by the Synoptists. The next important theory was that of Gieseler, A.D. 1818, who preferred *oral tradition* as the explanation of the similarities and divergences of the Gospels. He held that oral tradition had taken two main forms in Greek, that of S. Paul as represented by Luke, that of the Galilean apostles as represented by Matthew and Mark. The remarkably retentive memories of many peoples, both Eastern and Western, in periods when books were scarce, can reasonably be appealed to in support of such an oral tradition. At this day there are Christians in Asia Minor who can recite large parts of the Church services in Greek, though they speak Turkish and are almost wholly ignorant of Greek. And two generations ago the Irish and the Scottish Highlanders could repeat quantities of legends and poems which they had never read. The oral theory has been popular in England, where it was defended by Bishop Westcott, and has recently been well presented by Mr. A. Wright.

In A.D. 1820 the authenticity of S. John's Gospel was called in question in Germany by an able work of Bretschneider. He afterwards showed that he accepted it, and for a time the popularity of this Gospel was secured by the brilliant influence of Schleiermacher. Celebrated alike as a preacher, a writer, and philosopher, Schleiermacher endeavoured to rescue German Protestantism from ruin by representing faith in Christ as independent of all historical reports of miraculous events. He regarded the doctrines of His miraculous birth, His resurrection, ascension, and return to judgment as having no connection with Christ's redeeming activity, and it is on this activity alone that faith was said to depend. A large amount of semi-Christian thought in Europe to-day can be directly traced to these opinions. With regard to the Gospels, Schleiermacher held that the three Synoptists composed mosaics from fragments such as are apparently mentioned in Luke i. 1-4, and that S. Matthew wrote not *our* Gospel according to S. Matthew, but a collection of sayings of Christ subsequently embodied in that Gospel. He strongly upheld S. John's Gospel as the work of an eye-witness, feeling it to be in harmony with his own personal experience of religion.

In A.D. 1831 there came to Berlin to complete his studies a young man who called upon Schleiermacher, and explained that he had come to hear not Schleiermacher, but the philosopher Hegel, who was just dead. That young man was David Strauss, the founder of the Judaeo-German scepticism which has waged a ceaseless war against Christianity for eighty years. In A.D. 1835 he published his *Life of Jesus*.

Strauss in his *Life of Jesus* rejects the now widely accepted view of Schleiermacher that Papias, when he mentions the Logia composed by Matthew, means a collection of the sayings of Jesus. He prefers to think that it was ' an entire Gospel,' but not identical with our first Gospel. He declares that ' our second Gospel cannot have originated from recollections of Peter's instructions,' and, like Evanson, holds that it is a compilation drawn from the first and third Gospels. With regard to the third Gospel and Acts he says, ' The companion of Paul may have composed his two works at a time and under circumstances when he was no longer protected by apostolic influence against the tide of tradition.' With regard to the Fourth Gospel he says, ' We meet with it first among the Valentinians and the Montanists about the middle of the second century.' He left to our Lord only the position of a gifted genius whom legend had gradually deified. He repudiated the doctrine of the incarnation, and the variations in the different editions of his *Life of Jesus* showed that he knew that to grant the authenticity of the Fourth Gospel would be to overthrow the foundation of his theory.

Strauss made every student of the Gospels ask, Is the life of Jesus only historical in the sense in which the life of Socrates is historical, or was it supernatural? Did miracles happen? He replied that they did not happen; they are legends born of the spirit of mythology. The people believed Jesus to be the Messiah; they expected the Messiah to work miracles that would equal or surpass the miracles wrought by the ancient prophets, therefore legend created story after story of His wonderful works. Sailing through the dim haze which he had projected from his study, Strauss was unable to give any satisfactory explanation of the non-miraculous incidents in the life and words of Christ. He was not sure whether the cleansing of the temple happened or not, he left it an open question whether the Baptist sent to Jesus to inquire 'Art thou He that should come,' and he asked how we can tell where the title 'Son of Man' is genuine in the sayings of Jesus and where inserted by the writer from habit. Strauss was not logical enough to see the fact which has been a corner-stone in the more extreme antichristian criticism of later years. It is that wherever we seek for Jesus in primitive Christian literature we find the supernatural as well as the natural traits recorded together. 'Never and nowhere,' as Kalthoff said in 1880, 'is He . . . a purely natural man.' The result of treating the Gospels as something from which everything supernatural can be drawn, leaving only a natural Christ, leaves us no Christ, but a myth only. Strauss did not get so far as this. His Christ was a religious genius, a Jew of human parentage, who thought that He would be taken up into heaven and come again to inaugurate His kingdom. Jesus thought that He would on His return to earth come in the glory of the Messiah to rule over a people free from bondage to a foreign power. The new era would be ushered in by a catastrophe at the command of God. Strauss seems to have thought that Jesus was in some uncertainty as to whether He was the Messiah or not, but that on the whole He came to the conclusion that He was, and that after His death His Messianic office, which was now potential, would be actual.

In the Judaeo-German portrait of Jesus drawn by Strauss we can recognise most of the traits of a very modern form of infidelity. But he was not consistent. He afterwards dropped his strong insistence on the Jewish element in Jesus, in which everything centres in the idea of a coming catastrophe, and in his *Life of Jesus for the German People*, published in 1864, Strauss veered nearer to the ordinary Christ depicted by what now calls itself 'liberal Protestantism.' The latter portrait is much less Jewish, much less influenced by the Jewish eschatology of the first century than by the rationalism of the nineteenth. Strauss was quite conscious of the fact that he was not a Christian. Schweitzer thus sums up the belief of Strauss : ' To the question, " Are we still Christians ? " he answers, " No." But to his second question, "Have we still a religion ? " he is prepared to give an affirmative answer, if the assumption is granted that the feeling of dependence, of self-surrender, of inner freedom, which has sprung from the pantheistic view of the world, can be called religion.'[1] And in the sad melancholy of the verses which he composed upon his deathbed there is not a trace of religious faith.

Ferdinand Christian Baur, whose work Strauss himself turned to account in the popular *Life of Jesus for the German People*, is the next great critic that claims our attention. He and his 'Tübingen School' began a new method of treating Church history, a method intended to explain how a visionary Jew, who had been followed by twelve other Jews, came by the close of the

[1] Schweitzer, *Von Reimarus zu Wrede*, p. 75 (English translation, p. 76).

second century to be regarded as essentially divine and the founder of a universal Church. The special type of philosophy which dominated Baur was that of Hegel. The Hegelian doctrine taught that underlying all nature there is an innermost essence, a spiritual principle, and nature itself should be regarded as a system of stages in which one stage necessarily proceeds from the other, not, however, in such a way that one is necessarily *produced* by the other, but produced in the inner idea which constitutes the ground of nature. Baur applied this principle to the history of Christianity, and found in it a clue to the origin of the New Testament. Believing as he did that Jesus was not divine, he supposed very naturally that His immediate disciples did not believe Him to be divine. Like Toland, the English Deist, he fastened his eyes on the semi-Christian Jewish sect of Ebionites, which is first definitely mentioned in early Christian literature considerably more than one hundred years after the death of Christ. These Ebionites, said Baur, represented primitive Christianity ; their religion was the religion of the first apostles, though evidently not the religion of S. Paul. And the Catholic religion as it existed about A.D. 200, a religion which taught less definitely than S. Paul the doctrine of justification by faith, a religion with sacred laws and institutions, is an amalgam of Jewish Christianity with S. Paul's Christianity.

According to Baur, the original apostles believed in the Messiahship of Jesus, but were otherwise orthodox Jews in doctrine and ceremonial. They intended to confine their missionary work to Jews. But S. Paul chose the world for his mission field ; he was convinced that the Gentiles would not come to Christ by the way of circumcision, and so he proclaimed salvation by faith in Jesus without circumcision and the works required by the Jewish law. The result was that

CRITICISM OF THE GOSPELS

S. Paul quarrelled with the Twelve. And after his dispute with S. Peter at Antioch there was a complete rupture between the two parties. The struggle between the Petrine and the Pauline Christians continued until the appearance of a common foe, the Gnosticism of the second century. The two parties in the Christian Church were then forced to draw closer to each other, and our present New Testament was the result of their alliance. Of its twenty-seven books only five were really genuine, the Epistles to the Galatians, Corinthians, and Romans, which show us the author fighting against the Petrine party, and the Judaistic Revelation, which attacks S. Paul under the name of Baalam. All the other books of the New Testament either were forgeries or were revised in such a way as to obliterate the feud of earlier times. S. Matthew's Gospel was Judaistic and Petrine, but retouched; S. Luke's Gospel, Gentile and Pauline, also retouched and altered. S. Mark's Gospel was composed later, in order to remove the contradictions which can still be traced in the other two Synoptic Gospels in spite of the restorer's artful aid. The Acts is a reconciling book which makes S. Peter and S. Paul speak with one another's tones. The remaining Epistles of S. Paul, like the Epistle of S. Clement of Rome and the First Epistle of S. Peter (so-called), are all forgeries which softened S. Paul's teaching in order to make it acceptable to the other party. Finally, there is the Gospel according to S. John, written about A.D. 170, with its essentially divine and therefore universal Saviour, and its identification of believing, loving, and keeping the commandments. This marked the close of the conflict and the coronation of Catholic Christianity as supreme.

Baur's hypothesis was the work of genius. It placed the Gospels and the whole of the New Testament in connection with a movement which every one recognised to be in some degree historical, and which some imagined to be entirely historical. The New Testament appeared to be a living body of literature, just as organic as it had appeared to the Christian who placed it all in the apostolic age and attributed it all to the guidance of the Holy Spirit. We may observe that of recent years there has been a tendency on the part of non-Christian writers, whether they are called 'radical' or merely 'liberal,' not to explain how much of their creed they owe to F. C. Baur. This habit of ignoring him, whether conscious or unconscious, is at any rate intelligible. In logical power he was infinitely superior to the great mass of succeeding rationalistic critics. He saw how the origin of Christianity and the Person of Jesus might be explained on a basis which left no real room for a miracle or an incarnation. It was the best possible explanation of its kind, and yet it is an acknowledged failure. The fatal weakness of Baur's scheme is its artificial symmetry. Even the four Epistles of S. Paul to which he appealed do not really support his theory as to the relation between S. Paul and the other apostles. But every addition of an Epistle to that list, and every subtraction of an Epistle from that list, alike undermines his theory. And it is now admitted on all sides that we must either add or subtract. The reckless imputation of forgery to every document which cried out against his reconstruction of the early Church has brought its own nemesis. There are now critics who, while they disbelieve in the authenticity of S. John's Gospel, do not dispute the genuineness of the Epistles of S. Ignatius, written near A.D. 110, or that of S. Clement of Rome, written near A.D. 96. And none of these Epistles could possibly have been written at these dates if Baur's theory of the quarrel between the apostles was correct. The publication of Harnack's great volume on early Christian literature in 1897 at least showed that from a literary point of view Baur's criticism was hopelessly shattered. This fact had been realised even by A.D. 1875. But in spite of it the Christ of Strauss and Baur has been again and again produced on the stage with new paint and new clothes.

§ 3. *Renan and his Contemporaries.*

Renan made the cleverest, though not the most learned, effort to make this figure walk. He introduced to the Latin races the rationalism of Germany. His famous *Life of Jesus*, which was published in A.D. 1863 and ran through eight editions in three months, was written in exquisite French and execrable taste. The Jesus of German scepticism was like a collection of bones, but the hero of Renan's romance is like the wax image of an Italian saint in which the bones are concealed under a smiling face and smart vestments. Our Lord is described with an astonishing lack of moral insight. Renan said that 'Jesus was charming,' and that 'in His general physiognomy He was such as the Synoptic Gospels represent Him to us.' In one passage Renan says that 'in Him was condensed everything that is good and elevated in our nature'; in another we are elaborately informed that we must not expect to find among Orientals, as in 'our rigid consciences,' an absolute opposition between 'good faith and imposture.' The value of this explanation becomes evident later, when we are told that Jesus was not able 'to moderate the greediness of the crowd and of His own disciples for the marvellous,' and consequently allowed Lazarus and his family to perform a burlesque resurrection. Renan invites his readers to admire a Christ of whom he says, 'Desperate, pushed to an extremity, He was no longer His own master. His mission weighed upon Him, and He obeyed the stream,' and 'sometimes His ill temper at all resistance led Him to inexplicable and apparently absurd actions.'

We are told to 'divest ourselves of the instinctive repugnances which are the fruit of a purely reasonable education,' and then to venerate a Jesus who first grew dissatisfied with the title of Rabbi, then with that of Prophet, and finally 'wished that people should regard Him as having a higher relation towards God than that of other men.' The Jesus of Renan is a conceited sentimentalist, and even in Gethsemane He is redolent of the perfumes of Paris.

Though Renan failed in moral insight, his literary insight was clearer than that of many of his school, and many of the views which he adopted have been subsequently ratified. He maintained that S. Mark's Gospel was written before all the eye-witnesses of the life of Christ were dead, and was derived from the tradition of Peter.[1] Then he held that the writer of our Gospel 'according to Matthew' took that of S. Mark as the basis of his own work, and transferred to it the discourses of Christ, which he found already arranged in 'packets' written in Aramaic, and a large number of stories current among the Christians. He rightly regarded the author as a Jewish Christian who was strongly anti-Pharisaic, and points out the 'charming state' and 'exquisite transition' and the 'excellent moment for art' that is revealed to us by a conscience which has become Christian without ceasing to be Jewish. S. Luke's Gospel was held by Renan to have been written about A.D. 95. The author, he believed, made use of S. Mark's Gospel but did not know our first Gospel; he plunged into tradition and drew from it freely; he had no record of the sayings of Jesus arranged in a long connected series; and those sayings which he found in the sources which he had collected he separated and polished to insert in his 'delicious stories.' Renan loved S. Luke as an artist; he speaks of him as we might speak of one of the

[1] *Les Évangiles*, p. 125.

fashionable French painters of the period of Louis xv., a Boucher or a Fragonard. Unlike the more paradoxical modern rationalists, he regards S. Luke as essentially Pauline, holding views in 'perfect conformity' with those of the apostle of the Gentiles,[1] and says that his Gospel 'forms a sort of intermediary between the first two Gospels and the fourth.' He declares its historical value to be inferior to that of the other two Synoptic Gospels. But he acutely remarks that the contrast between the speeches attributed to the apostles in Acts, a work by the same author, and the speeches attributed to Jesus in the third Gospel, prove that the Synoptic Gospels 'really contain an echo of the word of Jesus.'[2]

Renan's treatment of S. John's Gospel is very characteristic. It was hardly to be expected that he would entirely despise such a treatise on 'the delicious theology of love,' and his aesthetic feeling made him sure that many of the historical traits of the fourth Gospel are convincing. He boldly adopts 'the system of John, according to which the public life of Jesus lasted three years';[3] and with regard to the close of Christ's life he again says, 'We follow the system of John.' Renan's *Life of Jesus* was accompanied and followed by a number of important German works dealing with the criticism of the Gospels and the life of Christ. Among these works are included those of Schenkel, Weizsäcker, Heinrich Julius Holtzmann, and Keim. They have much in common with Renan; they are deeply infected with rationalistic views of Christ's Person, but they speak with admiration of the character of Jesus and of His attempt to found an inward and spiritual kingdom. It is significant that Strauss accused Schenkel of using, in a 'sodden' condition, the materials of Tübingen theology, and of want of frankness in clinging to orthodox phrases

[1] *Op. cit.* p. 266.   [2] *Op. cit.* p. 284.   [3] *Vie de Jésus*, p. 270.

which did not represent his real views. Like Renan, these writers were inclined to draw upon the fourth Gospel in order to supplement the other three. Schenkel adopted the teaching of S. John with regard to Christ's second coming; Holtzmann, while basing his work on the ministry of Christ as recorded by S. Mark, did not wholly exclude S. John; Weizsäcker directly asserted that the fourth Gospel contains 'genuine apostolic reminiscences.' They were struggling with a dilemma. They instinctively felt that S. John's Gospel really adds to our knowledge of the ministry of Christ, but they were resolved not to accept it, because it teaches His Divinity. Weizsäcker in his later book on the *Apostolic Age of the Church*[1] shows this quite plainly. He says, 'It is impossible to imagine any power of faith and philosophy so great as thus to obliterate the recollection of the real life, and to substitute for it this marvellous picture of a Divine Being.' It is assumed that 'the real life' could not have been divine, and the gradual abandonment of the fourth Gospel has been the result. Keim denied the possibility of using it as a historical source, and though a few later rationalistic writers have endeavoured to weave together S. John and the Synoptists, they have on the whole gone back to Strauss and Baur. They consistently ignore the fourth Gospel, or allude to it in order to make the most of the differences between it and the earlier Gospels, and to declare that the Synoptic traditions must be preferred. These arguments would be considerably more plausible if the same writers did not proceed to treat the Synoptic Gospels in precisely the same way as the Fourth. For having attempted to persuade us that the Synoptists are historical whenever they seem to disagree with S. John, they now strain every nerve to prove that they are unhistorical whenever they

[1] Vol. ii. p. 211 (English translation).

record anything that favours S. John's account of our Lord's ministry and Person. At the end they present us not to S. Mark's 'Son of God' but to a 'man of God' of their own creation.

If the authenticity of S. John's Gospel had really been disproved, it would have been incumbent upon every sincere student to reject it. But during the very period when its rejection became an axiom with the critics who presupposed that the New Testament picture of Christ is incredible, its genuineness was defended both in England and on the Continent by scholars of the highest rank, such as Lightfoot, Westcott, Zahn, and Godet.

§ 4. *Present Day Criticism and Rationalism.*[1]

It would be impossible to give in this chapter even the shortest outline of all the history of the criticism of the Gospels during the last thirty years. Broadly speaking, the followers of Baur have been forced to go much further in one direction or another. On the one hand, they have become nihilist, denying that Jesus ever existed, or affirming that we can know practically nothing about Him, and deriving Christian teaching from Buddhism or some esoteric Oriental philosophy. On the other hand, they have become 'fragmentists,' lacking Baur's massive originality, and surrendering his views piecemeal, accepting the genuineness of several of the books of the New Testament which he rejected. Those that have desired to retain the name of Christian have involved themselves in a view of Christianity more pessimistic than that of Baur. According to Baur, Christian doctrine can be held to

[1] It should be observed that a large number of modern non-Christian and semi-Christian writers, though not all, object to the term 'Rationalist' as applied to themselves. They prefer the term 'Liberal,' and give a new sense to the word Rationalism, applying it to certain types of intellectualism in theology.

represent a genuine development of the human mind, though marked by many serious aberrations. But the more recent 'liberalism' is apt to assume that Christianity as taught by Christ was pure, but that as taught by the apostles and the Church of their age, it was exceedingly corrupt. Greek influence upon Christianity is too often regarded as almost entirely evil, and the contribution of the Greek race to Christian thought and life as little better than a pollution. With regard to the origin of the Gospels, the 'liberal' school, by concentrating attention upon the Gospel of S. Mark as our earliest source for a knowledge of the ministry of Christ, has achieved a distinct success. It has taken up the argument advanced in 1837 by C. H. Weisse, that the priority of S. Mark's Gospel can be demonstrated, and that the other two Synoptic Gospels have been based on that of S. Mark and a document or documents containing the sayings of Jesus. This theory is now so widely accepted that at present it completely holds the field. It is regarded as proved by Harnack and von Soden in Germany, by Batiffol and Lagrange in France, and Dr. Sanday and Professor Burkitt in England. The first of these scholars calls for mention as having published valuable monographs on the Synoptic Gospels, as well as large and important works dealing with other departments of theology, and a notable exposition of his own conception of the essence of Christianity. He may be fairly regarded as the most prominent, most learned, and one of the most reverent exponents of a religion which derives its impulse from Christianity though rejecting all its distinctive doctrines. While not accepting the genuineness of S. John's Gospel, he places it at a far earlier date than Schmiedel, who has tried to bring it down again to a date nearer to that selected by Baur. He attributes the third Gospel to S. Luke, the companion of S. Paul, while regarding him as much more artistic than exact. He also assigns the second Gospel to its traditional author, and even dates the first Gospel near the time of the destruction of Jerusalem. He holds that Jesus was conscious of a unique moral nearness to God, a kind of sonship which prompted Him to believe that He was the Messiah. But he has shown a strong tendency to declare spurious, or interpolated, or unhistorical, passages in the Gospels which do not favour his own 'reduced Christianity.' A religion of this type is on the Continent of Europe ordinarily described as 'Liberal' or 'Modern' Protestantism.[1] It is now being propagated so widely and so systematically that it is worth while stating what amount of Christianity the average type of 'liberalism' leaves more or less unquestioned.

There is a Founder whom the 'liberal' theologians call 'Jesus' but not 'Christ.' He was not born of a Virgin, but was the son of Joseph and Mary. He was not divine, but may perhaps be called 'Son of God' in a titular sense, on account of the close moral union which existed between Himself and the Father. His mind must be studied by the ordinary rules of psychology. He gradually developed a sense of His sonship towards God, and then came to believe that He was the Messiah expected by the Jews, and the supernatural 'Son of Man' foretold in the seventh chapter of Daniel—this, however, is not conceded by all 'liberal' critics. He is especially regarded as a Teacher. The prophetic side of His office, like the kingly or Messianic side, is apt to be neglected. He did not at the beginning of His ministry realise that He would be put to death by the Jews; afterwards He saw that He

---

[1] The Modernism which has arisen and been condemned within the Roman Catholic Church has done so little original work in the region of New Testament criticism that it is not necessary to describe it in this chapter.

must die, and believed that the kingdom would come when that death was accomplished. He attributed no propitiatory character to His death. It was a self-denying act, a fine moral example, not a means of atonement between God and man. With this reduction of the doctrine of the Atonement there is usually to be found in 'liberal' theology a reduced view of the guilt of sin and man's need of a Saviour. Christ's bodily resurrection and ascension are emphatically denied, and the testimony of the evangelists to these events explained as mere legend based on certain phantasms of Him which the disciples saw or imagined, or on the belief that Jesus was living with God, because of His moral union with God, or the belief that He must be alive, because He had before His death declared that He would return.

Like the Gnostics of ancient times, the modern 'liberals' treat as Jewish fables the teaching of Jesus about His second coming, the resurrection of the dead, and the judgment. 'Liberalism' is satisfied to think of a continuous growth of the good which is already in us. And it dislikes all notion of an interference, any interposition of God in the work of redeeming man, any cataclysm in establishing the reign of righteousness. Hence while reverent epithets are often given to Christ, 'liberal' Protestantism, when it is honest and outspoken, always denies that He is God. Consistently with this denial, even its best representatives, such as Harnack, denounce as 'sub-Christian,' *i e.* semi-pagan, the whole idea of man being made partaker of the divine nature through union with Christ. This doctrine, which is rooted in the teaching of S. Paul and S. John, and was so magnificently developed by the Greek Fathers of the Church, is elaborately attacked or ignored as a fiction. With this denial goes the whole doctrine of the sacraments. Instead of efficacious means by which God acts morally upon the human soul, the sacraments are nothing but bare symbols, and sometimes it is denied that Jesus instituted Christian baptism or desired His disciples to continue any celebration of the meal which He ate with them the night before His death. 'Liberalism' has valued Christ's teaching about the kingdom of God, so far as that kingdom is regarded as inward and as a moral bond between believers. But the Christian conception of the Church vanishes. If there is no divine Saviour, it is seen that there cannot be a body through the members of which He acts upon the world. Baur objected to S. Paul's Epistle to the Ephesians because it contains 'the material conception of the Catholic Church'; Julicher finds in the high priestly prayer of our Lord in S. John xvii. a forged utterance inspired by a later idea of the unity of the Church; Harnack repudiates Christ's mention of the Church in S. Matt. xvi. He is copied by Dr. James Moffatt in his *Historical New Testament*, where we are told that 'to suppose that Jesus contemplated a visible church as the embodiment of His gospel is almost to be guilty of a historical atrocity' (p. 269).

The Protestantism of the sixteenth century constantly appealed to the doctrinal teaching of S. Paul. But the so-called 'modern Protestantism' is intensely hostile to it, attacking the very roots of S. Paul's teaching about our Lord's divinity, His past and present atoning work, as well as the Pauline doctrine concerning the Church and the sacraments. This hostility is sometimes masked by praises of the apostle, especially where his name is honoured as it deserves.

It should lastly be noticed that with a repudiation of Christian eschatology, 'liberal' Protestantism has decidedly, though not universally, tended to minimise the ascetic element in Christ's teaching, and to lay a rather one-sided stress on the joyful and genial nature of Christian ethics.

That 'liberal' Protestantism is hardly distinguishable from a modernised form of Judaism is self-evident. And it has lately been treated as such in the remarkable commentary on the Synoptic Gospels composed by a leading English Jew, Mr. Claude Montefiore, published in 1909, and in his work, published the next year, on *The Moral Teaching of Jesus*. These books were marked by an enthusiasm for the teaching of our Lord so genuine as to create a profound impression on English Judaism. The learned author believes that Jesus supposed Himself to be the Messiah, though he does not accept as genuine the crucial passage in which Jesus declares that 'no man knoweth the Father, but the Son.' Mr. Montefiore's work is built on the foundation of Gentile rationalism of a pronounced though not extreme type. It must therefore stand or fall with that system.

§ 5. *The Eschatological Critics.*

Recently this comfortable Christianity, so carefully reduced by the professor in his study to fit the capacity of the man in the street, has received some very rude shocks. First Wrede assailed it with his negations. Then the new 'eschatological' school, represented by Johannes Weiss, and more brilliantly by Schweitzer, attacked it as trenchantly as the 'modern' school has ever attacked orthodox Christianity. They have fastened their arguments to the eschatology of the Gospels, that is, the teaching about the last things, the end of the world, the future resurrection, the judgment day, and the kingdom to be founded when that judgment is complete. They claim to show that the attitude of Jesus towards these articles of the Jewish faith of His time prove conclusively that He was not 'modern.' Paradoxical as some of the utterances of this school have been, and meagre as is their portrait of Christ, they have done some useful work, both destructive and constructive.

Jesus, they assert, shows no such mental development during His ministry as the 'liberal' Protestant professors have declared. And the Synoptic Gospels cannot be treated as waste paper whenever they happen to conflict with a conception of Jesus created in the nineteenth century. He knew that He was the Messiah, and appears in the Gospels throughout as a prophet preaching that the kingdom of God would come. He believed that there would be a great catastrophe at the end of the world, and the title 'Son of Man,' which He so frequently employed, cannot with any degree of sanity be treated as an interpolation. It actually forms a strong guarantee of the primitive and trustworthy character of the passages in which it occurs. It was unintelligible to Greeks, and goes back to the old Hebrew stage of Christianity.

The kingdom of God is not a mere union of hearts and the reign of a gradually spreading morality. Its coming will be outward, open, supernatural, operated by God and His angels. Man is to prepare for it by repentance, by passive patience, and not by effort or active organisation. It will be established in this present world. When Jesus announced it, He announced it as something still future, but all in the immediate future. It did not come when He began His ministry, though He at first expected that it would come during His ministry. When He met with opposition and rebuffs (here the eschatological school agrees with some of the 'modern' theologians), He believed that it would come after His death. He also believed that His death had a highly supernatural significance, for He thought that in Himself there would be summed up all those woes which the Jews believed would be the painful prelude of the golden age. He understood, like Caiaphas, that it was expedient that one should die for the people, nay for the world, for by His death others would be saved from dying.

Further, the eschatological school insists that the moral teaching of Jesus is not of that genial and joyful character which attracts the German bourgeois. It contained a strongly ascetic element, it was predominantly 'other-worldly,' the precepts delivered in the Sermon on the Mount being intended for the brief interval between the time when they were delivered and the new miraculous existence. The beatitudes are not exhortations, but mere serious statements that those who possess certain qualities are shown by this very fact to be predestined to be members of the coming kingdom. Jesus does not found the kingdom of God, He waits for it, and the 'mystery of the kingdom' is the secret that the movement of repentance, begun by the Baptist and furthered by Jesus, will be quickly followed by the dawn of the kingdom. It is impending, and human prayer and repentance are causing it to come quickly.

Lastly, the eschatological school repudiates the 'modern Protestant' conception of the sacraments. It asserts that if this conception were true, the Church would never have continued the use of sacraments. We may indeed ask why should a Church which repudiated circumcision continue to use a merely symbolic baptism, and why should it commemorate by a feast the death of its Founder if the feast only spoke of a pitiful tragedy? From the eschatological point of view Christian baptism is intelligible. John baptised 'unto repentance,' giving to his adherents a provision for securing that forgiveness of sins, that salvation, which they could only secure from the Messiah. To use a favourite metaphor of the early Christians, John's baptism 'sealed' the recipients to secure them against condemnation. But the baptism of the Christian Church was more than this. It was 'with the Spirit' as well as 'with water.' And the object of being baptised with water at the hands of John the Baptist was not only to secure forgiveness but also to secure future baptism with the Spirit. Since Pentecost the Spirit has been present with the Church, and so, according to Schweitzer, the 'Christianising' of baptism consisted in nothing more than adding baptism with the Spirit both logically and in point of time to baptism with water.

As for the Eucharist, it was not a mere memorial, and had practically nothing to do with the satisfaction of hunger. 'The act of Jesus is an end in itself, and the significance of the celebration consists in the fact that it is He Himself who makes the distribution.' So says Schweitzer. His explanation is inadequate, for it does not do justice to the fact that Jesus used the words, 'This is My body' and 'This is My blood,' but it at least implies that the meal was Messianic, and that it had a definite reference to an immediate future when Jesus and His disciples would be once more united at the same table. Jesus believed that He, and He alone, could distribute in actual reality that feast which the Jews hoped to enjoy in the kingdom of the Messiah. In His mind, as in the mind of the primitive Church, His last meal was neither a mere meal nor a bare symbol of His death.

The eschatological school, which represents the last phase of Judaeo-German rationalism, is open to a no less severe criticism than the Teutonic rationalism which it has so roughly handled. History has told us very plainly what manner of man the eschatological enthusiast is wont to be. The frenzied utterances of the early Montanists, the wilder Anabaptists, the visionary Camisards, the gibbering early Irvingites, all contribute something to the picture. The New Testament shows us traces of the same spirit. In S. Paul's

Epistles to the Thessalonians we find a tender rebuke and correction of some earnest and excitable Christians who were expecting the immediate coming of Christ and end of the world. That they did not represent the normal tone of primitive Christianity should be obvious to any thoughtful student. A Church which so quickly organised its ministry, its worship, and its charity, a Church which at once set to work to evangelise first the Holy Land and then the Roman Empire, must have 'learned Christ' very differently. The mere survival of S. Paul's Epistles, with their deliberate moderating influence on the more excitable elements in Christian thought and practice, shows that the mind of the Church was sober. Otherwise his letters would have suffered the same fate as the prophetic roll thrust by King Jehoiakim into the flames. And so great and sane and moral a movement as early Christianity cannot have derived itself from a Christ who was intoxicated with the delusions which are attributed to Him by the latest form of criticism.

But both 'liberal Protestantism' and Judaeo-German rationalism are of value to the man who can estimate the positive elements which they contain. And the latter form of rationalism is a most useful corrective of the former. It has been right in showing, like the extreme infidel school, that the theories of Harnack, Wernle and others, make an incredible chasm between the religion of Jesus and that of S. Paul, or of the primitive Church as a whole. The more the 'liberals' have whittled away the consciousness which Jesus had of His divinity and ignored the ascetic element in His teaching, and the more they have denied that He taught the atoning efficacy of His death and the reality of sacramental grace, the more they have darkened the origin of Christianity for the modern inquirer. On the other hand, the 'liberals' are able to retort that the religion taught by Jesus is a religion for ordinary life, it was meant for this world before it was meant for the world to come, and the impression which Jesus produced upon His disciples was not the impression of 'an imperious ruler' but a gracious Teacher. The kingdom was not primarily a kingdom of catastrophes. Jesus Himself taught that it was to work like leaven. Neither party has done anything like justice to the religion of the Gospels, or to that Person whose relation to His followers has from the first been understood by all true Christians to be something essentially different from that of Moses to Judaism, or of S. Francis to the Franciscans, or of John Wesley to the Methodists. By studying the writings of both parties one can learn how rash it is to make reckless concessions to the latest conjecture which may pose as critical. An enlightened orthodoxy has difficulties to face, but it has no such fatal difficulties as those which beset the schools which we have briefly described. And it will be an unfortunate thing for English scholarship and English Christianity if there is any great increase of the tendency to prefer what is smart to what is solid, and to make this country a home for the lost causes of unbelief.

In concluding our remarks on the course of modern criticism of the Gospels, it will not be narrow-minded if we strike a patriotic note. During the last forty years Englishmen have changed from one of the most insular to one of the most cosmopolitan of races. The new spirit has deeply affected religion, literature, and theology. It is a spirit which has hardly yet learnt self-control. It has shown itself in earnest but not always well digested plans for the reunion of Christendom, and in the enthusiastic study of certain classes of foreign books dealing with the earliest history of Christianity. Even students seem sometimes to forget what a large amount of the best critical work on the Gospels has been done in England. Any country might have been proud to have produced a Lightfoot and a Westcott, and passages which they wrote on the Gospel according to S. John are as well worth weighing as anything that has been written during the last twenty years on the same subject. The study of the same Gospel has been stimulated in the wisest way by Dr. Sanday's *Authorship and Historical Character of the Fourth Gospel* (1872), and his *Criticism of the Fourth Gospel* (1908).

The Synoptic Gospels have been discussed in England with a sense of responsibility and minuteness of investigation which is on a level with the very best German work, and sometimes above it. Thus in 1880 there was published Mr. Rushbrooke's *Synopticon*, side by side with which may be mentioned Dr. Arthur Wright's *Synopsis of the Gospels* (1896 and 1903).

Sir John Hawkins published his *Horae Synopticae* in 1899, and a second and improved edition of it in 1909. It is a work which is of the highest critical quality, and whether one is in entire agreement with it or not, he will find it difficult to mention any foreign book which is quite as good. Dr. Stanton has published two large volumes on the Gospels as historical documents (1903 and 1909), which are also of a very high quality. The commentaries on the Synoptic Gospels in the English language, such as those by the Venerable W. C. Allen, Dr. Plummer, and Dr. Swete, cannot reasonably be said to be inferior to any recent Continental works, and Dr. Sanday's *Outlines of the Life of Christ* (1906) is just what is wanted by those who know that we cannot have such a thing as a full biography of our Lord, but may learn enough to teach us His character. To this must be added the invaluable *Studies in the Synoptic Problem*, by Members of the University of Oxford, edited by Dr. Sanday (1911).

CHAPTER III

THE SYNOPTIC PROBLEM

§ 1. *Introductory.*

LET us leave the fourth Gospel for the present and concentrate our attention upon the first three Gospels. The first literary problem concerns the order in which they were written, and the dates. They do not appear in precisely the same order in all the old manuscripts of the Gospels and writings which mention the Gospels. S. Irenaeus quotes them in this order: Matthew, Luke, Mark, John,[1] and: John, Luke, Matthew, Mark.[2] Clement of Alexandria is said by Eusebius[3] to have mentioned an old tradition which placed first the Gospels with the genealogies, as written first, Matthew and Luke, and then Mark and John. But much the most usual order is that which we have in our modern Bibles. S. Irenaeus has it as well as the other arrangements just mentioned, and it is found in the Muratorian Canon and in almost all the Greek manuscripts. With one important exception, and this exception is not hard to explain, our order is almost certainly right. There is now an almost unanimous agreement among scholars that Mark is the earliest and John the latest of the Gospels. Opinions vary as to the relative dates of Matthew and Luke. But it is agreed that both are later

---

[1] *Adv. Haer.* iii. 10-11, § 7.   [2] *Op. cit.* 11, § 11.
[3] *H. E.* vi. 14.

than Mark. That the Gospel according to S. Luke was written, as was believed in the second century, by the author of Acts, and that this author was really S. Luke, the companion of S. Paul, is a view which is supported by abundant internal evidence, and is no longer confined to orthodox Christian circles. Some years ago it seemed to me that this conclusion was proved up to the hilt by Sir John Hawkins in his *Horae Synopticae*, and since the publication of that book it has increased in favour. If we assign the third Gospel to S. Luke, we can hardly place it later than A.D. 80, unless the author was very much younger than S. Paul. It may even have been written between A.D. 60 and 70. Our first Gospel raises more difficult problems than the third. As it stands, it was written in Greek and not translated from Hebrew or Aramaic, in spite of the Hebraisms which it contains. It is also composite, as will be shown in detail later. But that one of the largest constituent elements in it was a previous work written by S. Matthew can only be denied by an excessive scepticism. The antiquity of this original work gave rise to the idea that the Gospel based upon it is the oldest Gospel. Even in its present condition the perceptible Jewish tinge of the first Gospel, and the manner in which the destruction of Jerusalem is confused with the catastrophe which is to be the immediate herald of the end of the world, decidedly suggest that it was written before, but not long before, A.D. 70, when the Romans took 'the Holy City.' A later date can only be assigned to this Gospel on the hypothesis that the writer, who elsewhere carefully adapted his material to his purpose, left unaltered certain puzzling passages which must have been written before Jerusalem was destroyed. This hypothesis seems far from probable. S. Mark's Gospel as a whole must have been written not later than the sixties, perhaps early in the sixties. The

THE SYNOPTIC PROBLEM

date of the Gospels will be more fully discussed in the chapters dedicated to each Gospel.

The three earlier Gospels present us with a story marked by unity of arrangement. The order of events is similar, the events recorded are usually the same from the preaching of John the Baptist to the resurrection of Jesus Christ. The unity is so unmistakable that at least as early as the time of the celebrated early historian and critic Eusebius of Caesarea, A.D. 320, the three Gospels were arranged in parallel columns. The awkward but now indispensable name of 'Synoptic Gospels' has been applied to them for nearly a hundred years, because they can be so tabulated that the reader can simultaneously get a common view or synopsis of the three. And the 'Synoptic problem' consists in the difficulties raised by the similarity and dissimilarity of the three. It is because the similarity is often so astonishing that we find it all the harder to explain the dissimilarity when it exists. It is not as if another arrangement of material was impossible. The fourth Gospel alone is enough to show that the 'memoirs,' as S. Justin calls them, might have been edited very differently. It is conceivable that a most edifying 'Life of Jesus Christ,' or selection of incidents in His ministry, might have been composed on lines equally distinct from the Synoptists and from S. John. And the first answer that we can give to the Synoptic question is that either all three Gospels depend on one common source, or two of them followed the order which they found in the third. The latter solution is now seldom called in question. It is now the common opinion that S. Mark's Gospel was copied and followed by the author of the first Gospel and by S. Luke. They added to his Gospel from other precious sources; but they used his work in a form substantially identical with that in which we read it to-day.

To test the above statement let us notice some details of interest and importance, many of which can easily be examined by those who have enjoyed no long technical training in the study of the Greek Testament. The next chapter will contain an account of those 'Sayings of the Lord' which are found in our first and third Gospels. But there are points which concern the methods and motives of the Synoptic writers which may properly be mentioned here as corroborating the accuracy of the solution now so generally accepted.

§ 2. *Luke is based on Mark.*

The first indication of an answer to the problem is suggested at once in the prologue of S. Luke's Gospel. He says, 'Forasmuch as many have taken in hand to draw up a narrative concerning those matters which have been fulfilled among us, even as they delivered them unto us, which from the beginning were eye-witnesses and ministers of the word, it seemed good to me also, having traced the course of all things accurately from the first, to write unto thee in order, most excellent Theophilus, that thou mightest know the certainty concerning those things wherein thou wast instructed.' Now most of this is perfectly clear. It proves that other narratives of the ministry of our Lord had been written before S. Luke wrote; that oral instruction about that ministry had been given to Theophilus and apparently other converts to Christianity; that S. Luke had known eye-witnesses and ministers of the Word who knew our Lord's teaching from the beginning, but was not himself one of these eye-witnesses; that he was convinced that his narrative was accurate and in chronological order.

It will naturally occur to us to ask whether among the many writers to whom he alludes we can reckon the author of the Gospel according to S. Matthew. The answer is now almost universally given in the negative. Some early critics, who belonged to the Tübingen school, held that Luke was dependent upon Matthew, and maintained that Mark was the latest, and dependent upon the other two. The theory was intended to fit their attempted reconstruction of the early history of the Church, according to which Christianity, after passing through a stage of Jewish unitarianism and Gentile ditheism, became a Catholicism with elements derived from both. The three Synoptic Gospels were supposed to fit these three stages of progress or perversion. But in more recent years opinion has usually tended in another direction. There is no proof or even probability that S. Luke copied Matthew. At the very start he would have found in the story of the Magi coming from a heathen country to visit the Infant Jesus something which would have appealed to his deep poetic instinct and his desire to show that Jesus was ' a light to lighten the Gentiles.' But he shows no trace of any acquaintance with Matthew's account of the sacred infancy, nor does he enrich his story of the resurrection by copying the command of the risen Lord to ' make disciples of all the nations.' Besides such omissions, the linguistic similarity between Matthew and Luke is too slight to warrant the supposition of dependence.

Just as it is practically certain that Matthew was not one of the sources incorporated into Luke, so it is practically certain that Luke was not one of the sources incorporated into Matthew. Widely as the tone of Luke differs from Matthew, it is almost inconceivable that this difference of tone would have wholly prevented the first evangelist from employing the third Gospel if he had known it. At first sight we are surprised to find that Matthew and Luke occasionally agree with one another when they both diverge from

Mark, and this agreement was not long ago thought to point to the probability that S. Luke had a copy of Matthew. But in several of these cases the agreement is simply the result of corruptions in the manuscripts, and the above hypothesis therefore remains unproved. As no one supposes that Matthew and Luke are based upon the Gospel according to S. John, the plan of which is essentially different, we are left with Mark, the simplest and shortest Gospel. Did S. Luke use it?

The question falls under three divisions.

I. The question of style and language. Does the language of Luke show that it is derived from that of Mark?

II. The question of contents. Do the contents of Mark and Luke correspond so closely as to justify the belief that S. Luke knew the whole Gospel of S. Mark?

III. The question of order. Does the arrangement of material in Luke prove that the author found it arranged in the order found in Mark?

All these three questions are better answered by an affirmative than by a negative reply. This reply does not gain its full strength until the first Gospel is also utilised. It is only when three parallel passages are read side by side in Greek that it can be seen that the Greek of Mark frequently accounts for the Greek of the other two evangelists, a fact which can be effectively tested by underlining the words which the three Gospels have in common. And it is only by comparing the contents and order of these three Gospels that one can see that the order which underlies the three is Mark's. Where Matthew leaves it, Luke keeps it; where Luke deserts it, Matthew goes with it. Matthew and Luke never agree in deserting Mark.

But although the proof only approaches demonstration if we compare all three Gospels, a comparison of

THE SYNOPTIC PROBLEM

either Matthew or Luke with Mark gives us luminous indications. Luke omits the following important passages in Mark, besides making other smaller omissions:—

1. Mark iii. 20-21. Our Lord's friends say that 'He is beside Himself.'

2. Mark iv. 26-29. The parable of the seed growing silently.

3. Mark vi. 17-20. The death of John the Baptist.

4. Mark vi. 45-viii. 26. Walking on the water; healing at Gennesaret; the tradition of the elders; defilement; healing of the Syrophoenician woman's daughter; the cure of a deaf man with an impediment in his speech: a second miraculous multiplication of loaves; the demand for a sign; the 'leaven of the Pharisees'; and the cure of a blind man with spittle.

5. Mark ix. 11-13. The question about the coming of Elias.

6. Mark x. 35-41. The ambitious request of James and John.

7. Mark xi. 11. Our Lord's first visit to the temple after His entrance into Jerusalem.

8. Mark xi. 12-14, 19-21. The cursing of the barren fig-tree and the discourse about it.

9. Mark xiv. 3-9. The anointing at Bethany.

10. Mark xv. 1 (cf. xiv. 53). The second meeting of the Sanhedrin to condemn Jesus to death.

How are we to explain these omissions if we accept the hypothesis that S. Luke knew and used our Mark? Either the passages in question were not in his copy of Mark, or he left them out on purpose. The latter hypothesis appears to be true, for we can in many cases find an intelligible reason for S. Luke's omissions.

1. The statement that our Lord was 'beside Himself' is omitted as derogatory to His honour.

2. The parable of the seed growing silently has a parallel in the parable of the mustard seed in Luke xiii. 19, drawn from another source than Mark.

3. S. Luke knows the facts relating to the Baptist's imprisonment and death. He records them in iii. 19-20; ix. 7-9, and for the sake of brevity says no more.

4. Various texts in Luke suggest that the author knew Mark vi. 45-viii. 26. But he omits Christ walking on the water, possibly as similar to the stilling of the tempest in viii. 22-25.

The tradition of the elders and the matter of ceremonial defilement probably had little interest for Gentile readers.

The words of Christ to the Syrophoenician woman were liable to be understood as confining salvation permanently to the Jews, and are therefore omitted.

The cure of the dumb man and the blind man with spittle, may perhaps be omitted because the means used was one employed in heathen magic.

The miraculous feeding of the four thousand is omitted as similar to the miraculous feeding of the five thousand recorded in Luke ix. 14.

The demand for a sign from heaven is met later in Luke xi. 16, 29 ff., and the caution against the leaven of the Pharisees comes in a different connection in Luke xii. 1.

5. The question about Elias is probably omitted because Gentile readers tended to take less interest in the Baptist. The early Hebrew Christians, on the contrary, took a deep interest in him.

6. The ambitious request of James and John is omitted out of a tenderness towards these apostles.

7. This is omitted in accordance with S. Luke's special treatment of the narrative of the Passion. His account, which was probably derived from special oral sources, will be described in our chapter on S. Luke. Under the same heading we must include 10.

THE SYNOPTIC PROBLEM

8. The cursing of the barren fig-tree is omitted because of the parable resembling it in xiii. 6 ff.

9. The anointing at Bethany is omitted because of the similar anointing in the Pharisee's house in vii. 36 ff.

Now it is possible that S. Luke omitted all the above passages by accident, for we must remember that an ancient scholar was not in the position of a modern one, who, if he loses or injures a book, can usually buy another copy the same week. And a good case can be made for the theory that certain of these passages were not in the original edition of Mark. S. Luke may have only had at his disposal a Marcan Gospel which omitted the 'great interpolation,' as it is sometimes called—vi. 45-viii. 26—and this view does gain considerable support from the fact that almost the whole of it is found in Matthew.[1] The last explanation is simple, and to some students appears almost too simple. But whether we hold it or not, the fact remains that we are left with the result that S. Luke appears to have utilised almost the whole contents of Mark.

If S. Luke possessed a written collection of our Lord's sayings before he got a copy of Mark, he would naturally be inclined to omit similar or identical passages when he found them in Mark. And if S. Luke had any wish to abbreviate, he would omit facts which seemed to him to be unimportant, or which would puzzle the ordinary reader. This would specially be the case if passages seemed derogatory to the dignity of our Lord or the character of the apostles. The simple way in which S. Mark depicts the failings of the apostles, and the emotions of our Lord and the limitations of His power, raised difficulties. They are toned down in Matthew and Luke. To the sincere Christian the limitations under which his Saviour chose

[1] See *Studies in the Synoptic Problem*, edited by Dr. W. Sanday, pp. 60 ff., 417.

to live and work are 'the condescension of pity and not the failure of power.' But the Jew thought otherwise; and the well-educated pagans liked their wise men to show an apathy superior to emotion. Doubtless they ridiculed some of the passages in Mark. And S. Luke modified and left out such passages, just as he omits as unnecessary such touches of 'local colour' as the twice repeated statement in Mark that Jesus and His disciples had no time for their meals (Mark iii. 20; vi. 31), and the story of the young man who followed Christ when the disciples fled, and himself fled naked when about to be arrested (Mark xiv. 51, 52).

If we pass from comparing the contents of Mark and Luke to comparing the order of the narrative, we find our theory corroborated. There are, exclusive of the story of the Passion, only seven real variations in Luke from the order in Mark.

1. Mark iii. 7-19a altered in Luke vi. 12-19.
2. ,, iv. 37, 38 ,, ,, viii. 23.
3. ,, v. 3-8 ,, ,, viii. 28, 29.
4. ,, v. 42 ,, ,, viii. 42.
5. ,, v. 42b, 43 ,, ,, viii. 55b, 56.
6. ,, vi 44 ,, ,, ix. 14a.
7. ,, xii 8 ,, ,, xx. 15.

None of these are of apparent importance except the first, which was caused by S. Luke's wish to provide an introduction to our Lord's 'Sermon on the Level Place.' The order of Mark is better kept in Luke than in Matthew.

§ 3. *Matthew is based on Mark.*

The phenomena which we find in Luke we find, though with variations, in Matthew. The evangelist has utilised the work of S. Mark. Like S. Luke he alters the rough colloquial and semi-Aramaic language of S. Mark into something that is slightly more classical

THE SYNOPTIC PROBLEM

and elegant. As a very simple instance we may mention that in Matt. xii. 31 we have 'men' for the quite Semitic phrase 'the sons of men' in Mark iii. 28. It has also been noticed that he systematically obliterates those instances of the use of the present tense in which S. Mark delights. S. Luke, in spite of being influenced by the somewhat un-Hellenic language of the Greek version of the Old Testament, can write good Greek. When we compare parallel passages in the three Gospels we see that in some cases Matthew manifests a better style than Mark, while Luke has both a better style and better words. Nevertheless, the three evangelists often agree verbally, and Matthew, though it has some favourite distinctive phrases, such as 'the kingdom of the heavens,' sometimes follows Mark practically word for word. For this students should compare such passages as

Matt. ix. 6	with Mark ii. 10.
,, ix. 12 f.	,, ii. 17.
,, x. 21 f.	,, xiii. 12 f.
,, xvi. 23	,, viii. 33.
,, xix. 6	,, x. 8b f.
,, xix. 30	,, x. 31.
,, xx. 28	,, x. 45.
,, xxvi. 24	,, xiv. 21.

Matthew omits the following important passages in Mark :—

1. Mark i. 21-28. Jesus casts out an unclean spirit in the synagogue at Capernaum.

2. Mark i. 35-38. Jesus retires before preaching in Galilee.

3. Mark iv. 26-29. The parable of the seed growing silently.

4. Mark vii. 32-37. The healing of a deaf man with an impediment in his speech.

5. Mark viii. 22-26. The healing of the blind man of Bethsaida.

6. Mark ix. 38-40. The incident of the exorcist who had received no commission from Christ.

7. Mark xi. 11. The first visit of Jesus to the temple in the week of His Passion.

8. Mark xii. 41-44. The widow's mite.

An explanation of at least some of those omissions appears to be possible, though we ought to be cautious in advancing them.

1. Matthew omits the scene in the synagogue, with the subsequent amazement of the people, in order to introduce an allusion to the impression created by our Lord in vii. 28, 29, at the end of the Sermon on the Mount.

2. Matthew perhaps omits the retirement of our Lord because it would interrupt the triplet of miracles here recorded. We shall see later how constantly the first evangelist arranges his subjects in fixed numbers, probably because he had found this method useful in oral teaching.

3. The parable of the seed growing silently may be omitted because it has a parallel in the parable of the tares.

4 and 5. The miracles of healing the deaf and the blind man are omitted, as there are parallels in the great chapter of miracles, Matt. ix.

6. The sanction given by our Lord to the work of the exorcist who was not a disciple may have been omitted lest it should be quoted as a precedent by such vagabond exorcists as were found by S. Paul at Ephesus (Acts xix. 13).

7. The first visit to the temple may have been omitted for the sake of simplification. The evangelist wished to connect Mark xi. 11 with 15-18, describing Christ's entrance into Jerusalem, thereby also connecting Mark xi. 12-14, 20-25, the different verses concerning the barren fig-tree.

8. The incident of the widow's mite is omitted because in Mark it forms the conclusion of our Lord's

denunciation of the scribes. This is replaced by a longer denunciation, so that the story would be rendered less appropriate.

That all three evangelists, even S. Mark, did abbreviate and omit incidents which they knew, becomes more evident the more their Gospels are studied. And it is worth noting that the Gospels according to S. Matthew and S. Luke and the Acts are very nearly of the same length. And it has been reasonably conjectured that they were all alike intended to fill a roll of papyrus of some definite size. As these are the three longest books in the New Testament, we can say that if the above idea is correct, the authors were restrained from exceeding their limits by the most practical of all considerations. This is not mere conjecture. For there was a certain recognised length for books, a 'tome' or cut of papyrus. And by comparing these three books of the New Testament with certain great classical works, such as Homer's *Iliad* and *Odyssey*, we find that the former were of more than the average length.

While the contents of Mark are almost all to be found in Matthew, we find in some places a decided difference in order. From iii. 1 to iv. 22 Matthew follows the order of Mark i. 2-20. After this we find sharp divergences until Mark vi. We have noted above how Matthew postpones an account of the impression produced by our Lord upon His hearers, and we find no very close adherence to the Marcan thread until we come to Matt. xiii. 53-58 (= Mark vi. 1-6). Then we find that the mission given by Christ to His disciples in Mark vi. is omitted, having been previously anticipated by a long discourse of Christ to the disciples in Matt. x. When Matt. xiv. is begun, the order of S. Mark is usually kept. At first sight the divergences are apt to conceal the agreements, and therefore the following table is inserted to show them both. The passages in italics come from other sources than Mark.

Mark.	*Matthew.*
	The story of the infancy.
The Baptist.	The Baptist and *his discourse.*
Baptism of Jesus.	Baptism of Jesus
The Temptation.	The Temptation
	Sayings at the Temptation.
Call of the Apostles.	Call of the Apostles
	Sermon on the Mount.
Miracles on the first day.	ix. Group of Miracles.
Miracles and Sayings on the Sabbath.	viii. *Centurion's servant.*
Appointment of the Twelve.	x. Appointment of the Twelve
	x. Sending out and *charge to the Apostles.*
	xi. *Discourse about John.*
	xii. Sayings on the Sabbath.
Satan divided against Satan.	xii. Satan divided against Satan.
	xii. *Sign of Jonah.*
Christ's mother and brethren.	xii. Christ's mother and brethren.
Parables.	xiii. Many Parables.
Miracles.	
In His own country.	In His own country.
Sending out the Apostles.	
Herod and John.	Herod and John.
Miracles, feeding, etc.	Many miracles, feeding, etc.
S. Peter's Confession.	S. Peter's Confession.
First Prediction of the Passion.	First Prediction of the Passion.
On Discipleship.	On Discipleship.
The Transfiguration.	The Transfiguration.
On Elijah.	On Elijah.
Dumb Epileptic Boy.	Epileptic Boy.
Second Prediction of the Passion.	Second Prediction of the Passion.
	Coin in the Fish's Mouth.
Various Sayings.	Various Sayings.
Blessing of Children.	Blessing of Children.
Renunciation of Riches.	Renunciation of Riches.
Third Prediction of the Passion.	Third Prediction of the Passion.
Request of James and John.	Request of James and John.
The Blind Man at Jericho.	Two Blind Men at Jericho.

After this the story of the Passion begins.

The above tables, necessarily abbreviated and imperfect, show that while Matthew is influenced by the order of Mark, the writer deserts that order in nearly a quarter of his Gospel, viz. in Matt. viii.-xiii., containing 252 verses. Yet even here he had before him either our Mark, or something equivalent to a large part of it, for out of the 252 verses there are 108 which are practically parallel with Mark.[1] If we could find no reason for the order chosen, we might seriously doubt if he had before him our existing Mark. But there are two reasons which appear to be quite evident. First, he wishes to add a large amount of material which is absent in Mark, and of this we shall speak presently. Secondly, he tries to put both his Marcan and his other material into compendious blocks. Christ's teaching is contained in five such blocks. Chaps. v.-vii., x., and xiii. comprise His teaching as to fundamental morality, missions, and parables, xviii. speaks of children and forgiveness, xxiii.-xxv. of the Pharisees and the Last Things. Further, chaps. viii.-ix. give specimens of His 'mighty' works, and chaps. xi.-xii. show how His words and His works were received. The writer tried to group the facts in such a way as to aid the memory of teachers and catechumens. So he takes miracles that are strewn about in Mark and places them together in viii.-ix. As our Lord's words about the Sabbath gain point when they are studied in connection with His denunciation of the Pharisees, the evangelist detaches them from Mark ii. and iii. and places them in a great anti-Pharisaic passage in Matt. xii. So the choice and the sending out of the apostles are placed together. We can see the same process at work in the later chapters, where there are omissions for the sake of

[1] See Sir John Hawkins, *Expository Times*, vol. xii. p. 471; vol. xiii. p. 20.

simplification (see above, p. 76) and important sayings that are not in Mark.

It seems then that the majority of modern scholars are justified in their belief that the first and the third Gospel in our New Testament are based upon the second. The authors sometimes corrected S. Mark's Greek, and sometimes considerably modified what he said. There has perhaps been too great a readiness to believe that they made these modifications to serve dogmatic interests which they had at heart. We must take into account the strong probability that the practice of oral teaching had done something to crystallise slightly different reports of the same incidents. And this theory is greatly strengthened by the fact that some of the widest divergences from S. Mark occur in the other narratives of the Passion. The death of Christ was so important, the story was so often repeated, additional details were so earnestly prized, that primitive Christian teachers had in their own minds enough to enable them to treat any written record with considerable freedom.

When we first realise how S. Mark's work was incorporated by the other evangelists into their own Gospels, it seems strange and very alien from the methods of respectable modern writers. Plagiarism, unacknowledged appropriation of another's labour, is nowadays not a recommendation but a condemnation. But all the evangelists regarded the matter on another plane. S. Mark does not call his Gospel his own, but simply that 'of Jesus Christ, the Son of God.' The Gospel was the common property of the Church. And it was still so much on the lips of those who knew either the Master or His apostles that the evangelists felt themselves free both to copy and correct what they found written. Less than a hundred years later S. Mark's work would neither have been copied nor altered in the same degree. To the Catholic it would have been

THE SYNOPTIC PROBLEM 81

too sacred, to the Gnostic it would have been too
carnal. The first would have left it reverently alone,
the second would have turned it into a Greek romance.

§ 4. *Non-Marcan Sources.*

In addition to the Gospel written by S. Mark,
Matthew and Luke show the use of written accounts
of our Lord's sayings. Mark contains comparatively
few of His discourses, the other two Gospels contain
them in rich abundance. And just as the two later
evangelists, in spite of the changes which they sometimes make in the style of S. Mark, have preserved
traces of his style, so they both show traces of another
document. More probably they used two different
versions of one document. From it were extracted
the Sermon on the Mount (Matt. v.-vii.; Luke vi.); the
sending out of the apostles (Matt. x.; Luke x.); the
discourse about the Baptist (Matt. xi.; Luke vii.);
and many other isolated sayings of our Lord. These
discourses and sayings of our Lord were written in
a simple and Hebraic style, such as we can readily
believe was His usual manner of speech. Luke has
kept what seems to be the more faithful reproduction
of the original order, Matthew has perhaps the more
original terms of expression. In Matthew the sayings
are arranged in large blocks, admirably adapted for
catechetical instruction. In Luke they are recorded
separately, and in some cases they are given in connection with the circumstances which led up to them.
If we read the Lord's Prayer (Matt. vi. 9-13; Luke
xi. 1-4); the treasure and the heart (Matt. vi. 19-21;
Luke xii. 33, 34); God and mammon (Matt. vi. 24;
Luke xvi. 13), we see how one evangelist combines
what the other keeps separate. In addition to sayings of our Lord, there was a certain amount of
history which linked those sayings together. Such

a blending of history and sayings is found in the preaching of the Baptist, the temptation of our Lord, and the Centurion's servant. All of these are found in a very similar form in Matthew and Luke.

With regard to the document or documents used in addition to Mark for the composition of Matthew and Luke, exact knowledge is impossible. Critics have given, and are still giving, the minutest attention to the subject, believing that here there exists a record of our Lord's teaching which is probably even more primitive than Mark. That S. Mark was himself acquainted with this source either because he had read it or because he had heard some of it, is probable if not certain. Important in this connection are his account of John the Baptist's preaching, the controversy between our Lord and those who accused Him of acting under the influence of Beelzebub, and the parable of the mustard seed. Here S. Mark appears to have used material which the other evangelists possessed both in a form distinct from Mark and also incorporated in Mark. Other and even more difficult problems are involved in the questions as to how much the non-Marcan document contained, and the relation of the document embodied in Matthew to the special source of information possessed by S. Luke. I think that Dr. Bartlet speaks correctly when he says that this source of information 'was a peculiar form of written memoirs elicited by our Third Evangelist *ad hoc*, not immediately for the literary purpose to which he finally put it, but rather as a permanent record of the most authentic tradition to which it had been his lot to obtain access, for use in his own work as an evangelist or catechist of the oral Gospel.'[1] This document we may call S, reserving for the other document the symbol Q, which is quite meaningless in English, as it represents the German Quelle or 'source.' The

[1] *Studies in the Synoptic Problem*, p. 351.

adoption of this latter symbol into English theological works at first deserved little but ridicule. But it now has the advantage of leaving the letter S free for employment in connection with Luke.

This special source used by S. Luke contained those exquisite passages which give to his Gospel much of its peculiar charm. We may believe that S. Luke had selected them because they were congenial to his soul, and that his own spiritual life was also greatly influenced by their revelation of the Master. Dives and Lazarus, the Prodigal Son, the Good Samaritan, and certain incidents such as the woman 'that was in the city, a sinner,' Zacchaeus, and Martha 'cumbered about much serving,' are drawn from this record. In it Jesus is specially represented as the Friend of sinners and the Consoler of the afflicted. The stories and sayings breathe the same spirit. They sometimes relate what was also to be found in Mark and in Q. But S. Luke regarded them as particularly authentic and important, and seems to have sometimes preferred this collection to Mark, otherwise he would not have inserted most of it bodily in one large block (Luke ix. 51-xviii. 14) into the midst of a narrative taken from Mark. Several eminent scholars who believe that S. Luke had this special source of his own, believe that it not merely related certain things which were also related in Q, but that it included passages directly copied from Q. I agree with Dr. Sanday in thinking that this was not the case, and that S. Luke was the first to fuse Q and S.

Having noticed S. Luke's special source, we now turn to inquire if the phenomena presented in Matthew and Luke really demand the explanation of a large common source other than Mark, viz. a collection of our Lord's sayings. In our next chapter we shall consider some external evidence which bears upon this matter, but here we shall confine ourselves to the internal evidence to be discovered in our first and third Gospels themselves.

First, it is evident that there is a large amount of most important material, nearly all records of our Lord's sayings, to be found in Matthew and Luke and not in Mark. It is conceivable that this might have been derived solely from oral tradition and teaching. No fatal objection to this view can be drawn from the fact that such oral tradition would have been originally in Aramaic while our Gospels are all in Greek. The two languages were often used side by side, like Welsh and English in some parts of Wales. But there is a more serious objection in the fact that a tradition cherished for the instruction of catechumens and Christians would almost necessarily have been formulated at first in Jerusalem, and would have told us more about our Lord's doings in Jerusalem. This is precisely what the Synoptists do not tell us until they come to the Passion. They tell us about the ministry everywhere else, they are rich in stories which go back to some witness or witnesses of His ministry outside Jerusalem. What is more is that, though Matthew and Luke give us their non-Marcan matter in two forms which are significantly different, they agree in one very striking particular. The arrangement in Matthew is coherent but artificial, its purpose is homiletical. The arrangement in Luke is more natural and equally coherent in another way. It suggests what seems to be a really genuine chronological outline of our Lord's ministry. Now, it is possible that S. Luke wrote down what he found traditionally preserved, and not written, and that the author of Matthew wrote down the same tradition in a different way. But would this tradition have consisted almost entirely of sayings of Jesus? Here the two Gospels agree. This is a real difficulty in the way of accepting the oral theory. It is far more reasonable to think that these sayings, with their intensely Palestinian and strongly primitive background, were written down at a time when there were

THE SYNOPTIC PROBLEM

still many who could remember the chief actions and sufferings of our Lord and the more important places which He visited, but knew that they were in danger of forgetting some of His gracious words.

Next, there is the style which we find in the non-Marcan passages in Matthew and Luke. Though both authors retouched S. Mark's style, and therefore, we may presume, the style of any other document that they copied, we find that the words which they employ point to the fact that each used a written source apart from Mark. When they follow Mark they both use their own favourite expressions less frequently than in those passages which are peculiar to themselves, and the same phenomenon occurs when they record discourses which are not in Mark. Various methods have been used for estimating the variations of style which occur in different portions of Matthew and Luke, but none is perhaps more simple and effective than that of Sir John Hawkins. He shows that in Matthew out of 1068 verses there are 338 which are 'peculiar,' having no parallel in the other Gospels. In Luke there are 1149 verses, and of these 499 which are 'peculiar.' But in Matthew there are 482 instances of the use of characteristic Matthaean words and phrases in the 'peculiar' division, and only 422 in the 'common' division. And in Luke there are 777 instances of the use of characteristic Lucan words and phrases in the 'peculiar' division, and only 706 in the 'common' division. That is, we find that in Matthew the characteristic words and phrases are scattered more than twice as thickly over the peculiar portions as over the other portions, and in Luke rather more than half as thickly again.

This certainly tends to show that both Matthew and Luke are largely derived from a written collection of our Lord's discourses. The two evangelists introduced their own favourite terms of expression into the narrative which they have in common with Mark, and also, though to a much less extent, into the sayings which they have in common with Mark. But both these classes of passages, and the sayings which are not in Mark, agree in showing a more sparing use of Matthaean and Lucan expressions. It is therefore reasonable to conclude that the non-Marcan passages common to Matthew and Luke, as well as the Marcan, have been mainly derived from written sources.

The above argument is immensely strengthened by the existence of the doublets or duplicate accounts of the same incidents or sayings in the same Gospel. An instance is in

Matt. xiii. 12.	*Matt.* xxv. 29.
For whosoever hath, to him shall be given, and he shall have abundance: but whosoever hath not, from him shall be taken away even that which he hath.	For unto every one that hath shall be given, and he shall have abundance: but from him that hath not, shall be taken away even that which he hath.

We may take another case from Luke:—

Luke viii. 17.	*Luke* xii. 2.
For nothing is secret, that shall not be made manifest; neither anything hid, that shall not be known and come abroad.	For there is nothing covered, that shall not be revealed; neither hid, that shall not be known.

In both these instances the first member of the doublet is apparently derived from Mark and the second not. The argument from the existence of doublets must be used with extreme care. We must not take for granted that whenever we find a doublet one member of it is necessarily an account of the very same incident as that recorded in the other member. Our Lord may have repeated the same sayings on different occasions. Nor need we fall under the same spell as those critics who, whenever they find two similar miracles recorded, regard one passage as a duplicate of the other, and having disposed of the genuineness of the one story, throw doubt upon the other. In this way the miraculous feeding of the four thousand is too readily declared to be the same as the feeding of the five thousand, the healing of the ten lepers in Luke xvii. 11-19 the same as the healing of the one leper in Luke v. 12-16, and the sending out of the seventy disciples in Luke x. is represented as a legendary duplicate of the sending out of the twelve apostles.

Putting aside the discussion of these points, let us return to solid ground. We cannot ignore the fact that in Mark, in great contrast with Matthew and Luke, there is only one doublet:

Mark ix. 35.	*Mark* x. 44.
If any man would be first, he shall be last of all, and minister of all.	Whosoever would be first among you, shall be servant of all.

It may be considered doubtful if this is a doublet of the stricter kind, for we can most easily believe that our Lord repeated such an injunction as this. Therefore it need not be the case that S. Mark has given us a duplicate account of the same saying. But a comparison of these passages with Matthew and Luke makes it very probable that one of these passages in Mark has been derived from Q. In Matthew some critics have reckoned no less than twenty-two doublets, of which we must mention the following eleven:

1. Matt. xiii. 12 and xxv. 29.
2. Matt. xvi. 4 and xii. 39.
3. Matt. xvi. 24 and x. 38.
4. Matt. xvi. 25 and x. 39.
5. Matt. xviii. 8 f. and v. 29 f.
6. Matt. xix. 9 and v. 32.
7. Matt. xix. 30 and xx. 16.
8. Matt xxi. 21 and xvii. 20.
9. Matt. vii. 16-18 and xii. 33-35.
10. Matt. x. 15 and xi. 24.
11. Matt. ix. 13 and xii. 7.

It is important to observe that in the case of the first eight of these doublets, the first member of the doublet, that in the first column, corresponds with a passage in Mark. The other members of the doublets, those in the second column, do not come from Mark. The doublets which are numbered 9 and 10 are of a rare kind, for both members of them seem to have been derived from Q, and 11 has no parallel in Mark or Q.

Next we can consider nine doublets in Luke:—

1. Luke viii. 16 and xi. 33.
2. Luke viii. 17 and xii. 2.
3. Luke ix. 3, 4, 5 and x. 4, 5, 7, 10, 11.
4. Luke ix. 23 and xiv. 27.
5. Luke ix. 24 and xvii. 33.
6. Luke ix. 26 and xii. 9.
7. Luke xx. 46 and xi. 43.
8. Luke xxi. 14, 15 and xii. 11, 12.
9. Luke xiv. 11 and xviii. 14.

The first eight of the members in the first column are parallel in position with similar verses in Mark. And all these eight have one member in that middle section of Luke (ix. 51-xviii. 14) which is derived from S. Luke's special source. Further, in 2, 4, 5, 6, and 7 the member of the Lucan doublet which corresponds in position with the similar passage in Mark is more like Mark than is the member which is in the middle section of Luke. In the case of the eighth instance, the preponderance of agreement is on the other side. No. 9 has both its members in the middle section. In addition to these doublets there are possibly others, and there are two which have neither member in that section. They are Luke viii. 18 and xix. 26, and ix. 46 and xxii. 24. Of these Luke viii. 18 is from Mark, and S. Luke has kept it after the explanation of the parable of the sower, whereas in Matthew it is placed before. Luke ix. 46 is

THE SYNOPTIC PROBLEM 89

also from Mark, and it is so likely that there were two disputes between the disciples as to who should be greatest that we may hesitate to call this a doublet.

To sum up this brief inquiry, one may say that in Matthew and Luke the contents, style, and duplicates make it certain that their origin is composite. They are based on Mark and on another document which they both used, and which can be denoted by the symbol Q. The same source was known to S. Mark, though he has made little use of it, probably because he deliberately wrote his Gospel to serve as a supplement to Q. S. Luke, in addition to Mark and Q, had another important source, which may be denoted by S.

§ 5. *The Stories of Christ's Birth.*

The narratives in Matthew and Luke concerning the birth and infancy of our Lord are obviously independent of each other They agree as to His birth at Bethlehem, the names of Mary and Joseph, the descent from David, and the residence at Nazareth. But the genealogies diverge widely, and the story of the birth in Matthew is told rather from the point of view of Joseph, that in Luke from the point of view of Mary. In Matthew we have no record of the presentation of the Holy Child in the temple, though the story would have been dear to any Jewish Christian's heart, and S. Luke says nothing of the Eastern sages coming to worship the light of the Gentiles, though this would have admirably suited the spirit and purpose of his Gospel. Plainly we here have two stories based on some independent sources. The second thing to notice is that neither of these stories can be regarded as a later addition to the Gospels such as the cruder class of critics used to maintain. The story in Matthew shows some of the evangelist's best-known characteristics. His love of artificial numerical arrangement is reflected in the genealogy, which contains three sets of fourteen generations, an arrangement which both assists the memory and makes use of the sacred Jewish number seven. His steady resolve to show that Jesus is the Messiah is shown throughout the story. And his defence of the character of the blessed Virgin is exactly in a line with his constant criticism of unbelieving Jewish adversaries. At least as early as the second century the Jews started a scandalous story about the paternity of Jesus. And the evangelist defends both Mary and her Son by not only asserting her virginity and His genuine Davidic descent, but also by introducing into the genealogy the names of Rahab, Tamar, and the wife of Uriah. These names alone were enough to prove that, in the providence of God, kings whom the Jews themselves regarded as members of the legitimate line were descended from women of irregular life. Thus the evangelist carries war into the enemy's camp.

Just as the story in Matthew is thoroughly Matthaean in form, so the story in Luke is thoroughly Lucan. Towards a real and inward Judaism S. Luke is always reverent, and there is therefore nothing un-Lucan in the reference to the throne of David and the obligations of the Law. The style is archaic but not un-Lucan. Here as elsewhere S. Luke has probably worked over a document which was either in Aramaic or translated from Aramaic. The author's consistent interest in women is here not merely illustrated but explained. And the artistic sense which marks the whole story is Lucan through and through.

No valid objection against the authenticity of these two accounts of our Lord's birth can be made on the score that the doctrine of the Virgin birth is a pagan importation into Christianity. Mythology, decent and indecent, has been ransacked to find the origin of the doctrine. But the fact remains that both accounts must have taken shape in Palestinian Jewish Christian circles. The tone is not Gentile, nor even that of Jews living in a Gentile environment. The bedizened legend of the miraculous birth of Buddha and a story of the Egyptian Isis supposed to have filtered into Christianity through Jewish legend have been appealed to in vain. It is not at all probable that the story of the Virgin birth was told at first except to those who were already convinced that Jesus was the Son of God. The apostles would be cautious in speaking of a matter which was open to such misinterpretation. S. Paul does not actually mention it, though his language about the sinfulness of all the descendants of Adam, except the sinless Jesus, cannot be explained if he did not believe in the miraculous birth of Jesus Christ. He gives clear expression to the idea of the solidarity of all mankind, and regards all men as infected with a taint derived from Adam by natural descent. But he regards Jesus Christ as the Second Adam, sinless in actual fact, free from the inherited taint of Adam's sin, and the Head of a renewed humanity, capable of communicating His life to others. In view of these connected ideas, it seems impossible to think that S. Paul did not believe that by a physical miracle Christ's birth was protected from the taint which accompanies our own. It is often said that S. John is silent as to the Virgin birth. But this silence cannot be taken for granted. For there is good ground for suspecting that in i. 13 the correct text is really ' who *was born*, not of blood, nor of the will of the flesh, nor of the will of man, but of God.' The reference is then to Christ, and not to Christians, and the text one of the strongest testimonies to the supernatural birth of Jesus. This view is corroborated by the assertion of His Jewish opponents in viii. 41. They say ' We were not born of fornication,' words which seem to imply a reference to the evil story about our Lord's mother based upon a perversion of the fact that He was not the Son of Joseph. This story is found in the Talmud, and was incorporated in a disgusting mediæval Jewish lampoon. It may have been current in S. John's time.

In the second century it is only where the apostolic faith concerning Christ was denied that we find the Virgin birth repudiated. Except among the semi-Jewish Ebionites and some more than semi-pagan Gnostics, we find that a profession of Christianity and a belief in such a birth went together, and we find this as early as S. Ignatius, A.D. 110. It is sometimes said that such writers as testify to this belief derived it from our Gospels. That is a double-edged argument. For, if it is true, it shows how universally and how early their account of Christ's birth was accepted. The virginity of Mary was asserted in the earliest forms of the creed. In other words, it was an 'article of faith' at least as early as the first quarter of the second century.

While it is now almost undisputed that the stories of Christ's infancy were as a whole written in their present form by our evangelists, it is still urged by some that they did not originally assert the Virgin birth. First, there is the difficulty raised by the strange variety of readings in Greek, Latin, and Syriac manuscripts in Matt. i. 16. The Old Syriac version has 'Jacob begat Joseph, Joseph, to whom was betrothed Mary the virgin, begat Jesus who is called the Messiah.' An elaborate comparison of the different forms of this text shows that the Old Syriac is here corrupt, but that it probably contains an older reading under later accretions. It is perhaps best to refer the reader to the discussion of the subject by Mr. C. H. Turner in the *Journal of Theological Studies* for January 1910. He holds that the best explanation of the existing variations is that the text which they have altered in different ways was :

Jacob begat Joseph the husband of Mary;
And Joseph begat (ἐγέννησεν) Jesus who was called Christ.

Mr. Turner is probably the ablest of all the critics who have defended the originality of the words 'Joseph begat Jesus.' It is, therefore, important to observe that he unequivocally asserts that it is 'quite certain' that the evangelist and his contemporaries 'accepted absolutely the Virgin birth,' and agrees with Professor Burkitt that 'since the Virgin birth is obviously of the essence of the narrative,' the above phrase, if it is genuine, 'must be interpreted in accordance with it.' That is, it must have been intended to establish a legal, rather than a natural, descent and heirship of Christ from David through Joseph. The adoption of Mary's Child by Joseph made the Child, according to Jewish law, a legal descendant of Joseph's ancestry, and proved his Davidic lineage.[1]

After long deliberation, I am unable to convince myself that the evangelist wrote, 'Joseph begat Jesus.' He takes such scrupulous care to impress upon his readers the truth of the Virgin birth that it is not likely that he would have used a phrase which they would have instantly felt to be inconsistent with such a miracle. In this short first chapter of Matthew the author explicitly teaches the miraculous birth in three separate verses (18, 20, 25). He reinforces the fact by a perfectly unambiguous quotation from the Greek version of Isaiah. And, as we saw above, he has the extraordinary boldness to hint at it in the genealogy itself by referring to three women, one of whom is Rahab. Not content with this, the evangelist in the second chapter carefully avoids describing the Holy Child as the child of Joseph in the very places where it would have been natural to do so, if he had

[1] See Dr. R. J. Knowling, *Our Lord's Virgin Birth.*

believed Him to be such. Is there then any other reading which will account for the variations in the manuscripts?

Mr. Turner has himself suggested such a reading:

Jacob begat Joseph the husband of Mary;
And Mary bare (ἐγέννησεν)[1] Jesus who was called Christ.

If the evangelist wrote this, all the phenomena can be naturally explained. The scribe of one manuscript, which must have been very early, and the parent of other copies, made a mistake which any copyist might make, writing 'Joseph' twice instead of 'Joseph' and 'Mary.' The mistake is natural, being of a kind which is so commonly made in rapid writing that it can excite no surprise. But whether this suggestion is accepted or not, the fact remains that belief in the Virgin birth is the evangelist's own belief and not an interpolation, it is Palestinian and not pagan, it is primitive and not late. This is so incontrovertible that Harnack, without accepting, it would seem, the doctrine of the Virgin birth, has recently said that it is 'beyond dispute that in the most important verses (i. 18-25) of the story of the Infancy in the first Gospel nothing is to be found that could not have been written about the year 70 A.D.'[2]

The case of S. Luke is slightly different. It has been recently argued by several critics, mostly very definitely rationalistic or anti-Christian, that the story in Luke could run quite smoothly and naturally if the two verses (Luke i. 34-35) were omitted. They are:—

And Mary said unto the angel, How shall this be, seeing I know not a man? And the angel answered and said unto her, The Holy Ghost shall come upon thee, and the power of the

---

[1] It is important to remember that in Greek the same word is used for 'beget' and 'bear.'

[2] *The Date of the Acts and of the Synoptic Gospels*, p 148 (English trans.).

Most High shall overshadow thee: wherefore also that which is to be born shall be called holy, the Son of God.

Here the evidence of the manuscripts is decisively against the omission of the verses in question. A sincere criticism compels us to say that the words above are part of the original text of Luke. Dr. Sanday has lately said of the first two chapters of Luke that 'there is nothing more intensely and primitively Jewish in the whole New Testament.'[1] Harnack also has lately said with regard to S. Luke's stories of Christ's infancy that 'S. Luke regarded them as proceeding from S. Mary; for his practice elsewhere as an historian proves that he could not have himself invented a fiction like this.' And he is satisfied that they too were written before A.D. 70.[2] It seems certain that S. Luke wrote the words as we have them. The manuscript evidence in their favour is overwhelming, they agree in style with the rest of the passage, and fitly attribute to our Lord a strictly supernatural birth, after attributing to His inferior and forerunner a birth attended by mysterious, though less miraculous, circumstances.

The hymns in this portion of Luke appear to have been drawn from an Aramaic source, though they contain Lúcan phrases. As S. Luke was in Jerusalem with S. Paul in A.D. 56 (Acts xxi.), it is quite possible that he may have found such a document there, and that he came to know some of the holy women who were friends of Mary. Among them was probably Joanna, the wife of Chuza, Herod's steward (viii. 3; xxiv. 10).

§ 6. *Valuable results of Criticism.*

While most of the above statements as to the Synoptic problem are such as meet with wide acceptance,

---

[1] *Miracles*, p. 14. [2] *Op. cit.* p. 155.

the problem is by no means entirely solved. Perhaps it never will be solved. The critics who write as though they had been at Rome and Antioch, and sat by the side of the evangelists while they composed their Gospels, are not to be wholly trusted. They are ready with an explanation for every word which the Synoptists changed, and they label each change with what they consider the appropriate motive. But it will be enough for most of us if we arrive at some well reasoned hypothesis which accounts for the origin of that knowledge of the life and teaching of Jesus Christ which we possess. We must be content if many details are unexplained, even after much searching. We must even welcome an entirely new hypothesis if it overthrows that on which we have spent much labour. And yet the results of the critical investigations of the last three generations have been substantial and valuable. Some of them may be mentioned.

(i) The practical certainty that the great bulk of the story in the Synoptic Gospels dates from the lifetime of persons who had seen and spoken with Jesus Christ. This is usually granted by non-Christian as well as Christian writers. The latest date to which Mark can with any plausibility be assigned is a little before A.D. 70. The sayings of the Lord which were written down before they were incorporated in Matthew and Luke were in all probability written earlier than Mark. An adverse critic may urge that this does not prove that everything in these documents is true. But it does at least give us ground for treating them with respect. The figures of a date do at least count for something. The proverb rightly warns us that two and two do not make five, but it can be maintained with equal confidence that two and two make more than three. The value of an earlier as compared with a later record has been strikingly shown during recent years in the case of the 'Lives' of S. Francis of Assisi. Sometimes with irreverence, and sometimes

THE SYNOPTIC PROBLEM

with sincerity, S. Francis has been considered the saint who was most like Jesus. His later biography, the official biography put out to the world in A.D. 1260 by the order of friars who regarded him as their father, is a valuable book. But the earlier books—the *Speculum Perfectionis*, written just after the death of S. Francis by brother Leo in A.D. 1226, and the *First Life of S. Francis*, written in A.D. 1229—are universally regarded as the truer picture of the saint who brought the Gospel once more to the people of the highways and the hedges.

A closer study of Jewish and Gentile life as they were in the first century of the Christian era has led to the conviction that the 'local colour' of the Synoptic Gospels is true to the alleged period and place. In the course of this book we shall consider many illustrations of this, and will also notice similar indications in the Fourth Gospel. The rugged Greek is the common Greek of the Mediterranean, with that Jewish flavour which we should expect from men living in a Jewish atmosphere. It is Greek which a schoolboy of seventeen is apt to despise, for it is no such literary idiom as that of Thucydides and Plato. But learned men now know what dialects are worth. They can value the poetry of the best Scottish ballads, and the crisp wit of the now dying Yorkshire dialects. And the Greek of the Gospels has its own magic. It is pithy and expressive. And it is this in spite of the fact that the underlying thought is usually not Greek at all, but thoroughly Semitic. The Christians made comparatively few converts among the Jews after the earliest years of apostolic preaching. It is certain that as early as A.D. 120, or earlier, the Christians were mainly Gentiles speaking Greek. And yet we find enshrined in the Gospels such Semitic words as *Amen, Abba, Talitha cumi*, and *Eli, Eli, lama sabachthani*. And these are not like antique gems set in reliquaries of a later and alien time. For some of the most vital phrases of the Gospels, such as the 'kingdom of the heavens,' or 'kingdom of God,' and 'the Son of Man,' 'the Christ' or 'Messiah,' and even 'righteousness' and the 'resurrection,' are not in the least Greek. To the Greek they were probably less intelligible than the phraseology in the *Analecta* of Confucius. They are fundamentally Hebrew, and Hebrew of the first century.

The geography of the Holy Land gives a local colour of very great importance. It is held by critics that S. Mark did not write his Gospel in that country, and yet the journeys of our Lord are sketched in such a manner that we obtain an intelligible outline of His missionary work. A skilful modern novelist might, no doubt, construct a story which fitted the geography of the Hebrides or the Pacific, and print a map to elucidate his hero's wanderings. But in the case of S. Mark we have a very rough writer who, without the slightest appearance of art, gives an outline which is too meagre to be fictitious. It is meagre, but it fits a precise historical situation. Our Lord avoided certain places because they were in the dominions of Herod Antipas, and S. Mark knew from an eye-witness that Jesus had to avoid some districts on account of the opposition of the civil as well as the religious authorities. S. Mark knows much about the Holy Land. S. Luke knows much about Asia Minor and parts of the Mediterranean. The apocryphal Gospels and Acts know very little. A writer who had to rely upon a vague tradition of the past, or upon the Old Testament alone, would hardly have mentioned Capernaum or Chorazin, both of which names occur in the Talmud but not in the Old Testament. A Gentile of inventive mind would also almost certainly have represented our Lord as teaching in some Gentile town, just as the Buddhists of Ceylon represented the Buddha as visiting their holy island. But none of the four Gospels definitely represents our Lord as preaching in any Greek city of Palestine. He only pays brief visits to non-Jewish districts. This is a negative but very real proof of the early date of the Christian tradition.

Again, the whole attitude of our Lord towards the religious authorities and institutions of Judaism fits a particular time. It is presupposed that the worship of the temple is still being offered. It is presupposed that there exists a class technically called the 'poor,' despised for their ignorance of the law as well as for their natural poverty. The existence of this class, we may almost say 'caste,' is proved by Jewish evidence. The Herodians, a party mentioned in the Gospel story, were at the close of the first century more dead than the Jacobites at the close of the nineteenth. In Rome and Ephesus at the close of the first or the beginning of the second century there would have been no need to compose discourses with Sadducees, who were already crushed or extinct. Pharisaism still lived, but the Pharisaic rules about cleanness and uncleanness fell into disuse, and the Church was already strong enough to make rules of her own such as we find in the manual known as the *Didaché*.

In short, the words of our Lord, like the journeys of our Lord, belong to Palestine previous to A.D. 70. Recognition of this fact is now so general that no moderate critic is likely to repeat concerning the Gospels the words once used by Dr. Jowett, that 'they are an unauthenticated fragment belonging to an age absolutely unknown.'[1]

(ii) We are reaching sounder principles in determining what is well attested and what is less well attested. So long as the theory that the Synoptic Gospels were three different forms of oral traditions

[1] Abbott and Campbell, *Life and Letters of Benjamin Jowett*, vol. ii. p. 341.

held the field, it was natural to say that if anything occurred in two Gospels it had two independent witnesses in its favour, and if found in all three, it had three witnesses. This theory, which itself is of modern origin, may contain a considerable element of truth. All the evangelists probably wrote with a large amount of subject-matter in their minds, even when they made use of books such as S. Luke expressly mentions at the beginning of his Gospel. But the fact remains that when all the first three Gospels relate the same thing, the witness may only be that of S. Mark, whose work is copied by the other Synoptic writers. There is no reason to regret this fact. It shows the very high estimation in which S. Mark was held at a very early period, apparently between A.D. 65 and A.D. 80. It also helps us to explain certain silences in the Gospels, gaps in the story. To take boldly one of the most important of all, it enables us to understand why the Synoptists do not mention the raising of Lazarus. This omission, if it occurred in three absolutely independent Gospels, would be so startling that we might feel inclined to agree with those who say that the story is a fiction. But its omission in the primitive collection of our Lord's *sayings* is natural. And though we should expect to find it in Mark, the repeated omissions in that record, and its great incompleteness, will make us too cautious to say that if the miracle happened he must have known it, and that if he knew it, he must have written an account of it.

With regard to the written collection of our Lord's sayings, it can justly be said that anything which has the double attestation of Mark and this other document, has very strong support. There may be, and are, many acts and sayings recorded by one evangelist only which are thoroughly historical and told in a manner which we deeply feel is worthy of the Saviour. But if we find that Mark and the sayings leave on our minds the same impression of Jesus Christ, that impression is one which we must retain. We may be sure that it does not tell us everything, but it tells us what no later age would ever have invented or could invent. Thus we are aided in dealing with the greatest problem of all. 'Who do men say that I, the Son of Man, am?' The question is always coming back. It is as fresh to-day as it was during any of the great Christological controversies which racked the Church of bygone days. He appears as more than Poet, more than Prophet. He utters the hardest words, such as 'Let the dead bury their dead,' 'He that hateth not father and mother cannot be My disciple,' and 'He that saveth his life shall lose it.' Yet He took the little children in His arms, pardoned the penitent woman, and said, 'Come unto Me, all ye that are weary and heavy laden, and I will give you rest.'

CHAPTER IV

THE SAYINGS OF OUR LORD

§ 1. *'The Lord Said'*

THE modern world has witnessed the rise and history of numerous Christian communities which in one way or another have been the product of the New Testament. Here or there an individual has derived from it his own ideal of what Christianity ought to be, and has founded a society to embody that idea. On the contrary, the Church of primitive times was not the product of the New Testament, but the New Testament was the product of the Church. That Church had sacred books which she called 'scripture,' or 'the scriptures,' and when quoting from these scriptures the Christians were accustomed to introduce their quotation with the phrase 'it has been written.' But these scriptures were at first simply and entirely the Old Testament. The Old Testament had a more elastic list of books in some quarters than in others, for at Alexandria books were accounted canonical which did not satisfy the more rigorous requirements of the Jews of Palestine. But for a long time 'scripture' was always the Old Testament. In the New Testament the solitary approach to an exception is to be found in 2 Peter iii. 15, 16, where the letters of 'our beloved brother Paul' are compared to 'the other scriptures.' This is an exception which proves

THE SAYINGS OF OUR LORD

nothing against our rule, for the late date of 2 Peter is on other grounds so likely that we cannot argue from this text that the first Christians gave the name of scripture to any New Testament writings.

What the first generation of Christians valued, and the next generation, was tradition. It is evident from various passages in the New Testament itself that many of them expected our Lord to return visibly within their own lifetime. They said Marantha, 'the Lord cometh,' and prayed 'Even so come, Lord Jesus,' expecting Him speedily. In the meantime, for a knowledge of His doctrine they relied upon the teaching of the persons whom Christ had commissioned to teach. Early and late in his Epistles, S. Paul speaks of 'the traditions' which were 'received' and 'handed on.' He has no New Testament to quote. If he has a book, he does not call it a 'Gospel.' With him the 'Gospel' is still one message of good news. It is not a book. The Thessalonians are bidden to 'hold the traditions' (2 Thess. ii. 15), the Corinthians are congratulated on keeping the traditions in the shape in which he gave them to his converts (1 Cor. xi. 2). As he had 'received from the Lord' what he had handed on to the Corinthians, so he tells Timothy to 'keep the deposit safe' (1 Tim. vi. 20, cf. 2 Tim. i. 13-14), and to commit it 'to such trustworthy men as will be competent in turn to teach others' (2 Tim. ii. 2).

S. Luke, the companion of S. Paul, refers to such a tradition, when at the very beginning of his Gospel he mentions 'the word' and 'the words.' Matter of important interest had been 'delivered' to him by those who 'from the beginning were eye-witnesses and ministers of the word,' and he writes that Theophilus may 'recognise the certainty concerning the words' in which he was 'catechised' or 'taught orally.' These *logoi* or 'words' would evidently comprise more than a group of sayings of our Lord, but it can hardly be doubted that such sayings were included in these *logoi*.

For a considerable time it was the custom of the early Christians to refer to these *logoi* of Jesus Christ as things which He 'said,' rather than things which He 'says.' When the position of the Gospels as the most authentic mine for Christ's sayings was fully established, we find that they began to employ the present tense, for it was understood that the writer meant that Christ 'says' this or that in His written word. We find this usage in the so-called Second Epistle of Clement about A.D. 140. But in Acts xx. 35, S. Paul, when quoting an unwritten saying of our Lord, speaks thus: 'Ye ought to help the weak, and to remember the words of the Lord Jesus, how *He Himself said*, It is more blessed to give than to receive.' This manner of speech is to be found in some other primitive Christian documents. The early Church manual called the *Didaché*, the letter of S. Clement of Rome, and that of S. Polycarp, writings composed between A.D. 95 and A.D. 115, say, 'The Lord commanded,' 'the Lord said.' These expressions originated at a period when there either was no written Gospel, or when living tradition was more valued than the written page. No doubt some Christians would naturally be more conservative than others, and would tend to retain such a habit later than others. Papias, bishop of Hierapolis in Phrygia, was a man of this type. About A.D. 140 he published his 'Expositions of the Lord's Oracles' (*Logia*). Many years before this he had collected traditions about the Lord, and he says, 'I did not suppose that the contents of books would profit me so much as the utterances of a living and abiding voice.'[1] From the fragments of his works preserved by Eusebius, the Church historian of two hundred years later, it is

[1] Eus. *H. E.* iii. 39.

THE SAYINGS OF OUR LORD

plain that when Papias collected these traditions the apostles were dead. Two of our Lord's personal disciples survived, probably at a very advanced age. They were named Aristion and John the Presbyter. Whether Papias actually met them or not is uncertain, but he derived information from them which he welcomed as of unique value. We are not justified in saying that he regarded the contents of the Gospels as less true than the sayings which he learnt orally. But the living tradition was still in his estimation so excellent that it was indispensable, and he was eager to secure this living tradition before it was gone for ever.

§ 2. *Was there a Collection of Sayings?*

The word *Logia* occurs in another connection in Papias, besides forming part of the title of his own work. And it is this other passage which nearly secured for the word *Logia* an entry into the English language. Papias says:—

Matthew then made an orderly arrangement of the *Logia* in the Hebrew dialect, and each one interpreted them as he was able.[1]

Some modern students who observed the similarity of the sayings of Jesus recorded in Matthew and Luke, and not derived from Mark, held that Papias was speaking of a document called the *Logia* which the two later Synoptic writers copied. That they did copy such a document is very probable, as we have seen in the last chapter. But it is by no means certain that Papias is here specifically speaking of it. In the New Testament *Logia* signifies the 'oracles' or utterances of God contained in the Old Testament, or the inspired utterances of prophets. At a rather later period *Logia*

[1] Eus. *H. E.* iii. 39.

means the 'commandments' or precepts of our Lord. It is used in this sense by S. Clement of Rome, A.D. 96, and also by S. Polycarp, the contemporary of Papias.[1] It seems probable that Papias also used the word *Logia* as equivalent to 'the commandments delivered by the Lord to our faith' in contrast with 'alien commandments' of heretics.[2] Now there is no reason whatever why we should not speak of the short pregnant sayings of our Lord as *Logia*, whether we use the word in the sense of 'oracles' or, in accordance with the more classical Greek meaning, understand it as equivalent to 'brief utterances.' But we have no evidence to show that the early Christians ever gave the name of *Logia* to any compilation of Christ's sayings employed by the evangelists. Papias himself speaks of the Lord's words, *Logoi*, in a manner which implies that he identified these words, and not a document, with the *Logia* that he knew.

But though we hesitate in saying that any book was called *Logia*, we have to ask if any written collection of our Lord's sayings did exist in the apostolic age, and if so, what this collection contained. The opening chapters of Acts, which abound in primitive touches, give us an exact idea of the general character of the earliest manner of preaching the Gospel. This preaching must usually have been in the Aramaic language, then commonly called Hebrew, though differing considerably from real Hebrew. The Gospels themselves show that our Lord spoke Aramaic. The Acts show us that it was the popular language of Jerusalem, for the mob which threatened S. Paul calmed down when they heard him begin to speak in Aramaic. The preaching of the apostles was 'preaching Christ.' They explained that Jesus of Nazareth was the Christ, the Messiah; they spoke of the signs and wonders which God had worked by Him, of His death

---

[1] *Ad Philipp.* 7. [2] Eus. *loc. cit.*

THE SAYINGS OF OUR LORD 107

as part of God's plan for man's salvation, and of His resurrection as an incontrovertible fact proving that He was truly the Lord. They testified to what they had 'seen and heard' (Acts iv. 20). Any one who reads S. Peter's speeches in the Acts will feel certain that the earliest tradition handed down by the apostles consisted primarily of some great facts of the story of Jesus combined with appropriate passages of the Old Testament which the apostles interpreted as referring to the Messiah. And some tradition as to the words of the Lord must have accompanied this preaching, for the apostles beyond all question preached to the unconverted about the second coming of Christ which He had foretold. Converts were apparently not required to repeat sayings of the Lord before they were baptised, and we have no trace as yet of any written sayings. But the new morality and teaching of the Christian Church demanded such sayings as their basis.

Here let us return to S. Paul. One very great advantage in dealing with his writings is that we know the dates at which most of his letters were written, at any rate within a year or two. We are unable to prove that any Gospel existed when he suffered martyrdom at Rome in or near A.D. 64. S. Irenaeus places the publication of the Gospel of S. Mark 'after the departure' of Peter and Paul, and appears to mean soon after their departure from this present world. Clement of Alexandria holds that S. Peter knew of it, and S. Peter died near the same time as S. Paul. It is therefore possible, though by no means certain, that S. Paul had seen our earliest Gospel before he died. But he certainly knew a 'guaranteed' tradition (2 Tim. ii. 2), and we must leave room for the hypothesis that he may have known some written documents about our Lord's teaching and life some years before he wrote his letters to Timothy and

Titus. S. Paul knows of Christ's poverty, His obedience to the law, His self-effacement and refusal to please Himself, His meekness and gentleness, His sinlessness. He appeals directly to the command of the Lord that a husband and a wife may not separate and remarry (1 Cor. vii. 10), and to His direction that those who preach the Gospel should live by the Gospel (1 Cor. ix. 14; *cf*. Matt. x. 9-11). Several other passages show reminiscences of Christ's sayings. The references to our Lord's death, the circumstances of it and of His resurrection, are numerous. Two passages are of special importance, that in which he writes about the institution of the Lord's Supper (1 Cor. xi. 23-26), and that in which He enumerates the appearances of Christ after His resurrection (1 Cor. xv. 3-8). The former has points of contact with Luke, the latter, it has been conjectured, *may* correspond with the list of appearances recorded in the original, now lost, ending of Mark. At least, the appearance to Cephas in 1 Cor. xv. 5 should be studied in connection with the words 'but go tell His disciples and Peter,' which come almost at the end of the genuine portion of Mark xvi. We cannot expect to solve the problem to our complete satisfaction. But the phenomena of these two passages in 1 Cor. are suggestive. Their detail and precision encourage us to think that the apostle was drawing from a considerable storehouse of information, probably written. And yet his source, if written, was not one of our Synoptic Gospels, for 1 Cor. is older than any of them. We have already noted that in Acts xx. 35 S. Paul is mentioned as quoting a saying of our Lord not in our Gospels, 'It is more blessed to give than to receive.'

On the whole, it is more likely than not that S. Paul had some written account of our Lord's ministry and possibly a written account of His sayings.

That S. Peter and S. James also used some written records is a tenable view. The First Epistle of S. Peter shows no acquaintance with our Gospels which can be called certain. But the apostle's idea of His Master, of His self-denial, and of His death as God's suffering Servant, is very closely parallel to that found in the Synoptists. While S. Peter recalls the Synoptists' portrait of our Lord, the Epistle of S. James shows us a very interesting kinship with the Sermon on the Mount. It has several points of contact with both Matthew and Luke, and yet does not actually quote any of our canonical Gospels. Its condemnation of 'hearers only,' of critics, and of worldliness, and its teaching about prayer, poverty, and humility, are apparently based on a familiar knowledge of some record of our Lord's sayings. These passages contain one remarkable variation from Matthew. S. James in v. 12 writes, 'Swear not . . . but let your yea be yea, and your nay, nay; that ye fall not under judgment.' Matt. v. 34, 37 has, 'Swear not at all . . . but let your speech be Yea, yea; Nay, nay; and whatsoever is more than these is of the evil one.' S. Justin Martyr in his First Apology, Chapter xvi., written about A.D. 152, says that Christ enjoined 'Swear not at all; but let your yea be yea, and your nay, nay; for whatsoever is more than these cometh of the evil one.' The agreement between Matthew and S. Justin Martyr in diverging from S. James is obvious. And it rather points us to the conclusion that there was some document other than our canonical Matthew from which S. James is quoting, and that this document influenced certain manuscript copies of our canonical Matthew more than others. S. Justin Martyr may be combining the words in Matthew and James. But when we consider this passage in James in connection with other verses similar to those in the Sermon on the Mount, it remains probable that S. James is quoting a certain book. If we acknowledge his Epistle to be genuine—and the grounds for denying it seem to be quite inadequate—we get some light on the date of the book that he quotes. For it is practically certain that S. James suffered martyrdom at Jerusalem in A.D. 62.

We can sum up the evidence of S. Paul, S. Peter, and S. James, by saying that it is probable, though not certain, that these three great disciples possessed written documents about our Lord. It is also probable that the first preaching of the Gospel as recorded in Acts was aided by some written account of our Lord's ministry and sayings, and a collection of quotations from the Old Testament. But there is not any absolute proof of the existence of any such documents. The first proof of any written documents that we get is in the prologue of S. Luke's Gospel, which can with most safety be dated between A.D. 75 and 80, and this prologue can be profitably studied in the light given to us in the words of Papias:—

Mark, having become an interpreter of Peter, wrote exactly whatever he remembered of the sayings and actions of Christ, not however in order. For he neither heard the Lord, nor accompanied Him, but afterwards, as I said, accompanied Peter, who gave instruction as occasion demanded, but did not make any ordered arrangement (σύνταξιν) of the Lord's sayings. So that Mark made no error in thus writing some things as he recalled them. For he had one object only, to omit or falsify nothing of the things which he heard. . . . Matthew then made an orderly arrangement (συνετάξατο) of the *Logia* in the Hebrew dialect, and each one interpreted them as he was able.

These two passages are part of a single tradition current at the end of the first or beginning of the second century. They do not refer to Matthew in its present form, for it is not in Hebrew, nor is it a transla-

THE SAYINGS OF OUR LORD

tion from the Hebrew. It can be proved that our present Matthew was composed in Greek, and it is only based partly on Hebrew or Aramaic writings. The question then arises, Does Papias refer to our present Mark? He speaks of the want of systematic order or arrangement in S. Mark's writing. And yet Mark is arranged chronologically and, in spite of the gaps which it betrays, we can from this Gospel determine a large part of the history of our Lord's ministry. The great majority of modern critics, nevertheless, hold that Papias is referring to our Mark. For this Gospel bears plain tokens not only of being very early in date and written under Petrine influence, but also of being an original work, not based on a previous Gospel by S. Mark. We must therefore ask if by 'ordered arrangement' Papias meant chronological arrangement. Probably he did not. Like Lucian (*de hist. conscrib.* 6 f.) he meant by 'order,' orderliness. He meant a system of instruction such as S. Matthew arranged in Hebrew.[1] S. Mark, though he used other sources, wrote down a faithful record of the evangelistic preaching of S. Peter, a preaching of Christ's words and Christ's actions. On the other hand, the original work of S. Matthew was serviceable and often translated, because it provided in an orderly fashion what Papias elsewhere calls 'the commandments delivered by the Lord to our faith.'

The distinction made by Papias between Matthew and Mark is made still clearer if we turn to Luke. The valuable little prologue by the author shows that he was not satisfied with previous narratives of our Lord's ministry. His investigations had yielded fruit. He had accumulated a large store of material, and his aim was to write 'a narrative in consecutive order' ($\delta\iota\eta\gamma\eta\sigma\iota\varsigma$ $\kappa\alpha\theta\epsilon\xi\hat{\eta}\varsigma$). The expressions used are quite

---

[1] Papias may also refer to the contrast between the artistic arrangement of S. John's Gospel and the shape of S. Mark's.

different from those used by Papias in reference to the original work of S. Matthew. S. Luke is giving us a new history partly based on Mark, and he records those discourses of Christ which he has in common with Matthew, in a historical setting, and not cemented together for the purpose of aiding memory and instructing catechumens. Two of our Gospels are evangelistic, those of S. Mark and S. Luke. Of the other two, one at least is catechetical, and very probably the other. For the Gospel according to S. John shows, like Matthew, distinct traces of grouping facts according to numbers such as would aid the memory of teacher and learner. And its relation to the Synoptic Gospels is such that it may have been used as an additional spiritual manual for those who had already been baptised, and had grasped some simple moral teaching and the outlines of our Lord's life.

It is then reasonable to conclude that Papias believed that S. Matthew's original collection of our Lord's sayings was not so much a narrative as an arrangement of groups of discourses and sayings. They were rearranged in different groups when *our* Gospel according to S. Matthew was written. They were not rearranged in this second form when S. Luke read them. S. Luke did not break up these blocks of marble to scatter over his garden and intersperse with plants. It was, on the contrary, the writer of our first Gospel who arranged the different groups together in their final shape. And the question is how we can separate the sayings of Jesus from their context in these two Gospels, compare them, and arrive at their most primitive form. The only safe way to begin is to take out of these Gospels those sayings which they both have and which S. Mark does not record. The first problem is to determine when sayings are, or are not, sufficiently parallel to justify us in holding that they ultimately came from one written source. It can hardly be expected that critics will ever entirely agree about this. But we shall not be far wrong if we agree with Sir John Hawkins in holding that these sayings include about 191 verses in Matthew, rather more than one-sixth of the whole Gospel, and about 181 verses in Luke, which make less than one-sixth. These parallels may be better described as consisting of 74 passages. And of these there are 56 which are placed differently in the two Gospels. It is very doubtful whether they were ever in exact chronological order. But there is some chronological order, for they begin with a short account of the preaching of the Baptist and of our Lord's temptation, and end before His Passion. They are predominantly concerned with conduct and character. But they are not only ethical. They show exactly how Christ dealt with Pharisaism, and the exact relation between the Baptist and the Messiah. And they throw a vivid light on the primitive Christian conception of the Messiah (see below, p. 126).

§ 3. *The Contents of the Collection.*

The sayings fall into five groups. The first, which we may call A, *contains an account of the Baptist's preaching, and of our Lord's temptation* (probably also His baptism), then *deals with the righteousness that God requires in the subjects of His kingdom.* Let us compare the record of such sayings as are found in Matt. v.-vii. and Luke vi. 20-49.

(*a*) Blessed are *the* poor *in spirit*: for *their's* is the kingdom of *heaven.*	Blessed are *ye* poor: for *your's* is the kingdom of *God.*
Blessed are *they* that *mourn*: for *they* shall be *comforted.*	Blessed are *ye* that *weep now*: for *ye* shall *laugh.*
Blessed are *they* that hunger *and thirst after righteousness*: for *they* shall be filled.	Blessed are *ye* that hunger *now*: for *ye* shall be filled.

Blessed are ye, when men shall reproach you and *persecute* you, and *say all manner of* evil *against you, falsely,* for *My* sake.	Blessed are ye, when men shall *hate* you, *and when they shall separate* you *from their company,* and reproach you, and *cast out your name as* evil, for *the Son of man's* sake.
Rejoice, and *be exceeding glad*: for great is your reward in heaven : for *so persecuted they* the prophets *which were before you.*	Rejoice *in that day,* and *leap for joy*: for, *behold,* your reward is great in heaven : for *in the same manner did their fathers unto* the prophets.
Agree with thine adversary *quickly,* whiles thou art with him in the way ; lest haply *the adversary deliver* thee to the judge, and the judge deliver thee to the officer, and thou *be* cast into prison. *Verily* I say unto thee, Thou shalt by no means come out thence, till thou have paid the last *farthing.*	As thou art *going* with thine adversary *before the magistrate,* on the way *give diligence to be quit* of him ; lest haply *he take* thee unto the judge, and the judge deliver thee unto the officer and *the officer shall* cast thee into prison. I say unto thee, Thou shalt by no means come out thence, till thou have paid the *very* last *mite.*
(b) Whosoever smiteth thee on thy right cheek, turn to him the other also. And if any man would *go to law with thee,* and take away thy coat, *let him have* thy cloke also.	To him that smiteth thee on the *one* cheek, *offer* also the other ; and from him that taketh away thy cloke, *withhold not* thy coat also.
Give to him that asketh thee, and from him that *would borrow of thee turn not thou away.*	Give to *every one* that asketh thee ; and of him that *taketh away thy goods ask them not again.*
Love your enemies, and pray for them that *persecute* you ; that ye may be sons of *your Father which is in heaven*: for He *maketh His sun to rise on* the evil and *the good, and sendeth rain on the just and the unjust.* For if ye love them that love you, what *reward* have ye ? *do* not even the *publicans the same*? And if	Love your enemies, *do good to them that hate you, bless them that curse you,* pray for them that *despitefully use* you . . . and ye shall be sons of *the Most High*: for *He is kind toward the unthankful* and evil. And if ye love them that love you, what *thank* have ye ? for even *sinners love those that love them.* And if

ye *salute your brethren only*, what *do* ye *more than others?* do not even the *Gentiles* the same? Ye *therefore* shall be *perfect*, as your *heavenly* Father is *perfect*.	ye *do good to them that do good to you*, what *thank have* ye? for even *sinners* do the same. . . . Be ye *merciful*, even as your Father is *merciful*.

Our Lord's teaching about the right and the wrong method of Almsgiving, Prayer, and Fasting here follows in Matt. vi. 1-8, 16-18. This seems to be in its proper place, but the Lord's Prayer, which is found in Matt. vi. 9-13, is in its original position in Luke xi. 1-4, where we find that our Lord taught it in response to the direct request of His disciples that He would teach them as John taught his disciples. S. Luke makes no mention of the Pharisaic customs of sounding a trumpet before giving alms and disfiguring the face on fast days.

It is probable that our Lord's saying that 'the lamp of the body is the eye, and when the eye is single the whole body is full of light' (Matt. vi. 22-23 = Luke xi. 34-36) is also in its proper place in Matthew. Then there comes the saying that 'no man can serve two masters' (Matt. vi. 24 = Luke xvi. 13). The next section, with its command to trust God for the necessaries of life, learning from the birds and the lilies (Matt. vi. 25-33 = Luke xii. 22-31), should probably be placed in section D below, before the command to watch, where S. Luke places it. The character of the member of the kingdom of God towards his neighbour is resumed in the saying

(c) Judge not, *that* ye be not judged. *For with what judgment ye judge, ye shall be judged*.	And judge not, and ye *shall* not be judged: and condemn not, *and ye shall not be condemned*: *release, and ye shall be released*: *give, and it shall be given unto you*; *good measure pressed down, shaken together, running over, shall they give*

And with what measure ye mete, it shall be measured unto you.	*into your bosom. For* with what measure ye mete, it shall be measured to you *again*.
And why beholdest thou the mote that is in thy brother's eye, but considerest not the beam that is in thine own eye? Or how *wilt* thou say to thy brother, Let me cast out the mote *out of* thine eye ; *and lo,* the beam is in thine own eye ? Thou hypocrite, cast out first the beam out of thine own eye; and then shalt thou see clearly to cast out the mote *out of* thy brother's eye.	And why beholdest thou the mote that is in thy brother's eye, but considerest not the beam that is in thine own eye ? Or how *canst* thou say to the brother, *Brother,* let me cast out the mote *that* is in thine eye, *when thou beholdest not* the beam *that* is in thine own eye ? Thou hypocrite, cast out first the beam out of thine own eye, and then shalt thou see clearly to cast out the mote *that is in* thy brother's eye.
Ask, and it shall be given you ; seek, and ye shall find ; knock, and it shall be opened unto you : for every one that asketh receiveth ; and he that seeketh findeth ; and to him that knocketh it shall be opened. Or what man is there of you who, if his son shall ask him for a loaf, will give him a stone ? Or if he ask for a fish, will he give him a serpent?	Ask, and it shall be given you ; seek, and ye shall find ; knock, and it shall be opened unto you. For every one that asketh receiveth, and he that seeketh findeth ; and to him that knocketh it shall be opened. And of which of you *that is a father* shall his son ask a loaf, and he give him a stone? or a fish, and he *for a fish* give him a serpent? *Or if he ask an egg, will he give him a scorpion?*
If ye then, being evil, know how to give good gifts unto your children, how much more shall your Father *which is in heaven* give *good things* to them that ask Him ?	If ye then, being evil, know how to give good gifts unto your children : how much more shall your *heavenly* Father give *the Holy Spirit* to them that ask Him ?
All things therefore whatsoever ye would that men should do unto you, *even so* do ye also unto them :	*And as* ye would that men should do to you, do ye also to them *likewise*.
for this is the law and the prophets.	[Cf. Matt. xxii. 40 :— On these two commandments hangeth the whole law and the prophets.]

(d) We may next read Matt. vii. 16-21, and xii. 33-35 with Luke vi. 44, 43, 45, 46, where we find a rough but substantial identity in the records of our Lord's teaching that a tree is known by its fruits, and then His words about empty profession of belief.

Not every one that saith unto Me, Lord, Lord, *shall enter into the kingdom of heaven*; *but he that* doeth *the will of My Father which is in heaven.*	*And why call ye* Me, Lord, Lord, and do *not the things which I say?*

This is followed by the vain plea made at the last judgment by those who, having disobeyed the Lord, declare that they 'prophesied in His name' (Matt.), or ' did eat and drink in His presence' (Luke). After this our Lord speaks of the two kinds of hearers, the man who built his house 'upon the rock' and the man who built 'upon the sand.'

And *every one that* heareth *these words of Mine*, and doeth them not, *shall be* likened unto a *foolish* man, which built his house upon the *sand*: *and the rain descended, and the floods came, and the winds blew, and smote upon that house*; and it fell: and great was the *fall* thereof.	But he that heareth, and doeth not, *is* like a man that built his house upon the *earth without a foundation*; *against which the stream brake,* and *straightway* it fell *in*; and the *ruin* of that house was great.

This first great section of the sayings began, as we saw, by explaining the work of John the Baptist and the position of the Messiah, and it is followed by two most remarkable passages. The first of these contains the account of the Gentile centurion, who came to our Lord with the prayer that his servant might be healed, and was confident that law and order would be the marks of any supernatural work that the Messiah might do for him (Matt. viii. 5-10, 13 = Luke vii. 1-10).

The words of Jesus that He had not found so great faith ' no, not in Israel ' must have sunk deep into the hearts of His first Jewish disciples. And the second passage contains the message of the Baptist, and our Lord's significant reply as to the Baptist's character and His own mission (Matt. xi. 2-11, 16-19 = Luke vii. 18-28, 31-35).

B. *The second group of our Lord's sayings is concerned with His disciples.*

(a) Commands to His disciples (Matt. viii. 19, 20, 21, 22 = Luke ix. 57, 58, 59, 60). The harvest is declared to be plenteous, but the labourers few (Matt. ix. 37, 38 = Luke x. 2).

(b) Directions to those who preach the Gospel (Matt. x. 7-16, 24, 25-38, 40 = Luke x. 3-12; vi. 40; xii. 2-9, 51-53; xiv. 26, 27; x. 16). The order here differs considerably in the two evangelists.

Closely connected with these directions are sayings about the rejection and reception of the truth. Woe is pronounced on Chorazin, etc. (Matt. xi. 21-24 = Luke x. 12-15). Christ pronounces a thanksgiving to the Father that He has revealed to the simple what is hidden from the wise (Matt. xi. 25-27 = Luke x. 21, 22), and utters a blessing on His disciples (Matt. xiii. 16, 17 = Luke x. 23, 24). He teaches them the Lord's Prayer (Matt. vi. 9-13 = Luke xi. 2-4).

C. *The third group of our Lord's sayings is concerned with His antagonists.*

Jesus is accused of casting out devils with the help of Beelzebub (Matt. xii. 22-30 = Luke xi. 14-23).

He speaks of the good tree and the corrupt tree (Matt. xii. 33-35 = Luke vi. 43-45).

He describes the man whom the unclean spirit leaves for a time only (Matt. xii. 43-45 = Luke xi. 24-26).

He is asked for a ' sign ' and says that the sign He gives will be like that of Jonah (Matt. xii. 38-42 = Luke xi. 16, 29-32).

THE SAYINGS OF OUR LORD   119

He denounces the scribes and Pharisees (Matt. xxiii.
1-36 = Luke xi. 39-52, but much fuller).

D. *The fourth group consists of various exhortations
to the disciples in view of coming trials.*

Jesus tells His disciples to watch lest the Son of Man
should come as a thief (Matt. xxiv. 43, 44 = Luke xii.
39, 40).

The servant set over the household is to act as a
prudent steward (Matt. xxiv. 45-51 = Luke xii. 42-46).

Encouragement is to be drawn from the fact that
the kingdom of God spreads like a grain of mustard
seed and like leaven in meal (Matt. xiii. 31-33 = Luke
xiii. 18-21). For the mustard seed, compare Mark iv.
30-32.

Jesus foretells that there will be occasions of stumbling (Matt. xviii. 6-7, 15 = Luke xvii. 1-3).

He utters the parable of the lost sheep (Matt. xviii.
12-14 = Luke xv. 4, 5, 7).

E. *The fifth group speaks of the doom of Jerusalem
and of the end of the world with the Messiah's return.*

Jesus foretells that Jerusalem, which has slain the
prophets, will be left desolate (Matt. xxiii. 37-39 =
Luke xiii. 34, 35).

He foretells His return (Matt. xxiv. 27, 28, 37-41 =
Luke xvii. 24, 37; 26, 27, 34, 35).

A consideration of these passages leads us to results
which cannot be called certainties, but at least are very
sound probabilities. The correspondence of considerable passages in both Gospels and the use of a number
of peculiar expressions go to prove rather cogently that
the two evangelists used a written source. There is
no reason why S. Matthew may not have written in
Aramaic a document which roughly corresponded with
the collection of sayings which we have briefly described
above. The sayings were put into a Greek dress before
they were incorporated into our first and third Gospels.

It is quite possible that there was more than one translation into Greek, or different recastings of one translation. S. Matthew himself may have written such a translation of his own work. It may be urged that nothing necessitates an Aramaic original, and that the very first report of our Lord's sayings may have been in Greek. But so long as there were Christian converts from Judaism of the humbler classes—and converts appear to have been mainly of the humbler classes—it must have been desirable, if not necessary, that the words of Jesus should be accessible to them in their own language.

The actual entire contents of the original document will probably never be determined at all minutely. It was apparently rather a handbook than a Gospel, and contained nothing like all the teaching which even the oldest and truest tradition attributed to our Lord. It contained few, if any, parables except that of the Lost Sheep, that of the Leaven, and the Mustard Seed. Possibly some critics are right in ascribing to it the partially similar parables of the Marriage of the King's Son (Matt. xxii. 1-10), and the Great Supper (Luke xiv. 15-24), and the parables of the Talents (Matt. xxv. 14-30), and the Pounds (Luke xix. 11-27). These, however, must be regarded as quite doubtful. It is commonly held that the sayings of our Lord which belong to the period covered by the narrative of the Passion were entirely absent from this document. If we could be certain that this view is correct, we might well be content with the theory of Sir W. Ramsay, that it was actually written before the close of our Lord's ministry. Wellhausen has assigned it to a later date than S. Mark's Gospel. But the general consensus of opinion is on the other side, and acute as Wellhausen sometimes is, his critical theories rest on a view of the origins of Christianity which is assumed rather than proved. If the non-Marcan elements in S. Luke's story of the Passion were taken from the sayings, then it still remains possible that the sayings were compiled while the first generation of disciples was still living. If, on the other hand, the sayings contained no story of the Passion, they must either have been compiled before the death of Jesus Christ, or at a time when there were so many persons who actually remembered His death and resurrection that it was not yet thought necessary to write the story. The latter theory is the most probable. The memory of Christ's death was never utterly overpowered by a belief in His immediate return. The early chapters of the Acts prove conclusively that it was not overpowered. But it was much less necessary at first to write down a history which many carried in their minds than the sayings which might be remembered by one or two.

The question whether Matthew or Luke has preserved the sayings of our Lord in the more correct and original form remains a difficulty. To some extent we can control one form of a saying by the other form. But there is not sufficient linguistic evidence to show fully the exact style of the source which they employed. It has been worked over by our first and third evangelists to such an extent that we cannot detect its flavour in the way in which an able Old Testament critic can detect certain strata in the Pentateuch or the Book of Isaiah. The safest clue as to the original form of the document is to be found in the sequence in which we find the sayings in Matthew and Luke. Sometimes they agree; more frequently they do not agree. More than two-thirds of the passages are differently placed, so that one or both dealt very freely with the order of Q. They most nearly agree in our Lord's sermon (Matt. v.-vii.; Luke vi. 20-49). Here each evangelist probably had before him the sermon in four similar sections. And on the whole the order of Q seems to be best preserved in Luke. We should expect this, because it is in harmony with S. Luke's regard for the order of Mark. And if the document was a collection of sayings, it is necessarily almost certain that they must have been arranged according to topics. And Luke furnishes indications of that kind of arrangement. He provides the sayings with introductions, some of which are vague, some more definite and apparently based on a sound tradition. If S. Luke had found the sayings in his source identical in order with the sayings which we find in Matthew, it is hard to see why he should have altered the order. But we can see both that in Matthew they are grouped according to a certain plan, and that the evangelist would have no scruple in following this plan if the sayings in his source were connected with little or no historical narrative.

§ 4. *An Authentic Account of Christ.*

We now touch one of the most fundamental questions, one which cannot be properly handled without a considerable training in biblical criticism. It is whether the evangelists, when quoting from Q, have preserved the sayings of Jesus in an authentic form. Did our Lord speak as they represent Him speaking? Was He such as they depict Him in His sayings? There are several ways in which the evangelists enable us to answer this question. In the first place, their account of His sayings is such that we can call it 'objective.' Just as the local colour in the narrative of the Gospels is true to a particular time and place, so the record of the sayings shows very little indeed of those interpretations and modifications which betray a later date. The negative evidence fits the positive. In spite of that subjective element without which any writing would be an impossibility, the Synoptists tell a faithful story. Each has his own ideal of Christ, but it affects his book to a much less degree than the ideal Christ of many modern writers affects their account of primitive Christianity. Take any popular modern description of the life of Jesus—Renan's, Farrar's, Harnack's, whose you will—and then ask if their ideal is as all-embracing as that of the three Synoptists. The evangelists lived through times of controversy. The Church was harassed, first by Jews, then by Judaising Christians, and then by heathens. And yet how little there is in the Gospels which betrays the times of battle, except the first battle with the Jews.

For instance, we know that the primitive Church was agitated by the question whether a convert to Christianity must become a Jew before he became a Christian. Must he be circumcised? A similar difficulty has begun to be felt in modern Judaism. Progressive Jews are asking if their children cannot be regarded as children of Abraham though they remain uncircumcised. But in the first century of our era it was assumed by the Jews that to be a true child of Abraham circumcision was essential. The fact that the early Church was troubled by the question is certain. But none of the Synoptic Gospels represent our Lord as saying a word which would decide the question. Matthew is the work of a cultivated Jewish Christian, and some think that he displays actual pro-Jewish tendencies. The most probable instance of this is in v. 32 and xix. 9, where he adds to our Lord's absolute condemnation of divorce an exception which is allowed by the Jewish Mishna. But the teaching of the Messiah is set far above the Mosaic law, even when it openly contradicts it. The writer assuredly had much of the mind of Christ. He gives us an account of our Lord's description of the judgment day, when 'the nations,' the Gentiles, are gathered before Him. They will be saved, not by works of the law, but by acts of love and mercy done towards the needy, and therefore done to Jesus, who Himself had not where to lay His head. Some have thought that the world-wide commission given by Jesus to His apostles at the end of this Gospel is inconsistent with His hard saying to the Syrophoenician woman, and that Jesus did not really mean the Gospel to be carried to the heathen. But the object of the evangelist in recording this saying was probably quite different. It was not to show that Jesus intended His followers to be Jews, but to show that He publicly yielded to the prayer of a Gentile, even at a time when He had wished to remain unnoticed.

Then let us consider the sayings of our Lord in Luke. S. Luke writes at a time when it was possible to hope that the Roman government would treat the Church with fairness. It is difficult to read the Acts without seeing how this hope pervades his writing. Moreover, S. Luke has a Greek and more than Greek joyfulness in his temperament. He discards as unnecessary in a Gentile environment some of the anti-Pharisaic utterances of our Lord that are kept in Matthew. Yet he records the startling saying that 'it is easier for heaven and earth to pass away, than for one tittle of the law to fail' (Luke xvi. 17). The whole temper of his book shows that he did not believe this to be true in a verbal sense. He must have found the saying in his records, and he copied it honestly, believing Christianity to be God's own fulfilment of Judaism. In the second century Marcion regarded Luke as the essentially Pauline Gospel. And it is true that it shows Christ as the Saviour of the Samaritan and the heathen, and all the sons of Adam. But the writer does not make either his own personality or his friendship for S. Paul in any way prominent. S. Paul insisted, and had to insist, on the truth of God's mercy to the Gentile world. But S. Luke prefers to lay stress on the love of Jesus for sinners. The evangelist is no mere echo of the apostle, still less his 'shadow.' If he told the story of the compassion of Jesus, he did not tell it to further any party interest, but because he had sufficient grounds for believing that He so spoke and acted. That S. Luke did probably here and there omit incidents which might be stumbling-blocks to the weaker brethren we have noticed above (p. 71). But his general attitude towards Jews and Gentiles alike is neutral while sympathetic. What do these sayings teach us with regard to the claims made by Jesus Christ? What do they show that He believed Himself to be? It is impossible for us to put aside all the discussions of the last three generations with regard to this momentous subject. We are confronted by every type of scepticism, each with its different answer, and united in nothing but their denial that the Christ of the creeds is the Christ of history. On the one hand, we have the Jesus who was born of a virgin, who claimed to be 'the Son of Man' in a new sense, as though mankind were in some way included in Himself, who claimed also to be the Son of God both by moral union of purpose and by a metaphysical union of life, and who, because He was the Son of God in a unique sense, claimed to fulfil the Jewish expectation of an ideal King, the Messiah. On the other hand, we are presented with a number of new Christs, who, from the point of view taken by the creeds, are all false Christs. There is the Christ who, we are told, never claimed any divine prerogatives, and who, if He ever called Himself even the Son of Man, did not mean that He was Son of Man in any representative or inclusive sense any more than S. Peter. There is the Christ who never claimed to be the Messiah, and there is the Christ who claimed to be the Messiah near the end of His life. There is the Christ who never claimed to be the Son of God, and the Christ who, when He made this claim, only meant that He was a human Messiah. There is the Christ who was literally the Son of Joseph, and there is the Christ who is only a sun-myth.

The investigation of the sayings incorporated in our Gospels touches these theories and shrivels them up. For it leaves us with a luminous proof that the oldest Christian tradition represented our Lord as consistently supernatural. We cannot find our way back to a Jesus who was not supernatural. There is no evidence for such a Jesus having existed. And the evidence for the supernatural Jesus is all the more cogent because it is mainly rather implied than taught. It is never thrust upon the reader. Nevertheless Q certainly recorded the preaching of the Baptist and probably the baptism of Jesus by John. The first was recorded to show that the ascetic who had produced so profound an impression on the people had done a work which was only preliminary and inferior to that of Jesus. The second would show how the divine Sonship of Jesus was ratified before His ministry began. And the story of the temptation was also in Q, and shows that Jesus at the very beginning of His ministry was tempted as the *Messiah*. If a Jewish inquirer asked, 'How can Jesus be the Messiah when He lived in poverty and hunger, and not in wealth and splendour?' the Christian reply was, 'Jesus was tempted to choose the latter, but showed His true Messiahship by choosing the former.' He is tempted to use His power in order to acquire that authority over the world which He had resolved to establish by meekness, service, and love. In the great words of S. Leo, 'that self-humiliation was not the failure of power but the condescension of pity.' This is what our oldest sources for the life of Jesus imply. He did not cry aloud to the public, 'I am the Messiah, obey Me.' If He had done this, the people would have made Him a King, and the real spiritual kingdom which He claimed would never have been founded at all. Jesus came forward openly as a Prophet, preaching repentance. But He also regarded Himself as 'the beloved Son' of the Father, as the Messiah, and as the mysterious 'Son of Man,' who is *the* Man who will judge and will represent and, as it were, include His people. When the Baptist sent two disciples to inquire whether Jesus was the Messiah who 'was to come,' He did not say, 'I am.' But His reply rivets together His miracles, His message, and His Messiahship (Matt. xi. 2-11; Luke vii. 18-28). The words which He adds, 'Blessed is he whosoever shall not be offended in Me,' can only be explained by the fact that He claims to be the Messiah, and knows that He is not such a Messiah as was expected by the debased Judaism of the day.

The visible reign and outward splendour of the Messiah belong to the future, but His sayings are issued in a tone which is that of neither the rabbi nor the mere prophet. Jesus instinctively takes up an infinitely higher position. He abrogates not only the ethics of the rabbis, but those of the Pentateuch. He asserts, 'Not every one that saith unto Me, Lord, Lord, shall enter into the kingdom of heaven; but he that doeth the will of My Father' (Matt. vii. 21 = Luke vi. 46). An orthodox confession of belief is not enough. But the very form of assertion indicates that He is Lord, and that there is no difference between doing the will of Jesus and the will of the Father. 'Every one that heareth these My words and doeth them' is compared with the man who built his house upon a rock (Matt. vii. 24=Luke vi. 47, 48). Salvation is made to depend upon loyalty to Himself. 'Every one therefore who shall confess Me before men, him will the Son of man also confess before the angels of God; but whosoever shall deny Me before men, him will I also deny before the angels of God.'

He declares that it will be 'more tolerable for the land of Sodom and Gomorrha in that day' than for the city which rejects His teaching when delivered by His disciples. And He pronounces woes upon Chorazin and Bethsaida, 'for if the mighty works which were done in you had been done in Tyre and Sidon, they would long ago have repented in sackcloth and ashes.' Here the stress is laid upon His miracles. They are regarded as the natural manifestation of His Person, they are what might naturally be expected of one who really is what Jesus claims to be.

It matters little if Q did not contain the memorable confession of His Messiahship made by S. Peter and recorded by S. Mark and the other Synoptists. There is ample evidence for the historical fact of that confession. But Q contained quite as strong testimony to the nature of Christ's personality. He is 'more than Jonah' and 'more than Solomon,' removed from all those who preceded Him (Matt. xii. 38-42 = Luke xi. 29-31). He never confesses sin, never asks God for pardon, never expresses that sense of unworthiness which Isaiah and Jeremiah so deeply felt. He advances demands which from any other lips would appear intolerable: 'Follow Me, and let the dead bury their own dead' (Matt. viii. 22 = Luke ix. 60); 'He that loveth father and mother more than Me is not worthy of Me,' 'Whosoever doth not take his cross and follow after Me is not worthy of Me' (Matt. x. 37, 38 = Luke xiv. 26, 27). Such are the sayings recorded in Q. And they are in harmony with the judgment which He pronounced in the words, 'He that is not with Me is against Me,' and with His prophecies that He, the Son of Man and the Lord of His household, would return suddenly. To be watchful, to be ready, to be faithful is what He meanwhile requires of His servants. The Christian student has no need to exaggerate what Q records of the claims made by

Jesus. For the whole attitude which we have been considering denotes a demand upon our inmost moral life such as no created being can with any justice make upon a fellow-creature. And this attitude is illuminated by a passage which shows that there exists a unique fellowship between Himself and the Fountain of all life and goodness. This passage is that which speaks of the mutual knowledge of the Father and the Son. Long ago it was noticed that this passage teaches a doctrine like that of the Fourth Gospel. Fairly interpreted, it seems to cover all that S. John wrote about the unique nature of the Sonship of our Lord. It describes a reciprocal relationship between the Son and the Father: the Son alone has a true knowledge of the Father; the Son is Himself such that the Father alone understands Him. Now, at one time it was possible to assert, though impossible to prove, that this passage was merely a later interpolation inserted into the midst of the genuine sayings of Jesus. Dr. Martineau, for instance, disliked its 'dogmatic assertion.'[1] So he rejected it along with other statements of Christ, such as 'One greater than the temple is here,' and other authoritative utterances of Christ. Such sayings were pronounced 'out of character with His spirit,' it being assumed that Jesus could not have claimed to be divine. But more penetrating criticism has shown that the passage in question belongs to the most primitive stratum in the Gospels. It is found in almost the same words in Matt. xi. 25-27 and Luke x. 21-22. It is as follows:

Matthew.	Luke.
At that season Jesus answered and said, I thank Thee, O Father, Lord of heaven and earth, that Thou didst hide these things from the wise and	In that same hour He rejoiced in the Holy Spirit, and said, I thank Thee, O Father, Lord of heaven and earth, that Thou didst hide these things

[1] *Seat of Authority in Religion*, p. 582.

understanding, and didst reveal them unto babes: Yea, Father, for so it was well-pleasing in Thy sight. All things have been delivered unto Me of My Father: and no one knoweth the Son, save the Father; neither doth any know the Father, save the Son, and he to whomsoever the Son willeth to reveal Him.

Come unto Me, all ye that labour and are heavy laden, and I will give you rest. Take My yoke upon you, and learn of Me; for I am meek and lowly in heart: and ye shall find rest unto your souls. For My yoke is easy, and My burden is light.

from the wise and understanding, and didst reveal them unto babes: yea, Father; for so it was well-pleasing in Thy sight. All things have been delivered unto Me of My Father: and no one knoweth who the Son is, save the Father; and who the Father is, save the Son, and he to whomsoever the Son willeth to reveal Him.

Here as elsewhere a minute study of the two passages shows that, while the actual expressions used in the first clause in *Matthew* seem the more primitive, it is in *Luke* that we find the true historical setting of the passage. The seventy disciples have just returned from their first mission. Their success has been a means of revealing to them the divine authority of Jesus, and their Master gives thanks to His Father, the Lord of heaven and earth, for giving them this revelation. He goes on to say that all things have been delivered unto Him by the Father. He is God's Son, the Messiah, and He has entered on His spiritual reign as His birthright. The idea of *the Father* revealing the nature of the Son to the disciples of Jesus is exactly what our Lord teaches in Matt. xvi. 17, when S. Peter confesses that He is the Son of God, and it corresponds with S. Paul's statement that it pleased God 'to reveal His Son in me' (Gal. i. 16). We may say that though this passage represents one of the highest points of doctrine in the Synoptic Gospels, it is in harmony with the whole claim that Christ makes over the conscience of mankind. And the additional passage in Matthew, in which Christ invites the weary to come to Him, agrees with all that we know of His majesty and tenderness. 'The meekness and gentleness of Christ' must have produced a profound impression upon the first disciples, or S. Paul would not have alluded to these characteristics as he does (2 Cor. x. 1). We may doubt if any good man who was no more than a prophet could possibly have spoken thus of his own meekness. It would have been a piece of intolerable and irreligious conceit. But the words fall with the accents of grace and truth from the one who could describe Himself with equal justice as Son of Man and Son of God.

Now that the passage cannot be treated as a 'non-authentic' addition, attempts are being made to attenuate its meaning. O. Holtzmann and Harnack explain the 'all things' delivered unto Christ as the doctrine that He taught! Wellhausen regards '*and no one knoweth the Son but the Father*' as an early interpolation, which must indeed have been early, as it is found in all manuscripts and in all versions of Matthew, and in all of Luke except one (*Codex Vercellensis*). Harnack tries to prove the same thing with an imposing array of quotations from the fathers, and says, 'The canonical version in both Gospels is "Johannine" in character and indefensible.'[1] He grants that 'if' the first evangelist wrote the passage as we now read it, 'his own Christology approached very nearly to that of the Johannine writings in one of the most important points.' He therefore tries to restore the original 'complexion' of the passage by omitting the words which we have printed in italics, and by rejecting the present tense *knoweth* for the aorist *came to know* where the Son's knowledge of the Father

[1] *Spruche u. Reden Jesu*, p. 210 (English translation, p. 302).

is in question. The result would be to weaken the parallel and likeness between the Father and the Son, and to suggest that the Son's knowledge of the Father began in time, and was not eternal. If it was not eternal, it would of course follow that the Son is not eternal, but a creature.

We may first remark that it is doubtful, as a matter of Greek grammar, whether the latter result would be attained by substituting one tense for another. But it is enough to say that the present tense is far better supported by the quotations in the fathers as well as by the manuscripts of the Gospels, and Harnack's appeal to the fathers has to be heavily discounted, being wrong or doubtful in several instances.[1] With regard to the important clause, which makes, he says, 'a formal likeness' between the Father and the Son, it remains an integral part of the text. It is really less distinctively 'Johannine' than the other clause, which says, 'Neither doth any know the Father, save the Son,' but it is essential to the balance of the whole passage.

The passage is testimony of the very highest value as to the oldest belief in Jesus and His own self-consciousness. And it agrees closely with the teaching of S. Paul, of the Epistle to the Hebrews, of the fourth Gospel, and of the Apocalypse.

[1] See Dom Chapman, *Journal of Theological Studies*, vol. x. p. 552.

CHAPTER V

THE GOSPEL ACCORDING TO S. MARK

§ 1. *Mark a Roman Book.*

IF we have with any degree of accuracy succeeded in showing the nature of the collected sayings of our Lord, it is obvious that they did not form what we call a Gospel. To S. Mark, so far as we know, belongs the glory of writing the first Gospel. That he knew a collection of Christ's sayings is likely. A comparison of all three Synoptic Gospels leaves the balance of probability on the side of this theory. His use of Q is fairly plain in the case of the account of the Baptist's preaching (Matt. iii. 7-12 = Luke iii. 7-9, 16-17 and Mark i. 7-8), in the account of the temptation shortly afterwards, in the story where Christ is accused of working miracles by Beelzebub (Matt. xii. 22-32 = Luke xi. 14-15 and Mark iii. 22-30), and the parable of the mustard seed (Matt. xiii. 31, 32 = Luke xiii. 18, 19 and Mark iv. 30-32). Several other instances exist.[1]

As time went on it became necessary to write down more than the sayings of Jesus. One by one the men who had walked with Him in Galilee and Jerusalem were passing away, and the Lord had not visibly returned to earth again. The growing Christian family wished to have more of the history of its Founder recorded. S. Mark therefore wrote not so

[1] See Mr. B. H. Streeter in *Studies in the Synoptic Problem*, p. 166.

much to supersede the sayings as to supplement them. He was Peter's 'interpreter,' says Papias; 'he followed Peter.' 'After the departure' of Peter and Paul, says S. Irenaeus, 'he delivered to us in writing the things that had been preached by Peter.'[1] Clement of Alexandria says that Mark wrote at the request of those who wished him to write what Peter had spoken, 'which, when Peter knew, he neither forbade nor encouraged it.'[2] The testimony of Clement can be reconciled with that of Irenaeus if we hold that the Gospel was written while S. Peter was alive, and given to the Church after his death. Possibly it underwent some revision before this was done. As the martyrdom of the apostles was in or near A.D. 64, we find that the oldest tradition provides us with a perfectly reasonable explanation of the origin of our oldest Gospel. It was written by one who is shown by the New Testament to have known both S. Peter and S. Paul, both of whom spent some of their last days in Rome. Many subtle but strong lines of evidence corroborate the Roman origin of Mark. The history of early Christian worship, which is steadily becoming recognised as important for the whole history of Christianity, gives us one or two significant hints. The late Dr. Ceriani, one of the most learned of recent liturgiologists, observed that when the student of the canon of the Mass shall have reached a point when he can really compare what was originally common to both Eastern and Western liturgies, one of the differences which he will discern will be that in the West the words of the consecration of the bread and wine as the body and blood of Christ follow more closely the form given in Matthew and Mark; in the East that given by S. Paul and S. Luke.

Again, we find that, even when S. Paul wrote to the Romans, they were not inclined to be very tolerant

[1] Eus. *H. E.* iii. 39. [2] *Op. cit.* vi. 14.

towards the 'weak' brethren who had an affection for innocent Jewish practices. The famous controversy in the second century between the Churches of Rome and Ephesus proves that they were still apt to be intolerant in that direction. And the question is involved in some very intricate matters of New Testament criticism. The combined evidence of S. Paul and S. John, and numerous indications in early Christian literature, make it more probable that our Lord died on the 14th day of the month Nisan than the 15th, and that He did not celebrate His Last Supper on the night of the Passover. But S. Mark's Gospel, though its details about the Last Supper are not consistent, does in its present form assume that Christ died on Nisan 15th. And while the Church of Ephesus took its stand upon the Johannine tradition, the Church of Rome took its stand upon the tradition enshrined in Mark and copied by the other Synoptists.

The Roman Christians believed that the Eucharist was a substitute for the Passover, instituted by Christ on the same night as the Passover. But they did not commemorate the institution. They transferred their 'Pascha' to the Sunday following, emphasising Christ's resurrection rather than His death and the institution of the Eucharist. Or, to put the matter more exactly, they celebrated the death with the resurrection. The history of Easter, Christmas, and even Whitsunday shows that in early times men saw nothing incongruous in this. As Easter commemorated both the death and the resurrection, so Christmas originally commemorated both Christ's birth and His baptism, and Whitsunday both His ascension and the descent of the Holy Spirit. The Christians did not think that both events happened on the same day, but believed that it was well for them to celebrate the two events together.

So the Roman Christians dissociated themselves, as far as was consistent with an observance of any Pascha, from the practice of the Jews, who always kept the 14th day of Nisan as the Pascha. We know that by A.D. 154 the Roman Church held firmly, and by A.D. 190 vehemently, to her Paschal usage. But in Asia Jews and Christians alike observed Nisan 14th, though the Christians attached to it an immensely enhanced significance, as the commemoration of the sacrifice of the Lamb of God. Sometimes S. Mark's Gospel appears to side with the latter view, for it contains various details which suggest that Christ died on Nisan 14th rather than Nisan 15th. The most significant is in Mark xiv. 2, where we are told that the Jewish authorities took measures for arresting Jesus two days before the Passover, with the resolve that the arrest should not take place during the feast. And yet the chapter goes on to represent them as arresting Him and holding a solemn meeting on the sacred night of the Passover itself. And S. Mark represents our Lord as keeping His Last Supper at the time of the Passover. He says, 'On the first day of unleavened bread, when they sacrificed the Passover, His disciples say unto Him, Where wilt Thou that we go and make ready that Thou mayest eat the Passover?' (xiv. 12). The first meal at which unleavened bread was eaten by the Jews was after sunset, when the next day, Nisan 15th, was reckoned as having just begun. Therefore S. Mark in the latter verse excludes the view that Christ died on Nisan 14th, the date of His death according to S. John. We can only repeat that Mark contains several indications that S. John and S. Paul are correct; but in spite of these indications the narrative, as it now stands, is on the side of the Roman view that the Last Supper coincided in time with the Jewish sacred meal which it supplanted. And in all probability it was so before Matthew and Luke were written.

In the above fact we discover something that is

Roman, but presumably non-Petrine. We must interrogate the Gospel more closely if we desire to seek for proofs of the author's contact with the apostle. Such proofs are frequent. They repeatedly corroborate what we know to have been held by Papias and his friends about A.D. 100, viz. that 'Mark, having become an interpreter of Peter, wrote exactly whatever he remembered of the sayings and actions of Christ, not, however, in order' (see above p. 110).

§ 2. *S. Mark's Style.*

The vividness of this Gospel has long been noticed, and it gives the book a peculiar freshness and interest. It contains a multitude of details, little touches of the brush which make the air breathe and the figures move. We must be prepared to hear all these details described as so much artifice, and a proof of the untrustworthy nature of the record. For there is a school of critics which is inclined to pronounce any mere summary of facts as too lifeless to be first-hand evidence, and then to declare that any detailed account is the literary trick of an impressionist writer. S. Mark's story is now called too realistic to be real. The thoughtful reader must judge for himself. The effect of these details is cumulative. They are too numerous and too natural to be all lightly attributed to imagination—the imagination of a writer who is incapable of writing any Greek but the roughest. The evangelist is no wizard like Sir Walter Scott, able to turn in a moment from a pithy local dialect to an exquisite literary language, and able to give flesh and blood to the creations of his own brain. His style inspires confidence in his honesty. It is so Aramaic in character that some critics think that the Gospel must first have been written in Aramaic, or at least based upon some Aramaic original.[1] It contains Aramaic words: *Boanerges* (iii. 17), *Talitha cumi* (v. 41), *Corban* (vii. 11), *Ephphatha* (vii. 34), *Abba* (xiv. 36), which are all omitted in Matthew and Luke, as well as the actual Aramaic words spoken by our Lord in His extreme desolation on the cross, words also recorded in Matthew. All these phrases come in fitly, for the writer has a genuinely dramatic sense such as the unlearned not unfrequently possess. But a dramatic sense does not account for his frequent grammatical irregularities, his plebeian Greek words, his clumsy use of Greek participles, or the Latin idioms employed in v. 23 and xv. 15, and such Latin words as *speculator* for a soldier of the guard (vi. 27), a contracted form of *sextarius* for a drinking-pot (vii. 4), *centurion* (xv. 39), and the Latin names for the coins *denarius* (vi. 37) and *quadrans* (xii. 42). If this Greek is not the Greek of an early Christian Jew with an imperfect education, we must for ever remain at a loss to know how such a man would have written. It is vigorous, naïve, and unpremeditated.

Why should such a writer be suspected if he tells us of the green grass where the crowds sat, and the appearance of flower-beds which they presented when sitting in groups in their bright Oriental costume (vi. 39, 40); or of the stern of the boat and the pillow on which our Lord slept (iv. 38); of the Gerasene demoniac cutting himself with stones (v. 5); of the woman who was a Syrophoenician but spoke Greek (vii. 26); of Jesus taking the children into His arms (ix. 36; x. 16); of the door where the colt was tied (xi. 4)? It is the same with regard to the proper names that he mentions. We do not deny that at certain stages of

---

[1] See Ven. W. C. Allen in *Studies in the Synoptic Problem*, p. 295. The theory of an Aramaic original of Mark is criticised by Dr. A. J. Maclean, Bishop of Moray, in Hastings' *Dictionary of Christ and the Gospels*, vol. ii. p. 130.

thought there comes a natural desire to supply information which is lacking in earlier authorities. Legend cherished the memory of the repentant thief and the centurion who confessed that the dying Jesus was the Son of God. And legend gave to the first the name of Dismas and to the second the name of Longinus. These names appear long after the Gospels were written, and there is no probability that they are correct. But such fictions are no satisfactory reason for doubting that S. John is correct when he alone tells us that the servant whose ear Peter cut off was named Malchus. Nor should S. Mark be accused by us of inventing the name of Bartimaeus, the blind beggar, whose name is unrecorded by Matthew and Luke (Mark x. 46); Salome, the mother of Zebedee's children (xv. 40); and Boanerges, their surname (iii. 17); also the names of Alexander and Rufus, the sons of Simon of Cyrene (xv. 21), names which would have been quite pointless if they had not been familiar in the circle for which S. Mark was writing.

§ 3. *The last twelve Verses.*

The last twelve verses of Mark are widely different in style from the rest of the book, and some of the most ancient authorities end with the words ' for they were afraid.' A few critics think that this was the original ending, S. Mark having closed his Gospel thus either by accident or intentionally. A far larger number of critics hold that there was some longer ending, now lost. Some think it was deliberately torn off because it contradicted the other Gospels. Others, and in all probability rightly, believe that there was at first only one copy of the Gospel, and that the end of the roll was lost by accident. The present ending is very ancient, for it is certainly quoted by Irenaeus, and is probably referred to by Justin Martyr. The origin of it was quite unknown until 1891, when an Armenian manuscript of the Gospels, written in A.D. 986, was discovered, attributing it to the 'presbyter Ariston.'[1] Ariston is another form of the name Aristion. It has been conjectured that this was Ariston of Pella, who wrote after A.D. 135. But this conjecture is rendered improbable by the occurrence of the definite citation in Irenaeus, which seems to necessitate an earlier date. The author, therefore, is most likely the Aristion mentioned by Papias, and one of the last of our Lord's personal disciples. If so, it may be fairly assumed that these verses were written in Asia Minor. But the problem cannot be said to be absolutely solved.

§ 4. *The Disciples and the Mysteries of God's Kingdom.*

Let us notice the relation of Jesus to His disciples. It is depicted by S. Mark with peculiar force. No other Gospel shows us so clearly how He trained His disciples for their great future, and how slow they were in understanding His purpose. They had to un-learn as well as learn. It was necessary to instruct them thoroughly as to the nature of the kingdom of God and His own work in founding that kingdom on earth. After the Pharisees had become definitely hostile to Him and united with the Herodians, *i.e.* the Government and Erastian party, He withdrew with His disciples to the sea-shore, but being followed by a multitude from Galilee, Judaea, and other regions, He retired to the hills. With Him He took 'whom He Himself would.' And He appointed twelve 'that they might be with Him, and that He might send them forth

[1] Mr. F. C. Conybeare, *Expositor*, 4th series, viii. p. 241.

to preach, and to have authority to cast out devils' (iii. 14, 15). He again returns to His public work. The scribes from Jerusalem definitely accuse Him of casting out devils by the prince of the devils, and then He finds that even His friends think Him mad, and His mother and brethren wish to remove Him from danger. In reply to this anxiety, He simply says farewell to His own family. 'Whosoever shall do the will of God, the same is My brother, and sister, and mother' (iii. 35).

As He cut Himself free from the sympathy of home, so must His disciples. He utters in public the parable of the sower. And we find at once a separation between esoteric and exoteric teaching. Words addressed to the disciples only are distinguished from those meant for the people who are without. 'When He was alone, they that were about Him with the twelve asked of Him the parables' (iv. 10). So again, later, we read, 'When He was entered into the house from the multitude, His disciples asked of Him the parable' (vii. 17), and it is 'in the house' that His disciples ask Him about the nature of marriage and divorce (x. 10). The parable of the sower, the subsequent explanation of this parable in private, the parable of the seed growing while men slept, and the parable of the mustard seed, are placed near each other by S. Mark in chap. iv., as specimens of many parables which Jesus 'privately expounded.' To the Twelve He says, 'Unto you is given the mystery of the kingdom of God' (iv. 11). Those who are 'without,' the outsiders, do not understand this secret. They only see the parable, the illustration from natural life, with the result that while seeing they do not perceive, and are not converted.

We are not to think that the Twelve had as yet any deep perception of 'the mystery.' Our Lord's words imply the contrary. He says, 'Know ye not this parable' (*i.e.* of the sower), 'and how shall ye know all the parables?' (iv. 13). But He has chosen them that they may know. They have been called to preach and to do the will of God. They have believed in Him sufficiently to answer His call, as is instanced by the fishermen who left their nets to follow Him (i. 16 f.). And they are beginning to know. What was the first great secret imparted to those who had received the word, and were to bring forth fruit? It was that the kingdom or reign of God was not to begin by any outward catastrophe, but by a slow and gradual process. It was to be thoroughly supernatural, and yet largely natural. This is what the hearers of our Lord found so hard to understand.

What the ordinary Jew desired was a sudden miraculous deliverance from present misery and oppression. In the Jewish Apocalypses and in the New Testament we can see how the people yearned for the restoration of the sovereignty of their nation. At the head of the victorious Jews there was to be a great temporal prince. He was to appear suddenly and conquer quickly. They dreamed of a time like the golden days of Solomon. And the 'day of the Lord,' which the ancient prophets had foretold, was to be the dawn, not so much of righteousness as of revenge upon the Gentile. Every now and then some impostor took advantage of these national hopes. Such was the Theudas mentioned by Gamaliel in Acts v. 36 as the head of an unsuccessful rebellion of four thousand men, and such was Bar-cochba, who in A.D. 134 stirred up the last frenzied opposition to Roman rule. When Christ came and preached that the kingdom of God was at hand, and bade men prepare for it by repentance, and when He severed Himself from the official teachers of Judaism, the populace hoped that He would head that great rebellion which would usher in the new age. As the fourth evangelist says, they wished to make Him a king (John vi. 15). Only a few were prepared to believe that the kingdom would come by a slow moral growth in the hearts of men, and then find an outward expression in a new community before the time was ripe for the great final change. This is the first mystery of the kingdom.

We must connect with this mystery our Lord's injunctions to silence. In several cases we find that after some miraculous occurrence Jesus told the witnesses of His power to remain silent; they were to tell no one. Different interpretations have been put upon these injunctions by modern critics. It has been held that they are not really authentic, but invented by the primitive Church or the evangelist to account for the fact that the Jews among whom Jesus had worked did not become Christians. The disciples did not suppose that He was the Messiah until He was dead, and they believed that He had appeared to them. And it was imagined by the early Church that the Jews did not accept Him as the Messiah, because He had not claimed to be the Messiah or encouraged them to believe it. On the other hand, it has been held that these injunctions are truly historical, and that Jesus enjoined silence because it was not His purpose to found a church or even a new system of morality. He came forward to preach repentance in view of the sudden miraculous advent of the kingdom of God. He knew that He was the predestined Messiah, but His second advent would be His first coming *as* the Messiah. The first of these theories seems to me to be profoundly unhistorical, and the second, though much truer, to be very one-sided. It is impossible to avoid the belief that the stories with which these injunctions are connected go back to genuine reminiscences of an apostle and others whom the evangelist had personally known. Moreover, their relative positions in the narrative appear to be historical. No commands to 'tell no man' are given at the time of the first healings in Capernaum, nor do they occur near the end when publicity was inevitable. They come where they are deliberately intended to check a popular Messianic movement. Christ does certain miracles in public, such as the cure of the paralytic in ii. 1-12, and the man with the withered hand in iii. 1-6. Here, as in the case of the feeding of the five thousand in vi. 35-45, there is no command to keep silence. But in the two former cases Jesus withdraws from the town, and in the last case He sends the crowd away. He does not wish to make His cures the most vital part of His work or rely on them for the spread of His fame. He refuses to accept such an advertisement as might be given Him by persons, whether epileptic or otherwise mentally alienated, whose 'unclean spirits' He had driven out (iii. 10-12). Cries which the bystanders plainly believed to be a confession of His authority as 'the Holy One of God' (i. 24), or 'the Son of the most High God' (v. 7), prove that the afflicted persons were conscious of His influence, but He seeks no such acknowledgment from such a quarter. Even when a leper whom He had healed disobeyed His injunction to 'say nothing to any man,' the result was that Christ 'could no more openly enter into a city' (i. 44, 45). With this we may compare the command that the raising of the daughter of Jairus should not be made known (v. 43; cf. vii. 36; viii. 26). The injunction given to Peter, James, and John after the transfiguration is of especial interest, for a time limit is imposed on their silence. 'He charged them that they should tell no man what things they had seen, till the Son of Man were risen from the dead' (ix. 9). The vision appears to be intended to confirm their loyalty towards Him as the Son of God before the impending trial of their faith involved in His rejection and crucifixion.

We cannot be wrong if we interpret these commands to 'tell no man' by our Lord's own teaching with regard to His Person. He knew that time was on

His side, that through His death there would be a new era for the kingdom of God which He had already inaugurated. The certainty that this time would dawn was compatible with both His laying the foundation of a new society and His promulgation of a new and better moral law. But the society must be realised to be His own, and His authority over the conscience must be unquestioned. He is God's Son, He can wait. And as 'God is patient because He is eternal,' His disciples must be patient, and not proclaim the full mystery of His Person until His resurrection proves His divine Sonship.

S. Mark does not spare the failings of the Twelve, who were being won to this true idea of God's kingdom and of the Messiah's office. In the storm Christ has to say to them, 'Why are ye fearful? have ye not yet faith?' (iv. 40). And after the evangelist has recorded how Christ walked to them on the sea, he adds, 'They were sore amazed in themselves; for they understood not concerning the loaves, but their heart was hardened' (vi. 51, 52). Again, they are so slow to understand the true nature of defilement that Christ asks, 'Are ye so without understanding also?' (vii. 18). They seem to have put a childishly literal interpretation on His warning to beware of 'the leaven of the Pharisees and the leaven of Herod.' And He pleads with them. 'Do ye not yet perceive? . . . Do ye not yet understand?' (viii. 14 f.). They cannot yet believe that He is fully able to provide them with their daily bread, just as He knows when they need rest and refreshment (vi. 31). Nor can they see how corrupting and pervading is the spirit of vitiated religion and worldly politics.

After S. Peter's confession, Jesus draws them from the thought of the kingdom of God to the thought of His own death. It is not that He has altered His own conception of His work. S. Mark gives us no hint of such an idea. The 'Bridegroom' foresaw His death before the Pharisees determined to destroy Him (ii. 20; iii. 6). But He expands His teaching now that the Twelve are better established in their allegiance to His Person and know something of the nature of the kingdom of God. But they are still very slow and dull. The latter part of the Gospel lies under the shadow of the cross even before we reach the detailed story of the Passion. Many of His adherents expected that the last journey of Jesus to Jerusalem would result in some startling upheaval, some great manifestation of God. We cannot otherwise account for the scene of Palm Sunday. But the Master went up to Jerusalem knowing that He would die, and that the 'wicked husbandmen' would kill the Son of the Lord of the vineyard. He had tried to prepare the inner circle of His followers for that crisis.

This story, as given to us by S. Mark, harmonises well with the theory that it was written by a friend of S. Peter. We are under no necessity of supposing that S. Peter composed any outline of the whole book, or that he provided all the incidents that it contains. Some other matters connected with S. Peter and with S. Mark's picture of our Lord will be noticed later. What we can be content to say just now is that the account which this Gospel gives of the training of the disciples, and of the influence which Jesus exercised over those disciples, does account for their subsequent devotion to His cause. It therefore points us back to an eye-witness.

§ 5. *S. Mark's Geography.*[1]

If we turn from the training of the disciples to

[1] I owe much in this section to Professor Burkitt's *The Gospel History and its Transmission*, while attributing a much higher value than he does to the record of journeys implied in the Fourth Gospel.

their first travels with the Master, we shall be able to corroborate the theory that the evangelist had known a personal follower of Christ. The descriptions of His journeys have not the air of being invented by a foreigner. Nor would they be probable as the invention of one who knew the scene of Christ's ministry at a later age. The excursions are 'roundabout'; they imply a certain amount of opposition and failure, and they fit the political circumstances of the time of Christ. Let us consider the country where our Lord travelled, beginning at the north. To the north-east there is the heathen district of Tyre and Sidon, and almost due east of Tyre is the city of Caesarea Philippi. Southward of the district of Tyre is the Jewish region of Galilee, coming down to the west coast of the inland sea of Tiberias. Almost in the heart of Galilee is Nazareth. And by the shores of the sea are Tiberias, Capernaum, and Bethsaida. *Over Galilee ruled Herod Antipas*, 'that fox'; but Bethsaida was just outside his dominions. Far south of the sea of Tiberias is the other inland sea, the Dead Sea, and the Jordan joins the two seas. To the west of the Jordan, just under Galilee, is Samaria, the country of schismatics, half-Jew, half-heathen, and strongly hostile to the Jews. Opposite Samaria, on the other side, is the heathen region of Decapolis. South of Samaria, and lying between the coast of the Mediterranean to the west and the Jordan and the Dead Sea to the east, is Judaea with the cities of Jericho and Jerusalem. Opposite Judaea, and on the east of the Jordan south of Decapolis, is Peraea. *Over Peraea ruled Herod Antipas.* And in the south of Peraea was the castle of Machaerus, where, as Josephus the Jewish historian records, John the Baptist was put to death.

The above brief description shows us that there were within this small geographical area three openly opposed religions: Judaism, Samaritanism, and heathenism. We further know from Jewish books that within Judaism itself there were different types of thought. In addition to the Pharisees, the strictly orthodox nationalist party, and the more sceptical Sadducees, whose centre was Jerusalem, there were the 'people of the land.' These were simple country folk, despised by the Pharisees for their ignorance and disregard of Pharisaic ceremonial, but probably ready to give ear to an attractive teacher. The ascetic Jewish community of Essenes, which lived near the Dead Sea, is not important for our present discussion.

The political divisions of the country are of very great importance. Galilee and Peraea had in the person of Herod Antipas a vicious ruler, who had been rebuked by the Baptist for marrying Herodias, his brother's wife. Such a man would not be inclined to view with favourable eyes any teacher of renown who continued the Baptist's habit of rebuking vice. Bethsaida and Caesarea Philippi were ruled by Herod Philip I., whom Herodias had deserted. Decapolis had been annexed to the Roman province of Syria by Pompey, the ten cities from which the district derived its name being allowed a considerable amount of freedom under Roman rule. Samaria and Judaea were likewise part of the Roman province of Syria, ruled by a Roman procurator. The Romans, as is well known, were usually tolerant towards the religion of their subject races, and in Samaria and Judaea they had to deal with religions which took themselves seriously. The whole history of Jerusalem under Roman rule shows that it was animated by a fanaticism which embarrassed the government, and which Rome had either to humour or to crush.

Now the narrative of S. Mark, meagre though it is, fits in with the three religions and the three governments which I have described. And it is in substantial agreement with certain important indications furnished by S. Luke and S. John. These indications must be mentioned later. In the meantime we can observe the following points in S. Mark's account of our Lord's journeys:—

A. The basis of our Lord's missionary work is Galilee, starting from Capernaum, a town which was not far from His own home at Nazareth, and was probably identical with the modern Tell Hûm.

(a) *First missionary journey, in towns of Galilee: withdrawal to the hills.*—His first excursion is in the neighbourhood of Capernaum (i. 38; ii. 1). Afterwards He travels on the north side of the sea of Galilee, where there was a toll-house on the border between the land of Herod Antipas and that of Herod Philip, and returns to the synagogue (ii. 13; iii. 1). He makes an expedition on the left shore (iii. 7, 13). This expedition was the result of a break with the Pharisees. They were indignant at His disregard of their rules respecting Sabbath observance, and went off to make plans with the government party, 'the Herodians,' to suppress the new Teacher.

When He goes, Jesus is followed by an enthusiastic multitude. But He now desires to instruct the few rather than the many. So he departs to the hills, summoning only 'whom He would,' and He appoints twelve men to be His apostles (iii. 13).

(b) *Opposition at Capernaum.*—He returns to Capernaum, apparently with the intention of passing to the other, the right, shore of the lake (iii. 19, 20). People have talked about Him during His absence. The scribes hold that He works miracles with the help of diabolic power. His own friends think Him mad (iii. 22 ff.). Therefore He leaves the town and spends a day on the shore of the lake (iv. 1). (c) *Second missionary journey, on the eastern shore of the lake of Gennesaret.*—He crosses the lake to the country of the Gerasenes, who beseech Him to depart from their borders (iv. 35; v. 1, 17). (*d*) *Third missionary journey, in the western highlands: Herod's perplexity.*—He returns and goes to Nazareth (v. 21; vi. 1). In the meantime Herod has heard of Him, and thinks that the Baptist is risen from the dead (vi. 14). Therefore after the miracle of feeding the five thousand Jesus and His disciples start in their boat for Bethsaida, outside the jurisdiction of Herod Antipas. But they are driven back by a contrary wind to Gennesaret, within that jurisdiction (vi. 45, 53).

B. Our Lord visits pagan districts.

(*a*) *Fourth missionary journey, into Phoenicia and Decapolis.*—In Gennesaret He is met by crowds of people and by Pharisees and scribes from Jerusalem. So dangerous are the circumstances that He goes far off to the heathen district of Phoenicia, containing the cities of Tyre and Sidon (vii. 24), and then to the predominantly non-Jewish district of Decapolis (vii. 31). A long circuit was made, and the reason evidently was to avoid Herod Antipas. But He goes back once more to a place which seems to have been on the west side of the lake (Dalmanutha; probably Magdalunaya, a suburb of Tiberias). He is immediately met by the Pharisees (viii. 10, 11). (*b*) *Fifth journey, to towns of Caesarea Philippi.*—He goes once more to Bethsaida, and then to the non-Jewish district of Caesarea Philippi (viii. 22, 27). Here S. Peter confesses Him to be the Christ, and He definitely foretells His death.

C. Our Lord's last visits to Jerusalem.

(*a*) *Journey to Jerusalem through Samaria (or Peraea).*—Christ journeys slowly to Jerusalem. He goes back from Caesarea Philippi to Capernaum, but goes in secret (ix. 30 ff.). In travelling southward He would be obliged to pass either through Samaria, on the west of Jordan, or through Peraea on the east, or through part of both. Most unfortunately we here reach a crux in the text of Mark. Ancient students saw the difficulty, and tried to correct the reading, with the result that we are confronted with three different readings, each of which is plausible. The later Greek MSS., followed by the English Authorised Version, say in Mark x. 1, 'He arose from thence, and cometh into the coasts [*i.e.* borders] of Judaea by the farther side of Jordan.' The Greek of this is perfectly plain, and means that He came into Judaea, not by passing straight through Samaria, but by going through Peraea. On the other hand, the Vatican MS., a most important MS. of the fourth century, and other kindred MSS., followed by the English Revised Version, have, ' He arose from thence, and cometh into the borders of Judaea and beyond Jordan.' This is also quite plain, and quite different from the other reading. It means that our Lord came into Judaea—probably through Samaria, but the way is not specified—and then turned eastward into Peraea. If this is correct, then Mark x. relates to a visit to Judaea, followed by a ministry in Peraea, before Christ's final return to Jerusalem. At first sight this is a very attractive reading. It agrees in an unobtrusive way with the Fourth Gospel, where we find that our Lord went to Jerusalem, was bitterly opposed (John vii., viii., ix., x.), and then retired to the east of the Jordan (John x. 40). From thence He went to Bethany and Ephraim (John xi. 54), returning to Jerusalem to die. Jesus, according to S. John, went beyond the Jordan after the feast of the Dedication at Jerusalem in December A.D. 28, and returned to Jerusalem for the Passover in March A.D. 29.

Such are the two readings with which the modern student of the Bible is most familiar. But there is a ' harder' reading, and harder readings are proverbially to be ' preferred' to the easier, as it can be shown that they were frequently altered by well-meaning scribes. The best Greek text of Mark x. 1 may be that which agrees with the old Syriac and Latin versions.

It runs, 'He arose from thence, and cometh into the borders of Judaea beyond the Jordan.' Now the borders of Judaea could only be 'beyond the Jordan,' to a person who was himself east of the Jordan, and presumably travelling through Peraea. It is certainly most unlikely that any one would have invented this very ancient reading. It may possibly be corrupt. An 'and' may have dropped out before 'beyond.' But if it is genuine, it implies that the person who originally told the story which we have in S. Mark went through Peraea, though it does not necessarily imply that Jesus went with him. The whole journey cannot be traced. But we learn from Luke ix. 51-56 that our Lord, with James and John, was refused admission into a Samaritan village. S. Peter was apparently not with them at the time. Probably the little company had divided, some of them going by the road through Samaria, and some of them going by the usual Peraean road adopted by Jewish pilgrims for the very purpose of avoiding Samaria.

It is possible that Jesus, after encountering this opposition from the Samaritans, crossed the Jordan and travelled through Peraea until He came nearly opposite to Jericho, and then crossed the river and came into Judaea. This seems to me perfectly consistent with the difficult reading in Mark x. 1, though not necessarily implied by it. But if this was our Lord's route, we should be led to suppose that it was more dangerous for Him to go through Samaria than through the Peraean part of Herod's dominions. This is not what the Gospels generally suggest. It is more probable that He went through Samaria, and arranged to meet the main body of His disciples, probably including S. Peter, on the west side of the Jordan near Jericho. This view has two advantages. It gives a reason for the fact that S. Mark's Gospel, which seems to be rich in the personal recollections of S. Peter, especially near its end, tells us practically nothing about this journey into Judaea. It also agrees with the fact that S. Luke here supplements S. Mark by important additions, apparently derived from another companion of our Lord. Among these additions is the parable of the good Samaritan (Luke x. 25-37).

When Jesus did reach the frontiers of Judaea He was at least safe from Herod Antipas, and S. Mark says, 'Multitudes came together unto Him again.' He then visited Jerusalem as recorded in John vii. 10.

In the view which has been adopted above there is a difficulty which it would be disingenuous to ignore. It is that Mark x. mentions only one actual visit to Jerusalem (x. 32), and not the two, or even three, visits implied by S. John (vii. 10; ? x. 22; xii. 12). If S. Peter, who was with our Lord during at least part of the time recorded in this chapter (x. 28), narrated one such journey, why did he not narrate more? It is a mistake to try to cut the knot by simply dismissing S. John's record of the different visits to Jerusalem as a pious fiction.[1] The question can only be answered, if at all, by another question: Why does S. Mark omit the precious material contained in the middle section of S. Luke's Gospel? It is generally admitted by critics that this material does not belong entirely to the period following the final departure of Jesus from Galilee for the south. And it contains much teaching which bears every conceivable mark of genuineness. Did S. Mark's instructor or S. Mark himself know this, or did one of them for any reason, such as a desire for brevity, omit it? We cannot tell. But we can say that it is probable that some of this teaching belongs to the time when Jesus went once more beyond the Jordan, after the feast of the Dedication in A.D. 28. That such is the case is not only intrinsically probable,

[1] For the historical value of the Fourth Gospel on this point see Dr. Sanday's *Outlines of the Life of Christ*.

but is also strongly corroborated by Luke xiii. 31-35. Here we are told that the Pharisees came to Jesus, saying to Him, 'Get Thee out and go hence, for Herod would fain kill Thee.' Jesus is once again in Herod's territory. He knows His danger. But He also knows that He is in equal danger at Jerusalem. He goes thither resolved to die.

The result of this investigation is to show that S. Mark's account of our Lord's travels, though far from complete, is of very great historical value. In spite of his conviction that Jesus is the Son of God, he certainly does not represent Him as breaking down all opposition and meeting with triumphant success. He is hunted; He has not where to lay His head. He delivers His message, but again and again He withdraws from danger until the supreme hour has come. The bare outline of facts is more pathetic than any adventures and victories which a romancer of later times would have attributed to a popular prophet. The more critically we look at it the more likely we are to think that it was based on the experience of one who was with Christ for a large part, but most likely not the whole, of His ministry.

We cannot discover the same precision in either Matthew or Luke. In the former Gospel it is destroyed by the author's grouping of the sayings of our Lord, and we find vague phrases, such as, 'Jesus went about all the cities and the villages' (ix. 35), and 'He departed thence to teach and preach in their cities' (xi. 1). In the same way S. Luke in viii. 1 says, 'He went about through cities and villages.' S. Luke, who is particularly accurate in the geographical allusions made in Acts, is very uncertain as to the itineraries of our Lord. A good instance is to be found in the passage which prefaces S. Peter's confession that our Lord is the Christ (Matt. xvi. 13; Mark viii. 27; Luke ix. 18). The first two evangelists definitely mention Caesarea Philippi. S. Luke omits the name altogether and says, 'As He was praying alone, the disciples were with Him; and He asked them, saying, Who do the multitudes say that I am?' S. Luke appears to have deliberately omitted the name as one unknown to his readers. An equally interesting case is found after the story of the miraculous feeding of the five thousand (Matt. xiv. 22; Mark vi. 45; Luke ix.). S. Mark shows that Jesus and His disciples intended on crossing the lake to go to Bethsaida; in Matthew 'the other side' is mentioned, but not the town; in Luke there is no mention of either one or the other. From S. Mark also we gain a clearer view of the last week of our Lord's life before the crucifixion, for he seems to show, either directly or indirectly, that our Lord returned every evening to Bethany (xi. 1, 11, 12, 19, 20; xiv. 3, 12 f.). The anointing of our Lord by a woman in the house of Simon the leper at Bethany is perhaps inserted by S. Mark on the wrong day (xiv. 3-9). Here it appears to be two days before the Passover. In John xii. 1 it is six days before the Passover. Perhaps S. Mark did not know exactly when it happened, and therefore put it next to the story of the betrayal, in order to throw the action of Judas into a higher relief. As a final instance of the greater minuteness of S. Mark's topography we may note that whereas he states that the discourse about the destruction of Jerusalem was delivered by Jesus 'as He sat on the Mount of Olives over against the temple' (xiii. 3), S. Matthew says simply 'on the Mount of Olives,' and S. Luke omits both the reference to the mount and that to the temple.

§ 6. *S. Peter in Mark.*

S. Peter is the most prominent of the disciples of Jesus, both at the beginning of the Gospel, where he is mentioned first of the Twelve (iii. 16), and at the end, where 'the young man' seen by the holy women at Christ's tomb says to them, 'But go, tell His disciples and Peter' (xvi. 7). S. Peter's confession that Jesus is the Christ is as central here as in the other Synoptic Gospels (viii. 29), but Mark does not record, like Matthew, the fact that our Lord called Peter the rock on which He would build His Church. Indeed, the things told concerning Peter are rather of a nature to check any desire to venerate him as the prince of the apostles. Here we find the reprimand which he received when he criticised our Lord's mission (viii. 33), Christ calling him 'Satan,' a term copied in Matthew but omitted in Luke. Like the other Synoptists, S. Mark records S. Peter's fanciful suggestion to erect three tabernacles to Jesus, Moses, and Elias on the scene of the transfiguration, a suggestion to which he adds, 'for he wist not what to answer' (Mark ix. 4; Luke ix. 33). S. Mark alone notes that it was Peter who specially called our Lord's attention to the withering of the fig-tree which He had cursed, and possibly S. Mark understands Christ's reply, 'Have faith in God,' as in some sense a rebuke of S. Peter's action (xi. 21, 22). It was Peter whom Christ awoke in Gethsemane by uttering his name, 'Simon' (xiv. 37); and his denial of his Lord is shown in the least favourable light, for he does not repent until the cock crew twice, giving him a double reminder of Christ's warning (xiv. 72). The record of Mark, followed by Matthew, mentions both the imprecations and the perjury of Peter, 'He began to curse, and to swear, I know not this man of whom ye speak.' And if we go back to the scene where this fall of S. Peter was predicted by Christ, we find the same characteristics. S. Luke says nothing of the failure of the apostles as a body. But S. Mark, closely followed by the first Gospel, mentions both our Lord's prediction that all would be offended, and Peter's presumptuous double declaration that he would be loyal, 'He spake exceeding vehemently, If I must die with Thee, I will not deny Thee' (xiv. 31).

That S. Mark created these features of his narrative is scarcely probable. Either he wrote with an animus against all the original twelve apostles, especially S. Peter, or relied upon some early tradition in which the saints appeared as less impeccable and infallible than they were supposed to be by later generations. Now S. Mark may have had a very great admiration for S. Peter. He may have revered him both as a man and as a martyr of Christ, and thought that any failing shown by him in early days was atoned for by a life spent and laid down in the service of Jesus. Such a thing as this is so reasonable that we need not feel bound by any psychological necessity to think that S. Mark despised S. Peter. A coarser manner than that of the evangelist would have been employed by the ancient writer who wished to advertise to the world the inferior quality of the earliest type of Christianity. The Clementine romances, forged about A.D. 200 by a Judaistic Christian who disliked S. Paul, give us a good hint as to the nature of primitive powers of calumny. It is much too subtle to see in S. Mark an armoury of innuendoes against the Twelve and a hidden glorification of S. Paul in the prophecy, 'Many that are first shall be last; and the last first' (x. 31).

§ 7. *S. Mark, S. Paul, S. John.*

This Gospel, though largely derived from S. Peter, must not be called distinctively Petrine. Such a view is unbalanced, and has provoked the energetic efforts which have been made, and are still made, to find in it the most pronounced Pauline teaching. A well-known representative of this critical tendency is Professor B. W. Bacon of Yale. He holds that the book has been revised by an ultra-Pauline Roman Christian who wrote about A.D. 70-75. Professor Bacon belongs to the school of writers who hold that S. Paul held a fundamentally different conception of the work of Christ from that which Christ held Himself, and that he turned the original message delivered by the apostles into an alien Gospel. When they discover in the Gospels any passages which lay emphasis upon the saving value of Christ's death, they usually feel themselves compelled to say that these are mere interpolations. So Professor Bacon says, 'In very high degree Mark's narrative is dominated by theoretical considerations, often manifestly derived from the Pauline Epistles, especially Romans,'[1] and 'the Paulinism of Mark is supremely manifest in this evangelist's whole conception of *what constitutes the apostolic message.*'[2] The Christian can be grateful to any critic, however hostile he may be to the heart of Christianity, when he testifies in this fashion to the inward unity of the New Testament. The Church of the second century was correct in regarding the books which compose it as the work of the same Spirit. S. Mark's Gospel, rough and simple as it is, teaches the doctrine of the cross as certainly as the fervid arguments of S. Paul. S. Mark and S. Paul apprehended Christianity in a manner which is radically the same. Were they both mistaken? Were there no events which explain their ideas?

The decisive event which justifies the doctrine of the cross is the crucifixion. Jesus died, when He might have avoided death. As Professor Bacon himself says, ' For some reason Jesus *did* go up to Jerusalem,

---

[1] *The Beginnings of Gospel Story*, p. xv
[2] *Op. cit.* p. xxviii.

and throw down the gauntlet in the face of the priestly hierocracy in the temple itself. For some reason He *did* follow a rôle which led to His execution by Pilate as a *political* agitator. For some reason His followers, very shortly after, *did* ascribe to Him not mere reappearance from the tomb, but exaltation to the place of the Messiah "at the right hand of God"—attributes so exalted that it is difficult to believe they had no other foundation than mere reverence for an admired Teacher.'[1] It is indeed difficult. The credulity of an illiterate peasant is pure enlightenment compared with the credulity of the critic who thinks that Jesus deliberately courted an awful death without the idea that His death would save sinners, that He was executed as a political agitator, and yet never made the one claim which in Roman eyes would justify His execution, and that after His death His followers died for declaring that He was alive in heaven, when they really knew that His body was rotting in Jerusalem. According to S. Mark, Christ died with a purpose. He had taught that He would give His life 'a ransom for many' (x. 45). The phrase comes from the Old Testament, and Jesus in using it meant that the offering of His life would be a means towards liberating men from guilt. Historically it has had this effect. The verse agrees with other passages which are found in our other oldest sources copied in Matthew and Luke. It is in the same line with other words in which Christ foretells His death and subsequent resurrection. It is in harmony with what all the Synoptists record in connection with the Last Supper. In short, all that S. Mark says about the significance of Christ's death is coherent, and it stands the severe test of comparison with all the best authenticated passages in the New Testament. According to all known rules of evidence it must, at least in substance, be part of the teaching

[1] *Op. cit.* p. 106.

of Jesus. According to a rigidly conservative scepticism it was not, because it could not be; and it could not be, because Jesus was a 'plain mechanic.'[1]

Other alleged footsteps of Paulinism need hardly detain us. If the evangelist did not borrow from S. Paul a novel doctrine of Christ's Person, and a novel doctrine concerning His death, but merely recorded what was the common faith of the Church, the accusation that he borrowed S. Paul's universalism is worthless. It is said that he falsely represents Jesus as commanding that the Gospel should be preached to all nations, in all the world (xiii. 10; xiv. 9); that His words to the Syrophoenician woman are less harsh and therefore less genuine in Mark than in Matthew (Mark vii. 24-30; Matt. xv. 21-28); that He is represented as altering the law of the Sabbath (ii. 27) and of unclean meats (vii. 15-19), and exalting the command to love (xii. 32-34). S. Mark also speaks of the rending of the temple veil at the death of Christ (xv. 38), and of God's rejection of the Jews (iv. 11 ff.). The question, however, is not whether this is all in harmony with S. Paul, which the Christian Church does not doubt, but whether the evangelist teaches a partisan Paulinism which perverts history. Jesus Christ gave a mighty impulse to both an extensive and an intensive universalism. This is widely admitted even by non-Christian writers, and we therefore have no sure ground at all for saying that the evangelist is a Pauline partisan. It is worth noting in this connection that the vocabulary of S. Mark is to an extraordinary degree less Pauline than that of S. Luke, and to a small degree less Pauline than that of Matthew. There are 22 words found only in Mark and in Paul, 32 only in Matthew and in Paul, 103 only in Luke and in Paul.[2]

At the present time, when so much is made of any

[1] *Op. cit.* p. 108.
[2] Sir John Hawkins, *Horae Synopticae*, p. 189.

apparent contradictions and antitheses in the Gospels, it is a real aid to correct thinking if we ask ourselves in every case whether these contradictions truly exist. Sometimes the problem has only to be grasped in order to be at least partly solved. We have already seen that the idea of a lasting opposition between a Pauline and a Petrine party in the primitive Church gains no support from this Gospel. The sharpest criticism has never been able to determine whether this, the earliest Gospel, contains a preponderating measure of Pauline or Petrine elements. And we are at least encouraged by this fact to think that much which has been tabulated among the distinctive theories of this or that great apostle is really Christian in the truest sense of the word. It is 'of Christ,' and only in a secondary sense 'of Paul' or 'of Cephas.' But we may now fitly allude to another supposed antithesis. The fourth Gospel and the second are generally held to be more widely separated than any other two Gospels. In Mark the subjective element appears to be least, in John it is greatest. Mark is essentially realistic; John is at least accused of presenting us with an idealised and remodelled story of our Lord. Mark is practical, concerning himself with the notable deeds of Christ's life; John is symbolic. That John selects events which have an inner meaning, and sometimes even two inner meanings, is indisputable. And many critics assert that John abounds in scenes and persons and events which are merely invented to enforce a doctrine or suggest a hidden and mysterious truth.

Let us compare a few points in Mark and John. We may note in passing that Volkmar, a critic much in vogue some thirty years ago, interpreted the miracles in Mark exactly as the most recent rationalism interprets the miracles in John. For him the woman with an issue of blood was a picture of Israel under the influence of the rabbis, whose prescriptions were impotent to expel uncleanness. The dead daughter of Jairus was, according to his interpretation, a picture of Israel united to the synagogue, and dead in spite of this union. For the present this method of interpreting Mark appears to have fallen into abeyance. The book is too graphic, its style too artless, for this vaporising. And yet the question still remains whether S. Mark himself did not think that certain of the miracles of Jesus, and certain events connected with His life and death, had a symbolic meaning. Was not the cure of the leper something more for S. Mark than a sign of the power of the Son of God? Must he not have noticed that he wrote down the story of the healing of the blind man immediately after he had shown the dulness of the disciples, and immediately before Jesus begins to reveal the mystery of His death? Was he not aware that the healing of the man who was both deaf and dumb in a heathen country would suggest the future work of Jesus in the heathen world? Would he not think that the repeated miracle of Christ feeding the hungry would suggest to his readers, and was intended by Christ to suggest, the coming Eucharistic feast? Is it possible that he regarded the rending of the veil of the temple when Jesus died as a chance event with no significance as to a new relation between God and the world?

If such questions are fairly considered we shall at least lose confidence in the dogmatism which pits the Johannine spirit against that of the Synoptists, and does so with the dogmatic purpose of reducing the Christian conception of Christ.

§ 8. *S. Mark's Portrait of Christ.*

A notable proof of the historical accuracy of this Gospel is to be found in the childlike simplicity with which S. Mark describes the emotions of our Lord, and even writes down what others might conceive to be derogatory to His honour. In this respect the difference between Mark on the one hand and Matthew and Luke on the other is very great. S. Mark speaks of Christ as showing anger and grief (iii. 5) and wonder (vi. 6). These words are omitted in both Matthew and Luke. He also applies to Christ the following expressions:—*sternly charged* (i. 43), *sighed* (vii. 34), *sighed deeply in His spirit* (viii. 12), *was moved with indignation* (x. 14), *was greatly amazed* (xiv. 33). In vi. 5 S. Mark says that Jesus *could not*, but Matthew in xiii. 58 that He *did not* do mighty works at Nazareth. We may also compare the following phrases:—*He wished to pass by them* (vi. 48); *He did not wish that any man should know it, and He could not be hid* (vii. 24; cf. ix. 30), omitted in Matthew. In several passages our Lord is represented as asking questions (v. 9, 30; vi. 38; ix. 12, 16, 21, 33; xiv. 14). These are omitted in Matthew, possibly because they might be interpreted as implying ignorance on our Lord's part. The question asked by Jesus Himself in Mark x. 3 is put into the mouth of the Pharisees in Matthew. In Mark the completeness and the immediate effect of Christ's miracles are less prominent than in the parallel passages in Matthew. Thus in Mark i. 32-34 *all* are brought and *many* healed, but in Matt. viii. 16 *many* are brought and *all* are healed (cf. Mark iii. 10; Matt. xii. 15). In three places in Matthew (ix. 22; xv. 28; xvii. 18) we find inserted a phrase intended to make it clear that Christ's healing power took effect immediately. The case of the barren fig-tree is important. In Mark xi. 12 we find that our Lord on His way from Bethany to Jerusalem was hungry, and seeing a fig-tree in leaf *came if haply He might find anything thereon*, but found nothing but leaves, *for it was not the season of figs*. Both these phrases are omitted in Matthew. The first might seem to imply ignorance, and the second might seem to suggest that our Lord was mistaken in expecting good figs at such a season. In Matthew it is added that the tree withered immediately, and that the fact caused the disciples to wonder so much that they called their Master's attention to it.

Most important is the difference between our Lord's question, '*Why callest Thou Me good? None is good save one, even God*' (x. 18), and the form in which it appears in Matt. xix. 17, '*Why askest thou Me concerning that which is good? One there is who is good.*' The words were not a disclaimer of holiness or of Deity on the part of the Saviour. They were a repudiation of a man's empty compliment involved in the address, 'Good Master,' and were meant to turn his thoughts upward to the Source of all goodness. S. Luke leaves the words unaltered (xviii. 19), perceiving that S. Mark had written something true to the character of Him who 'humbled Himself.'

It is right and necessary clearly to place before us these passages which imply the limitations under which our Lord lived. But the practice of accepting these passages as if they were the only real clue, or the best clue to a correct interpretation of Christ's life, is most unreasonable. For the very fact that S. Mark so candidly narrates passages of this kind gives us a guarantee that his other statements are at least in the main historical. And it is beyond dispute that in his mind this second class of statements is far the more important.

S. Mark's particular titles for Jesus are 'the Son of God' and 'the Son of Man.' It is quite evident that this latter title means something very different from 'a mere man.' The title is apocalyptic. It goes back to Daniel vii. 13, where the four great empires of the world are represented by four beasts, but their dominion falls before the advent of 'one like unto a Son of Man.' This supernatural person is Israel, the saints of God united in one heavenly predestined figure. Gradually the name acquired the strictly Messianic meaning which it bears in the 'Similitudes' of the Book of Enoch (chaps. 37-70). Here the Son of Man is a superhuman Messiah, whose office it is to judge the world, to vindicate the righteous, and to crush the wicked. At the day of judgment 'the kings, and the mighty, and the exalted' will set their hope upon the Son of Man and implore His mercy. But only the righteous will be 'saved,' and 'the Lord of Spirits will abide over them, and with that Son of Man will they eat and lie down and rise up for ever and ever.' Without in the least disclaiming the idea of sovereignty and power which the name bears in the Jewish apocalyptic story, Jesus shows that He is sovereign of another and higher order. He fills it with a deeper meaning, as He filled the phrase 'kingdom of God.' And for S. Mark it is precisely the Jesus who walks upon the earth, hungry and poor, who is this heavenly being who has been exalted to heaven (xv. 62) and will come again with power and glory (xiii. 26). He represents Jesus as calling Himself the Son of Man even when He is speaking of His work on earth (ii. 10, 28; x. 45), of His sufferings (viii. 31), and His resurrection (ix. 9).

To S. Mark the life of Jesus was a sufficient and overwhelming proof that Jesus is the Messiah and the Son of God. Just as the fourth evangelist writes with the intention that his readers may believe that Jesus is 'the Christ, the Son of God' (John xx. 31), so S. Mark wishes to leave upon his readers an impression which he regards as vital to religion. It is the same as that of the fourth evangelist, though sometimes presented in other words. For him Jesus is the Christ, and the Christ is the Son of God. The dignity of Christ is attested at the beginning, at the central crisis, and at the end of Christ's ministry. His divine Sonship is attested by the Father at His baptism (i. 11).

His Messiahship is confessed by S. Peter, the representative of the disciples (viii. 29), and the centurion, whether he was heathen or proselyte, who stood by the cross of the dying Jesus, confessed that He was ' the Son of God ' (xv. 39). And Jesus Himself acknowledges to the high priest that He is ' the Christ, the Son of the Blessed ' (xiv. 61). These testimonies were not recorded by chance, or because the evangelist thought that he had nothing else to tell us. He recorded them deliberately, with the conviction that they are so important that he had nothing *better* to tell us. They are part of the essence of his Gospel.

With regard to the Baptism of our Lord, recent controversy has made it almost as necessary to see what S. Mark does not say, as what he actually says. Certain sects of the second century of the Christian era, more Jewish than Christian, taught that Jesus was only a man chosen by God, who became an *adopted* and titular Son of God, and the Messiah, at His baptism. Some even held that the Holy Spirit who then descended on Jesus was what they called the Son of God, a half-divine being who came to dwell in the man Jesus. In recent years such views have sometimes been considered primitive. But by no critical dexterity can the earliest Gospel be made to harmonise with such theories, any more than it can be made to harmonise with the somewhat similar view that Jesus first became the Son of God at His resurrection. S. Peter, in Acts x. 38, says that God anointed Jesus Christ ' with the Holy Ghost and with power.' This corresponds exactly with S. Mark's conception of the result of Christ's baptism. It does not exclude a divine Sonship existing before the baptism, and it does not exclude that outward demonstration of the divine Sonship which S. Paul connects with the resurrection (Rom. i. 4). The words heard by Jesus at His baptism, according to S. Mark, are ' Thou art My beloved Son, in Thee I am well pleased.' They combine the thought of two passages in the Old Testament, in one of which the royal Messiah is described, in the other the ideal suffering servant of God (Ps. ii. 7; Isa. xlii. 1). In the original the first passage runs, 'Thou art My beloved Son, this day have I begotten Thee.' If S. Mark had simply copied this verse,[1] it might have reasonably been argued that he held the 'Adoptionist' view of Christ's Person. Such is not the case. In Mark we do not gather that Jesus became the Son of God at His baptism, but that He knew that He was the Son of God. It does not follow from this that the baptism brought to Him no increase of spiritual power. But it is simply undeniable that the work of the Holy Spirit in equipping the Messiah for His mission is but little emphasised in Mark. It is much more prominent in Luke, where, however, the supernatural birth of Christ is recorded, and where the doctrine of His divine origin is unmistakably implied.

What meaning is attached to the phrase 'Son of God' can only be ascertained by a close study of the Gospel itself. His authority (i. 27; iii. 15; vi. 7) and His power (vi. 2, 5, 14) are repeatedly illustrated; His figure is commanding; His conquest over spiritual adversaries is continuous. The evil spirits obey Him (i. 27) and fear Him (i. 24, 34; v. 7; ix. 26). They do this because they recognise that He is the Son of God (i. 24, 34; iii. 11 f.; v. 7). He, the Son of Man, is able to forgive sins, and He regards the miracle of healing which accompanies this forgiveness as an easier matter than forgiveness (ii. 9 f.). He is 'Lord of the sabbath,' able to regulate the true observance of the day (ii. 28). He feeds five thousand with miraculously created bread (vi. 44); the sea and the winds obey Him (vi. 48 f.). He withers a fig-tree by His word (xi. 14, 20). He raises from the dead the daughter of Jairus (v. 42). When scribes from Jerusalem accuse Him of

[1] The verse appears in this form in some Western manuscripts of Luke.

working miracles by Satanic power, He treats this as blasphemy against the Holy Spirit, and S. Mark's comment shows that he regards the reply of Jesus as identifying calumny against Himself as a sin of this unpardonable nature (iii. 28-30). Even if we omit this comment of the evangelist, the passage as it stands in Mark exalts Jesus higher than the corresponding passage in Matthew (xii. 22 f.). For in the latter Jesus speaks of calumny against the Son of Man as pardonable, distinguishing it from blasphemy against the Spirit. In Mark xii. 1-12 we have a final parable of warning, in which Jesus expressly distinguishes Himself as 'the beloved Son' and 'the heir' from 'servants' of God, who had previously come to teach the Jews. If all these passages imply a merely human Messiah, we may well ask how the evangelist would have described the action and teaching of One who was by nature more than man. S. Mark certainly understood that Jesus is the Son of God, not merely in the lower theocratic sense of a human Messianic King, but because He is the sole Person among men who derives the essence of His being from God.

The author of this, our earliest Gospel, had no 'humanitarian' conception of Christ. It is worth noticing that Professor Harnack has lately stated that S Mark—for he believes that S. Mark wrote this Gospel—'has almost transformed our Lord into a spirit-being of divine power, or had found such a conception of Him already in existence . . . he and his authorities have modified the tradition concerning Jesus in accordance with the experience of the Christian Church.'[1] That S. Mark 'transformed' the conception of Christ's Person is easy to assert, but it is impossible to prove. For the principal documents in the New Testament, which are older than S. Mark's Gospel, such as S. Paul's Epistles, the Sayings, and the First Epistle of S. Peter, unite in representing Jesus as 'a spirit-being of divine power.'

[1] *Luke the Physician*, p. 122 note (English translation).

CHAPTER VI

THE GOSPEL ACCORDING TO S. MATTHEW

§ 1. *General Characteristics.*

ORIGEN, the genius and the defender of early Greek Christianity, saw that this Gospel was written for Christian converts from Judaism.[1] These converts, both in Palestine and beyond, would be anxious for information about the Messiah. They would be anxious to prove to Jewish inquirers and Jewish persecutors that the Scriptures prepared for the coming of a poor and persecuted Saviour. They were also confronted by the fact that Gentiles were pouring into the Church on the understanding that the law of Moses was largely abrogated. S. Paul had taught that national privileges as such were at an end, though he also taught that the Gospel really belonged 'to the Jew first.' They would therefore eagerly desire to know what the attitude of Jesus really was toward the Law, what was now to be done, and what was to be left undone. It was inevitable that these Christian Jews should ask, first, Did our prophets foretell such a Messiah as Jesus? and, secondly, Did Jesus destroy or fulfil the Law of Moses? To these two questions the evangelist endeavours to give a full answer. And it is throughout the Jew rather than the Gentile that he has in mind. The quotations in this

[1] Eus. *H. E.* vi. 25.

Gospel form by themselves a study of great importance. It was long ago observed that they fall into two distinct classes. The first class consists of quotations from the Old Testament used as comments on events connected with the life of Christ, and intended to show that in these events certain great prophecies have been fulfilled. They are all ushered in by the formula, 'in order that what was spoken by the prophet might be fulfilled' or by a formula nearly to the same effect. These quotations vary widely from the Greek version of the Old Testament. One of them, that which says that 'He should be called a Nazarene' (ii. 23) cannot be identified with any exact passage in the Old Testament. Perhaps the evangelist himself is playing upon Hebrew words which resemble 'Nazarene' and mean 'Branch,' the Messiah having been spoken of as a 'Branch,' or his meaning is, '*for* He shall be called a Nazarene,' and he thinks that by becoming an inhabitant of a specially despised town, Jesus fulfilled the prophecies which represent the Messiah as despised and poor. The other quotations of this same class are firstly, ii. 6; iv. 15 f.; viii. 17; xiii 35; xxvii. 9 f., which are translations, and partly paraphrases, of the Hebrew; secondly, i. 23; ii. 15; ii. 18; ii. 23; iv. 6; xii. 18, which are translations from the Hebrew, but eked out with the Septuagint. That in xxvii. 9-10, which speaks of the words of *Jeremiah* with regard to the thirty pieces of silver, like ii. 23 concerning the Nazarene, presents a special difficulty. Possibly it is from the apocryphal book of Jeremiah. These quotations from the prophets vary very much in the nature of their application to the event recorded by the evangelist. Sometimes the verse quoted is directly Messianic, such as 'The virgin shall be with child, and shall bring forth a son' (i. 23). 'Out of Egypt did I call my son' (ii. 15), which in Hosea applies to the Hebrew people, is in Matthew applied to the Messiah, because He is in an eminent degree representative of Israel's filial relation to God. The weeping in Rama over the death of the Israelites in the Assyrian invasion, quoted in ii. 18, and the quotation in iv. 15, 16 from Isaiah, about the darkness of the shadow of death in the land of Zebulon followed by the light when Sennacherib's forces were dispelled, stand on a different level. They offer merely poetical parallels to the lamentation over the murdered innocents and to the night-dispelling preaching of Christ in Galilee.

While the above quotations show a Hebrew background, the quotations which Matthew has in common with Mark are as a rule actually nearer to the Septuagint than those in Mark. The same is true of some non-Marcan quotations. This, when considered in connection with the facts described in Chapter III., adds to the numerous proofs of the composite origin of our first Gospel. The phenomena appear to be accounted for by the hypothesis that the author was a Christian Jew, who knew both languages, and quoted sometimes from memory and sometimes perhaps from a collection of Messianic texts.

The literary method of the author of our first Gospel is further illustrated by its frequent traces of a numerical arrangement of the deeds or words of Jesus Christ. This does not merely add to the effect produced upon the reader, but was also in all probability intended to aid the memory of teachers and catechumens. The common numbers so employed are three, five, and seven. The genealogy is artificially compressed into three divisions, each containing fourteen names. There are three main incidents in the holy Childhood, the coming of the Magi, the flight into Egypt, and the return from Egypt (ii. 1-23); there are three temptations (iv. 1-11); three examples of righteousness, viz. almsgiving, prayer, and fasting (vi. 1-18); three prohibitions—Lay not up treasure on earth; Judge not; Give not what is holy to the dogs (vi. 19.-vii. 6). These groups of three abound to such an extent that we have not space to mention anything like the whole list. But we may note that in viii.-ix. 8 there are three miracles of healing, viz. of leprosy, palsy, and fever; and three miracles of power over natural and supernatural forces, viz. a storm, demoniacs, and sin. In ix. 18-34 there are three short stories containing four miracles of restoration, viz. of health, life, sight and speech. In xii. 38-42 there are three signs given to the Pharisees, viz. that of Jonah, the Ninevites, and the Queen of the South. In xxii. there are three questions asked Him, by the Pharisees, the Sadducees, and the lawyer. The concluding chapters also abound in these groups. In xxiv. and xxv. there are three parables against negligence, viz. the Faithful and Unfaithful Slaves, the Ten Virgins, and the Talents. In xxvi. there are three prayers in Gethsemane, and three utterances of our Lord at the time of His arrest. In xxvii. 51-53 there are three signs to attest the Messiahship of the crucified Jesus, viz. the rending of the veil, the earthquake, and the resurrection of saints. In xxviii. there are three groups of witnesses to the resurrection of our Lord, viz. the women, the soldiers, and the disciples.

Comparison with Mark and Luke leaves no doubt that some of these groups were arranged by the evangelist himself.

The number *five* is also of importance in this connection. Matthew contains five great discourses of our Lord, each of which ends with such a formula as, ' It came to pass when Jesus finished ' (vii. 28 ; xi. 1 ; xiii. 53 ; xix. 1 ; xxvi. 1). These five discourses are : the Sermon on the Mount ; the charge to the apostles ; the collection of parables ; the discourse on the little child, with certain sayings that follow ; and the denunciation of the Pharisees, followed by the great discourse on ' the last things.' In chap. v. the Sermon on the Mount contains five corrections by our Lord of inadequate ideas about the Law of God, each beginning with the words, 'But I say unto you' (22, 28, 34, 39, 44).

With regard to the number *seven*, we have already noted the divisions of our Lord's genealogy, and we can add the seven parables in chap. xiii. and the seven woes in chap. xxiii.

That the above arrangement is based upon Jewish literary methods is clear. Three and seven are favourite numbers in the Old Testament, and the number five was equally classical. There are the five books of the Pentateuch, the five books of the Psalms, the five Megilloth or Rolls, and the five divisions of the *Pirqe Aboth* or Sayings of the Fathers.

This Gospel is, in the arrangement of its matter, artificial. Its numerical grouping of our Lord's sayings produces an effect of unity and solidity. It is like some masterpiece of architecture such as the cathedral church of the Holy Wisdom at Constantinople, in its grandiose and harmonious character.

The composite nature of this document, artistically welding together S. Mark's narrative with other sources, at once raises a question as to its authorship, such as is not so acutely raised in the case of the other synoptic gospels. Neither S. Mark nor S. Luke were numbered among the twelve disciples of our Lord, and they would therefore naturally have to depend upon such information, oral or written, as they were able to collect. On the contrary, S. Matthew was one of the apostles who was with Jesus during His ministry, and must have been in possession of abundant first-hand knowledge. Would he be likely to accept the framework of his story from S. Mark? It is difficult to think so; and it becomes all the more difficult when we realise that Mark, in spite of its inestimable value, contains certain gaps which S. Matthew in all probability would have been able to fill, and which are not filled by the Gospel which bears his name. So far as the date of Matthew is concerned, there appears to be no definite stumbling-block in the way of its apostolic authorship. Without attributing it to any extravagantly early period, we can say that it bears numerous marks which stamp it as a document written within forty or fifty years after the crucifixion. The fact that it is in some ways artificial is no adequate proof of a late date. The writers who think that a late and developed stage of thought is necessarily implied whenever they discover in any religion an elaborate ceremonial, or a deep theology, or a conscious literary skill, have to reckon with very stubborn facts. The magnificent worship which the Syrian Christians employed ages before an equal splendour was customary at Rome, the early but profound theology of S. Ignatius of Antioch, and the Syriac 'Hymn of the Soul,' are among the many monuments of the past which tell us that all is not late that shows a fulness of knowledge or of art. The Gospel according to S. Matthew, which I believe contains that apostle's own collection of our Lord's words embedded in it, reveals both an intimacy with the old religious culture of the Hebrews, and a very real skill in fitting his story to the needs of the growing Church of his time. The author is, in the words of Christ, which he quotes, a 'scribe who hath been made a disciple to the kingdom of heaven, like unto a man that is a householder, which bringeth forth out of his treasure things new and old' (xiii. 52).

In S. Matthew's original collection of our Lord's Sayings, for which we have adopted the symbol Q, the word 'Gospel' cannot now be discovered. But these 'good tidings' are implied in the answer given by our Lord to the disciples of John the Baptist (Matt. xi. 2-11; Luke vii. 18-28). 'The blind receive their sight, and the lame walk, the lepers are cleansed, and the deaf hear, and the dead are raised, and the poor receive good tidings; and blessed is he whosoever shall not be offended in Me.' The writer of the Sayings understood by these 'good tidings' the news of the coming of the kingdom of God to those on whom Christ's beatitudes were pronounced. They were the truly blessed, and such would not be offended in the stern and lowly Son of Man. S. Mark, writing somewhat later, reads into the word 'Gospel' its fuller meaning. With him, as with S. Paul, the Gospel cannot be separated from the Person of the Jesus who had been crucified and raised. That Jesus Himself had meant that His good tidings should be understood in this fashion when He had risen from the dead, seems implied in the authoritative claim which He made upon the souls of men. S. Mark records His saying, 'Whosoever shall save his life, shall lose it, and whosoever shall lose his life for My sake and the Gospel's, shall save it' (viii. 35); the nearest parallel to which in Q perhaps omitted *for My sake and the Gospel's* (Luke xvii. 33; but cf. Matt. x. 39).

Even if Q did not actually contain the word 'Gospel,' the author may have regarded the message of salvation in the same way as S. Mark. He firmly believed that Jesus was the Messiah, he knew that the Christian must take up the cross (Matt. x. 38; Luke xiv. 27), and, unless we have misinterpreted him, he only omitted the story of the Passion and the Resurrection because they were still imprinted on the minds of Christ's disciples. Both he and S. Mark speak of the 'kingdom of God,' and attach to the phrase the same meaning. It is a reign of God, both present and future, inward in the heart of the blessed, and to be manifested outwardly at the second advent in all its power.

The author of our 'Gospel according to S. Matthew'

did what S. Mark never attempted. By incorporating Q in his own book he practically terminated its existence as an independent work. And he applies to the teaching of our Lord a significant title not found elsewhere in the New Testament. He calls it 'the Gospel of the kingdom' (iv. 23; ix. 35; xxiv. 14). It urged repentance, but it also inspired joy, and he does not apply the name of Gospel to the preaching of the Baptist. The latter preached repentance and proclaimed that the kingdom was at hand, but the note of severity in his message was perhaps too marked for the evangelist to give the preaching of the forerunner the name of 'good tidings.' It is well known that the evangelist calls this kingdom the 'kingdom of the heavens,' a phrase which he uses thirty-two times, while he only once uses the phrase 'kingdom of God' employed by the other Synoptists.[1] It is merely an instance of the Jewish reverence which shrank from uttering the name of God, and used periphrases, such as 'the heavens,' in order to avoid the name itself. Possibly the Aramaic Sayings of S. Matthew used this same periphrasis, and we need not hastily conclude that the evangelist was the first Christian writer to employ it.

Our first Gospel might itself be called 'the Gospel of the kingdom.' Nowhere do we find a closer alliance between the new Christian joy and the old Jewish hope. The result is sometimes regarded as a contradiction, but chiefly by those who fail to see that all great and comprehensive truths contain something of this element of contradiction. Like S. Paul, the evangelist fights Pharisaism step by step. He is on his defence, and from the genealogy in the first chapter to his indictment of the chief priests for bribing the guard at the holy sepulchre, he is a critic of Judaism. Like S. Paul, he was proud of his Jewish race, and he

[1] Matt. xix. 24.

had a sympathetic insight into the antique world and could appreciate its prophetic inspiration. Those waves of expectation which Judaism had so long experienced found an answer in his heart. His Gospel is the most apocalyptic of our Gospels. Whatever injury Judaism had suffered in the grasp of an exaggerated legalism and literalism, it had not lost the hope of the great apocalypse, the revelation of God. Jews still believed that the ideal state of the world would be perfectly realised, and God would reign visibly on earth either by some manifestation of His own Person, or of His anointed Son. This advent would be the 'consummation of the ages.' Our first evangelist is the only evangelist who uses this phrase, and he uses it five times. He alone gives us the parables of the Virgins and the Talents, and the description of the Sheep and the Goats (chap. xxv.). They are to warn his readers to be completely ready for the coming of Him who is both the Bridegroom and the Judge of the soul. The kingdom is not a future one only. The series of parables in Matt. xiii. compare not the doctrine of the kingdom but the kingdom itself to the man who sows good seed, to a grain of mustard seed, to leaven, to a hidden treasure, to a merchant seeking pearls, to a dragnet. But the first and the last of these parables have a directly apocalyptic interpretation added. At the end there will be a separation not of Gentile from Jew, but of the wicked from among the just. It is implied that the kingdom will then be perfectly realised, and in Matt. vii. 21 it is shown that a man's right to enter that kingdom must rest upon his character and relation to God, 'Not every one that saith unto Me Lord, Lord, shall enter into the kingdom of heaven; but he that doeth the will of My Father which is in heaven.' It is worth noting that S. Luke, the more Gentile evangelist, does not mention the kingdom in the corresponding passage of his Gospel (Luke vi. 46).

§ 2. *Date of Matthew.*

The perceptibly Jewish colouring of this Gospel puts us at once on the right track when we seek to discover its date. The more radical critics of sixty years since tried to assign it to a date which is now generally regarded as impossible. Baur wished to fix it about A.D. 134, near the time of the second destruction of Jerusalem by the Romans. But the internal evidence points to a date much nearer A.D. 70, the year of the first destruction. Many critics are inclined to date it a generation or so later, mainly on account of its doctrinal teaching, a point which we must consider a little later. On the other hand, one of the ablest writers on this Gospel, and one who is by no means always conservative, has adopted the very early date of about A.D. 50.[1] It is difficult to reconcile this with the evangelist's use of Mark. And it appears equally difficult to assign it to a period between A.D. 75 and A.D. 100. For it is luminously clear that the visible return of the Son of Man is expected 'immediately after the tribulation of those days' in which Jerusalem will be laid desolate (xxiv. 29). Nothing can be more unlikely than that these words were merely copied by the evangelist from an older source after Jerusalem had been destroyed. They appear to be a modification of S. Mark's words in Mark xiii. 24, deliberately made by a writer who is uncommonly deliberate in all that he writes. He carefully removes various difficulties which the ordinary Christian would feel when reading Mark, but here as in xvi. 28 (cf. Mark ix. 1) he not only leaves, but actually emphasises, words in Mark which very soon after A.D. 70 would be among the most perplexing of all. We may compare the remarkable verse in which the evangelist, speaking

[1] Ven. W. C. Allen, *Expository Times*, July 1910.

of the potter's field bought by the chief priests, adds, 'wherefore that field was called, The field of blood, unto this day' (xxvii. 8), a statement much more likely to be true before the destruction of Jerusalem than after it. The verse about the bridegroom 'tarrying,' in the parable of the ten virgins (xxv. 5), and that which speaks about the 'long time' before the Lord cometh, in the parable of the ten talents (xxv. 19), seem in no way to prove a late date. Even before A.D. 70 many of the first believers in Jesus must have left this life, and those who had expected His speedy return would feel that they had waited long. Such verses cannot outweigh the evangelist's expectation of a great catastrophe which will follow upon the appearance of the 'abomination of desolation' in the holy place (xxiv. 15). This catastrophe is expected more definitely here than in any other Gospel. And the only natural explanation of the fact is that the evangelist, believing that the fall of Jerusalem was near, did, as a devout Hebrew Christian, believe that the destruction of God's city would be the herald of the destruction of the old world.

The external evidence, afforded by quotations from Matthew in early Christian writers, is decisively in favour of the theory that the date is much nearer A.D. 70 than A.D. 135. For it can be proved that the First Gospel was the popular Gospel of the early Church. It cannot be by mere chance that whatever order is adopted by early writers in arranging the Gospels, they almost invariably put Matthew first. Moreover, it cannot be that the Christians of the second century gave this pre-eminence to the Gospel because it showed most favour to their own predilections. The Church of the second century was vehemently opposed by the Jews. Jewish literature shows that the 'heretics' were illtreated in the synagogue and cursed in daily prayers. And Christian literature has recorded the part which the Jews played at the martyrdom of S. Polycarp in A.D. 155. In return, the Christians found it very difficult to do any justice to Judaism. They did not adopt the Antisemitic line of the Gnostics, who ascribed the Old Testament to an evil god inferior to the supreme Being. But many refused the name of Christian to Jewish converts, who, though sound in their faith towards Christ, still kept the Law. The so-called Epistle of Barnabas in A.D. 130 and Justin's dialogue with Trypho about A.D. 155 unite in adopting an almost defiant attitude towards the ceremonial Law of the Old Testament. In Barnabas we find the view that the Jews went astray in fitting a literal meaning to the laws about the Sabbath and circumcision. In Justin there is the view that the Sabbath was instituted because the Jews forgot God, and that circumcision was commanded that the Jews might be visibly marked out for punishment by the Romans.

In fact, the primitive Gentile Church had little sympathy with Judaism, and little understanding of the principles of continuity and development in religion. We have to be content with the fact that it had far more sympathy and more intelligence in these matters than the cultured heathenism and Gnosticism of the time. And we must not expect to find it tenderhearted towards Jewish exclusiveness. And yet, in spite of all this, the Gentile Church used Matthew most. The earliest certain instance of a citation of a saying of Christ as 'Scripture' is from this Gospel in the Epistle of Barnabas, iv. 14. Dr. Schmiedel has tried to make out that these words, 'many called, but few chosen,' are not from the words of the Gospel, which are identical, but from a version of the Book of Enoch which does not exist.[1] And Professor Burkitt suggests that the author 'had forgotten the reference.'[2] It is

[1] *Encyclopaedia Biblica*, vol. ii. col. 1828
[2] *The Gospel Story and its Transmission*, p. 320.

THE GOSPEL ACCORDING TO S. MATTHEW 181

more probable that the ancient writer means what he says, and intentionally quotes as Scripture the verse as recorded in Matthew. And this is made all the more probable by the fact that St. Ignatius about A.D. 110 shows, like Justin, a closer affinity with Matthew than with any other Gospel. I do not at all mean that they used no other of our four Gospels, only that they show the plainest traces of the first.

There is another phenomenon to be observed in the first half of the second century. S. Matthew was not connected with either of the two great centres of Christian life. He was a converted tax-gatherer, and very little is known of his life after the resurrection of our Lord. Perhaps the tradition existing at a later date was correct in saying that he went to Parthia. But legend also connects him with India and Ethiopia. At any rate we have no evidence of his ever visiting Rome and Ephesus. The first of these two cities did, even in the second century, glory in its connection with S. Peter, and it is fairly certain that S. Mark, the interpreter of S. Peter, wrote his Gospel in Rome. Ephesus had other noble traditions. The Church there gloried in the name of John, the disciple of the Lord, and possessed the Gospel which bore his name. Neither of these two Churches, nor any other great Church of the world that spoke Greek and Latin, claimed to have been founded by S. Matthew or to have enjoyed his instructions. Yet in the Far West as in the Far East the Gospel according to S. Matthew was accepted, and enjoyed a position of pre-eminence.

There is only one reasonable explanation of these facts. It is that this Gospel must have been written a considerable time before the close of the first century. Its whole tone suggests that it was written for Greek-speaking Jewish Christians in Syria and Palestine before A.D. 70, and its external history suggests that immediately after the destruction of the holy city it was carried to the Gentile Christians in Antioch, Asia Minor, and Rome.

§ 3. *Catholicism of Matthew.*

Against the above view a constant appeal is made to the alleged 'Catholicism' of Matthew. We find critics who declare it to be 'Catholic,' and therefore, as they hold that primitive Christianity was not Catholic, they are convinced that Matthew is late. In the meantime other critics assert that there is no Catholicism in it, and that there is therefore no reason to forbid us to believe that it is early. There is the third view, that the book shows a simple form of Catholic belief, and that such a doctrine is quite compatible with what we know of the state of Christianity before the catastrophe of A.D. 70 and the chasm that henceforth yawned between the Church and the Synagogue. The conception of the Church which this Gospel presents to us may, after all, be primitive, may be what Jesus Christ taught, and not an anachronism which has filtered into the record of His sayings.

As instances of these accusations of anachronism we observe that Wellhausen says with regard to Matthew that ' we cannot help recognising that the Ecclesia, the Church, is meant' (in certain parables), ' although the name is generally avoided on historical grounds. . . . This identification of the kingdom and the Ecclesia is entirely comprehensible, seeing that the Christian Society was undeniably the work of Jesus, and it was considered to be the porch of Heaven itself. But this kingdom, as it is set forth in Matthew, is altogether " Christian"; it cannot have been thus set forth, or rather presupposed, by Jesus Himself.'[1] Nearer home we find an English Non-

[1] *Einleit.* p. 105.

conformist, Professor Peake, saying, 'This rather Catholicised Gospel may have been written towards the close of the first century.'[1] Dr. J. Estlin Carpenter, an English Unitarian, says with regard to the idea of the Church in Matthew that it 'is in some sense present in the background much oftener than the term itself appears.'[2] We may cordially accept this view, without inferring that the Gospel has modified the teaching of Jesus in this particular. And we cannot with Dr. Moffatt think that the mere mention of the word 'ecclesia' and the parables which imply the presence of evil with the good in the visible Church, and the regulations with regard to discipline and baptism, point to a modification and corruption of the ideas of Jesus.[3] Such an argument begs the question, unless it can be proved that His Gospel excluded such a system.

If we bear in mind that Acts and the most widely accepted Epistles of S. Paul show that the impulse towards a definite Church organisation was potent long before the destruction of Jerusalem, we shall merely find in Matthew a corroboration of their testimony. In Matthew the community or corporation of believers who accept Jesus as the Son of God and Messiah is called 'Ecclesia' or Church; this Ecclesia is regarded as the embodiment of the kingdom of God on earth, and the individual disciples are called 'sons of the kingdom' (xiii. 38). The word 'Church' is first applied to the whole body of our Lord's disciples and is so applied by our Lord Himself (xvi. 18). It is secondly applied to a local body or church representing the larger body in a single spot; it is the society to which a particular offender belongs and under whose jurisdiction he falls (xviii. 17). S. Paul

[1] *Critical Introduction to the New Testament*, p. 123.
[2] *The First Three Gospels*, p. 375.
[3] *The Historical New Testament*, p. 269.

uses the word in both these meanings. As the name 'Ecclesia' was familiar to Greek-speaking Jews, being employed as the equivalent of the Hebrew word *qāhāl*, there is no reason whatever for suspecting that both the name and the idea did not belong to the most primitive period of Christianity. As for the precise organisation of this Church, it is remarkable how little Matthew contains. The position of S. Peter is that which he occupies in all the Gospels, in Acts, and in the Epistle to the Galatians, and his functions are described in strongly Jewish language. The twelve apostles are to sit on twelve thrones judging the twelve tribes of Israel (xix. 28), a figure of apocalyptic language of an obviously ancient character. There is no mention of bishops, presbyters, or deacons. Admission into the Church is by baptism. But this is no evidence of a late date. And though there are critics who hold that the mention of the Trinity in our Lord's command to baptise does prove a late date, a good deal can be said, and well said, on the other side. Allusions to a threefold nature in the Godhead are too numerous and too early in the New Testament for us to maintain that it was after A.D. 70 that 'Catholicism' first required the use of this formula in baptism. The organisation of the Church suggested in Matthew can no more safely be alleged as a proof of a late and degenerate period than the simple prophecy of our Lord that the city of his murderers would be burnt (xxii. 7) can be called a 'decisive' proof that the Gospel was composed after that event had taken place.

A Roman origin has sometimes been sought for the famous text in which Jesus declares that He will build His Church on the rock of Peter (xvi. 18). No doubt this text has been a favourite text in Rome. It has been valued there from the days when Pope Callistus irritated Tertullian by quoting it in the great controversy concerning the discipline of penitents about A.D.

215. It shines round the interior of the dome of S. Peter's basilica. It has become a controversial war-cry. But it is at least probable that this and the two stories in which S. Peter walks on the sea, and finds the shekel in the fish's mouth (xvii. 24-27), are derived from the Christians of Jerusalem. That S. Peter was peculiarly revered in the mother Church is certain. S. James presided at the momentous council there in A.D. 49, when it was decided not to exact circumcision in the case of Gentile converts (Acts xv.). But it was S. Peter who summed up the meaning of the council in his own words. And it was under the aegis of the name of ' Cephas ' that Judaising semi-Christians endeavoured to upset the work of S. Paul in Corinth and apparently in Galatia also. The same regard for Cephas is shown in the strange Judaistic romances about S. Clement which became popular in Rome in the third century, but were evidently not first devised in any Gentile atmosphere. It is practically certain, though the Tübingen school denied it, that S. Peter suffered martyrdom at Rome, and that he had some share in the organisation of the early Roman Church. But we know from S. Irenaeus, who wrote about A.D. 185, that in his day the share of S. Paul in that organisation was well remembered. He attributes the appointment of Linus as bishop of Rome to the two apostles jointly. And it was not until S. Paul's share in that work had been somewhat overshadowed by legend that the Christians of Rome would have been even tempted to invent such a text as the promise given by our Lord to S. Peter. Either the text is, as I believe it to be, the record of a genuine tradition, or it is the invention of an early Judaistic Christian circle.

There are other passages in Matthew which bear upon the Catholicism of the Church and must now be mentioned. They imply the admission of the Gentiles into the Church. And it is urged, on the one hand, that as they imply this universalism, they cannot be the genuine words of Jesus, and are later inventions. It is urged, on the other hand, that, although the admission of the Gentiles into the Church is taught by our Lord in the Gospel as one of the fundamental principles of the Christian religion, there is nothing to show that the Gentile, thus admitted to an equality with the converted Jew, will not be required to keep the Law of Moses. Now the Jews themselves made proselytes on that condition, admitting to a lower rank those who observed merely certain moral rules, and admitting to the full status of an Israelite those proselytes who undertook to observe the whole moral and ceremonial Law contained in the Old Testament. Even the triumph of rabbinism which followed the destruction of Jerusalem in A.D. 70 did not put an end to a Jewish missionary propaganda conducted on the principle that the Gentile who was circumcised, and undertook the obligations which circumcision involved, became one of God's people. In fact, the Jews of modern Europe are to a large extent descended from Tartar proselytes who were converted to Judaism in the eighth century of the Christian era in what is now part of Southern Russia.[1]

What, it is asked, is there to show that the Gentile converts, foreseen by our first evangelist, were not expected to keep the Law? They would differ from converts to the ordinary Judaism of the day by being required to confess that Jesus, the Son of God, is the Messiah, and that Jesus, through His death, resurrection, ascension, and outpouring of the Holy Spirit, was inaugurating the kingdom of God, and, unlike

[1] I am indebted to Professor Margoliouth for my first knowledge of this fact. Many details may be found in *The Jewish Encyclopaedia*, vol. iv. p 1 ff , article 'Chazars' (Funk & Wagnalls, New York and London, 1903).

converts to orthodox Judaism, they would be baptised into His Name, but it would be taken for granted that they would be circumcised and keep the Law. Therefore, it is urged, the first Gospel probably belongs to a period long before the destruction of Jerusalem.

Underneath this apparently simple suggestion there lie some very serious problems. In the first place, there is the question as to whether in A.D. 49 the Church at Jerusalem decided in a council not to lay upon Gentile converts the burden of the Law, excusing them from circumcision, and only demanding in addition to abstention from idolatrous and unchaste actions, that in certain regions where Jewish and Gentile converts came into daily contact with each other, the Gentiles should abstain from eating meat containing blood or killed in a cruel manner. The two latter practices were very offensive to the pious Jew. Acts xv. records that such was the decision of the Church. The older rationalism and the more extreme type of recent rationalism treat the story as a fiction. But it fits so admirably the other events which took place in the development of primitive Christianity, and it has gained such substantial support from the increasing mass of evidence which favours the view that Acts was written in the apostolic age, that we can safely assume that Acts has given a correct account of the main facts. The improbability of the story having been invented in the second century is conclusively shown by Dr. Sanday in his pamphlet on the *Apostolic Decree*.[1]

If we grant that the Church in A.D. 49 made such a decree with regard to the non-observance of the Law by Gentile converts, then it is almost inconceivable that S. Matthew's Gospel was written after that date in opposition to a decree so solemnly ratified. And since Antioch was one of the very first places to be

[1] Leipzig (A. Deichert'sche Verlagsbuchhandlung, Nachf.), 1908.

affected by the rule, and this Gospel was probably written in or near Antioch, the chance of such a contradiction is reduced to a minimum. Further, if this Gospel is earlier than A.D. 60 we must be prepared to assign to S. Mark's Gospel, which it has used so freely, a date which is opposed to all the best evidence.

§ 4. *Jesus Christ and the Law.*

A second problem which underlies the assumption that Matthew expects Gentile converts to keep the Law of Moses is this: Would such an assumption accord with the real teaching of Jesus Christ? What was the attitude of Jesus towards the Law? Three views are possible. The extreme sceptical view is that Jesus was only a religious Jew, observing the Law and expecting that His disciples would do the same, though it is not certain whether He claimed to be the Messiah or not. Such a Jesus could not have founded a universal religion. So we find that Professor Huxley, a protagonist of English agnosticism, said, 'If the primitive Nazarenes of whom the *Acts* speaks were orthodox Jews, what sort of probability can there be that Jesus was anything else? How can He have founded the universal religion which was not heard of till twenty years after His death?'[1] According to this view the Founder of Christianity regarded the whole Mosaic Law as binding on His followers. It is enough to say in reply that none of the Gospels nor the Acts support such a theory. It is quite inconsistent with the earliest Gospel, where Jesus Himself claims to be 'Lord of the Sabbath,' and where 'entrance into life' and 'inheritance of eternal life' are promised not to a mere keeping of the commandments, but to an imitation of the self-sacrifice of Jesus (Mark ix. 43, 45;

[1] *Science and Christian Tradition*, p. 302.

x. 17 ff.). It is inconsistent with the promise of Jesus that His yoke is easy (Matt. xi. 29), and with S. Peter's statement that the Law was a yoke 'which neither our fathers nor we were able to bear' (Acts xv. 10). That all these passages and all similar passages are fictions cannot be maintained when no critical evidence supports the assertion.

Another view with regard to the attitude of our Lord towards the Law is that of semi-rationalism. It is more plausible and perhaps more popular than the above. It holds that Jesus was inconsistent, though in a way nobly inconsistent. It is said that He observed the Law and intended that His followers should do the same, but that unconsciously He prepared for its destruction. His own teaching about the relation between the human soul and God slowly undermined the banks of stone by which Judaism had diverted righteousness into its own narrow channel, and prevented it from fertilising the world. His action is even compared with the first efforts of Luther, who, it is said, wished to remain within the borders of the Roman Catholic Church, assuming that it was his proper home, and that its rulers would eventually see that he loved the Church and take his side. The grounds for supposing that Jesus was unconscious of what He was doing merely reduce themselves to this, that there is an apparent contradiction between some of His sayings and actions affecting the Mosaic Law, and it is held that He would not consciously be guilty of such a contradiction. Now these supposed contradictions are more numerous and striking in the first Gospel than in any other, though some can be found even in the fourth. And, therefore, if it can be shown that in Matthew there is no adequate proof that our Lord intended His disciples to keep the Mosaic Law, the whole theory breaks down. If the record of *this* Gospel does not imply such an intention on His part, no

Gospel implies it; and if the evangelist did not think that His Master taught such a doctrine, he could not have intended that His Gospel should teach it. And, therefore, the attitude of Matthew towards the Jewish Law cannot point to a period when the disciples thought it necessary that every Gentile should be circumcised.

§ 5. *Marriage, Meats, Sabbath.*

In considering the attitude of Jesus Christ towards the Law as recorded in Matthew, it will be most practical first to consider certain passages to which a confident appeal is sometimes made on the ground that they prove that the evangelist believed that his Master thought that the Law would remain binding.

There is one matter where it must frankly be admitted that the influence of Judaism in opposition to Christianity seems to have left a plain trace upon this Gospel. It is conceivable that the passages in question have been interpolated by later scribes, but it is certainly quite probable that they were written by the evangelist himself. This grave matter is our Lord's teaching with regard to marriage. The laxer school of Jewish rabbis, that of Hillel, permitted divorce for the slightest provocation, such as even the Mosaic Law never contemplated. The stricter school, that of Shammai, by their interpretation of Deut. xxiv. 1, which allowed a man to divorce a wife 'because he hath found some unseemly thing in her,' allowed divorce when the wife had been guilty of adultery. As it is almost certain from the statements of S. Mark, S. Luke, and S. Paul that our Lord allowed no divorce in any circumstances whatever when a marriage had once been consummated, we can hardly avoid the conclusion that Christ's teaching in Matt. v. 32 and xix. 9 has been affected by a false, though unconsciously false, tradition. The clause about adultery is a direct quotation from Shammai, and it lowers our Lord's doctrine concerning divorce to the level of the higher of the two Jewish doctrines then current. It is doubtful whether the clause is consistent with the context in either of the two passages. For in both it is assumed that the woman who has been put away *continues to be the wife of her original husband*, a fact frequently overlooked by those who appeal to these verses as a sanction for the second marriage of an innocent person who has divorced a guilty spouse. But whether the clause is consistent or not, its Jewish origin is evident. And consequently the teaching of Christ about divorce in Matthew makes a useful starting-point for those who hold that the Gospel throughout assumes that the legalism of the Old Testament will remain in force. The other alleged proofs appear to me to be wholly inconclusive, but the most important must be mentioned.

The Jewish Law had prescribed in detail what kinds of food defiled the person who ate them. The Jews also had a most elaborate system of ablutions both of persons and vessels in order to avoid any possible contamination. What does the evangelist say about Christ's attitude towards such ceremonial defilement? He records our Lord's saying, 'Not that which entereth into the mouth defileth the man, but that which proceedeth out of the mouth, this defileth the man' (xv. 11), followed by a brief explanation given by our Lord to S. Peter. The verses in Mark and Matthew will now be added in parallel columns, the words peculiar to each being printed in italics.

S. Mark vii.	S. Matt. xv.
	Then came the disciples, and said unto Him, Knowest Thou that the Pharisees were offended, when they heard this saying?

S. Mark vii.	S. Matt. xv.
	But He answered and said, Every plant, which My heavenly Father planted not, shall be rooted up. Let them alone: they are blind guides. And *if* the blind guide the blind, both shall fall into a pit.[1]
And *when He was entered into the house from the multitude,* His *disciples* asked of Him the parable.	And *Peter answered* and said unto Him, *Declare unto us* the parable.
And He said unto them, Are ye *so* without understanding also?	And He said, Are ye also *even yet* without understanding?
Perceive ye not, that whatsoever *from without* goeth into the *man, it cannot defile him; because it goeth not into his heart,* but into his belly, and goeth out into the draught?	Perceive ye not, that whatsoever goeth into the *mouth*
This He said, making all meats clean.	
And He said, that which proceedeth out of the *men,* that defileth the man.	*passeth* into the belly, and *is cast* out into the draught?
	But the things which proceed out of the *mouth come forth out of the heart*; and they defile the man.
For *from within,* out of the heart *of men,* evil thoughts proceed, fornications, thefts, murders, adulteries, *covetings, wickedness, deceit, lasciviousness, an evil eye,* railing, *pride, foolishness*: *all* these *evil* things *proceed from within,* and defile the man.	For out of the heart come forth evil thoughts, murders, adulteries, fornications, thefts, *false witness,* railings: these are the things which defile the man: *but to eat with unwashen hands defileth not the man.*

Unfortunately the incident is not recorded by S. Luke, so that we cannot check the statements in Matthew and Mark by what might possibly have been a more correct account. But I find it hard to agree with the critics who, holding it certain that S. Mark's account

[1] Cf. Luke vi. 39.

is throughout the more primitive, and that the other evangelist had before his eyes S. Mark's words exactly as they stand in our present Gospel, believe that he deliberately altered them because he disagreed on principle with S. Mark. The words in Matthew which speak of the Pharisees being offended are extremely natural, as is the introduction of St. Peter's name. It seems, to say the least, unnecessary to attribute these divergences to the evangelist's consistent antagonism to the Pharisees, and to his special interest in S. Peter. In both Gospels the main point is quite clear, though it is rather more luminous in Mark. The Pharisees held that it was necessary to wash the hands before a meal, not to avoid being dirty, but lest any person eating with others should be ceremonially unclean and communicate this uncleanness to the food, which would then make every one who partook of it unclean. Our Lord teaches that there is no religious defilement in the matter at all. Nothing that goes into a man defiles a man; it is the things which proceed from him that may defile him. Of course, it would be possible to pervert our Lord's words by some form of rabbinism; and this was done by the powerful Russian sectaries in the time of Peter the Great, when they maintained that to smoke tobacco was condemned by this verse, but apparently were less ready to oppose the excessive use of brandy. If we found any gloss comparable to this in the words of Matthew, we might well say that it had perverted or Judaised S. Mark's statement. S. Mark added to our Lord's words a reflection of his own, viz. '*This He said, making all meats clean.*' To the modern Christian this appears to be a wholly legitimate inference from the words of Jesus. But they are not one of the 'words of Jesus.' And if they were in the copy of Mark that was used by the author of our first Gospel, it seems to me very unreasonable to say that he omitted them because he held, unlike the Council of Jerusalem of A.D. 49, that certain meats convey a religious defilement to those who partake of them. We may even go a step further than this. S. Paul himself, the apostle of Gentile freedom, held that there were circumstances in which it would be wrong to eat meat that had been offered to idols. An idol was nothing, and one might eat or not eat without any difference in God's eyes. But the use of such meat might injure another man's conscience, and to share in an actual idol sacrifice by eating the food offered to the idol he regarded as a heinous sin. It is doubtful whether S. Paul would have said that our first evangelist was at all wrong in omitting S. Mark's comment. And even if the evangelist had supposed that the Jewish Christian was bound to observe the Mosaic Law in reference to unclean meats, and there is not sufficient proof of such a belief on his part, this would not necessarily affect the case of the Gentile at all. We know that in the second century the two sects of Hebrew Christians who kept the Law themselves differed fundamentally. The Ebionites, or extremists, who were merely Jews believing that Jesus was a human Messiah, held that the Law was binding on all who accepted Jesus as the Messiah. The Nazarenes, the more moderate and orthodox party, believed that it was only binding on men of Hebrew blood, and not binding on the Gentiles. It was one thing to observe the Law like S. James while giving the right hand of fellowship to the apostle of the Gentiles, and another thing to hold that S. Paul and every one who did not keep the Law were destined to Gehenna.

After the law of marriage and the law of meats we must notice that 'rule of worship' which, as always, implies a 'rule of belief.' One of the most interesting passages concerned with worship in the New Testament is Matt. v. 23, 'If therefore thou art offering thy gift at the altar, and there rememberest that thy brother hath aught against thee, leave there thy gift before the altar, and go thy way; first be reconciled to thy brother, and then come and offer thy gift.' This has been fully explained by Mr. Israel Abrahams in his valuable contribution to *Cambridge Biblical Essays*. He shows that the passage refers to one who has to bring a sin-offering, 'and in the act of so doing remembers that he has not yet made amends for a wrong committed by him against another man, presumably for the very wrong which has been the reason for bringing the offering at all.' According to rabbinic law a sin-offering, in case of a theft, was useless until the stolen goods were restored. Not only so, but there is also a remarkable passage in the *Tosefta* which exactly fits the passage. It is, 'If one has brought his trespass-offering before restoring the stolen goods, the priest (though he has already slain the sacrificial animal) shall not go on to mix the blood (for sprinkling) until the offerer has restored the stolen goods.' So valueless was the gift considered that the animal, though slain, was not used as an offering, but taken outside the temple precincts and destroyed. Mr. Abrahams says, 'The parallel is exact. . . . To me it seems almost certain that Matthew has here preserved a genuine saying of Jesus.' Nothing, in fact, could illustrate more admirably our Lord's attitude towards the Jewish Law than this passage when considered in connection with the verses concerned with unwashed hands. One denies all merely ceremonial defilement; the other affirms that worship and ceremonial cannot be acceptable to God unless the heart is right. In the latter case Jesus takes part of the best rabbinical teaching, and gives it a simpler and wider form which will cover any sacrifice to God. He takes for granted that the Jews to whom He is speaking ought to frequent the temple and fulfil the temple rites. The same principle marks His command to the cleansed leper. He is bidden, 'Go thy way; show thyself to the priest, and offer the gift that Moses commanded' (Matt. viii. 4). The man was not to imagine that his miraculous cure made it superfluous for him to obey the Law. Further, our Lord adds that this is to be done 'for a testimony unto them.' The priests were to have an opportunity of seeing that the Messiah did not disregard the Law. If the ceremonial law came into conflict with the moral law, it must give way. But so far from being indiscriminately condemned, it was to be treated as valid when it fostered the right relation between the creature and his Creator.

The above statements with regard to sacrificial worship seem to be indisputably genuine 'sayings of Jesus.' And the record of them in Matthew, especially the mention of 'the altar,' favours the view that the Gospel was written while the altar was still undestroyed. To maintain the contrary view seems as paradoxical as the assertion that the Epistle to the Hebrews was written at the close of the first century, in spite of the fact that the author declares that the Jewish priest 'standeth day by day ministering and offering' (Heb. x. 11). But there is nothing to show that these words in Matthew might not have been written between A.D. 60 and A.D. 70 as well as twenty years earlier. And there is certainly nothing whatever to show that our Lord expected that the Gentile Christian would be under an obligation to obey the literal precepts of any Jewish ceremonial regulation.

Matt. xxiv. 20 contains an allusion to the Sabbath which is sometimes quoted as a clear proof that the author conceived that the observance of the Sabbath was binding on all Christians. Our Lord in this verse says, 'Pray ye that your flight be not in the winter, *neither on a Sabbath.*' Mark xiii. 18, in speaking of this flight from Jerusalem before the siege, contains a mention of winter but not of the Sabbath. It is therefore thought by some critics that the latter is a Judaistic interpolation, though it is not impossible that S. Mark may have known it and omitted it. That flight on a Sabbath might be fraught with disaster is shown by 1 Macc. ii. 32-38, where certain pious Jews, having retreated into the wilderness and been pursued by the forces of Antiochus, refused to do anything to defend themselves because it was a Sabbath day, and were butchered with their wives and children. In a community of Jewish Christians there might be many who would feel scruples about going more than a Sabbath day's journey on the Sabbath, or about taking any measures other than this short flight for the defence of themselves and their families. The injunction attributed to our Lord in Matthew is therefore perfectly intelligible without our supposing that either the evangelist or his Master considered that such scruples ought to be permanently fostered. It cannot be isolated from the actions recorded in chap. xii, where Jesus teaches that mercy is better than sacrifice, and that the method of observing the Sabbath practised by the Pharisees cut through the real purpose of the holy day. If the Sabbath rest every week has to yield to the necessity of preparing the temple sacrifices, much more can it give way to requirements of philanthropy. Such is the teaching of chap. xii., and it is hard to think that the evangelist who wrote that chapter would have thought it wrong for a man to save his wife and children from the Roman soldiers by moving more than three miles on a Sabbath day.

It may still be objected that in Matt. xxiii. 2 Jesus says, ' The scribes and the Pharisees sit [or, took their seat] on Moses' seat : all things therefore whatsoever they bid you, these do and observe ; but do not ye after their works : for they say, and do not.' The immediate context shows that this is not to be interpreted as a sanction of the rabbinical additions, perversions, and misinterpretations of the Law. Such were 'heavy burdens' wrongfully imposed. Perhaps I may illustrate this from my personal experience. Several years ago I was in the company of one of the most prominent and orthodox of English Jews. To my astonishment he asked me to open a letter for him. He explained that it was a Jewish festival, and that he might not open it, though he made it obvious that he might study the contents. Now it would surely be both possible and reasonable to hold that a Jew ought to observe what his rabbis could show him to be the Law with regard to the Sabbath without holding that he might indulge in such a form of casuistry. The observance of the Sabbath was not only natural but beneficial to the Christian Church until it became possible to spend a new space of twenty-four hours in worship and rest. But this passage, in which our Lord upholds the authority of the scribes and Pharisees at a time when the Christian Church existed only in embryo, cannot be fairly interpreted as binding on any Christian Jew after the day of Pentecost, still less as binding on Gentile converts.

§ 6. *Our Lord and S. Paul.*

Let us sum up. With the single exception of the modified tradition about marriage, the record given in Matthew appears to give a consistent picture of Christ's attitude towards the Law. He drew a deep line of cleavage between the actual Law of the Old Testament and the rabbinical *Halacha*, or 'tradition of men.' We have seen that He by no means despised all rabbinical teaching. But in the matter of ceremonial defilement, almsgiving, the Sabbath, prayer, fasting, and temple worship, He strove to lead men from false restraints to that mastery of self which only belongs to the true children of God. This involved not only a return to the Law, but a return to Him who gave the Law. The result is sometimes a verbal contradiction in His teaching. He says, 'Think not that I came to destroy the law or the prophets; I came not to destroy, but to fulfil. For verily I say unto you, Till heaven and earth pass away, one jot or one tittle shall in no wise pass away from the law, till all things be accomplished' (Matt. v. 17, 18). Evidently He knew, and the evangelist knew, that He was suspected of breaking the Law. And some of His commandments, especially with regard to revenge and marriage, do supersede the Law. The contradiction between this assertion of the permanence of the Law and His disregard of it can be done away if one condition is fulfilled. If there exists some law within the Law, so far-reaching as to penetrate all that the writers of the Old Testament directed to be done, and able to complete what they left incomplete, the contradiction disappears. This law within the Law is love. And the Old Testament itself testifies to this in its command that a man shall love the Lord his God, and love his neighbour as himself. All the Synoptists record that our Lord insisted upon this command as vital. But it is remarkable that in Matthew alone do we find the addition, 'On these two commandments hangeth the whole law and the prophets' (Matt. xxii. 40).

It is this recognition that there is a law within the Law which enables us to see that the teaching of Jesus is itself consistent, and that the teaching of S. Paul agrees with it. The elaborate attempts made to establish an opposition between 'Jesus and Paul' have not been successful either in this or any other direction. Of course, it is true that Paul, a converted sinner, a man who had writhed under the tyranny of the rabbinism in which he had been trained, and only found through Jesus 'peace with God,' could not possibly speak of the Law and of sin and atonement as Jesus spoke, He whose heart never needed 'reconciliation' and 'atonement.' Allowing for this difference, the unity of S. Paul's doctrine with that of His Master is complete. Behind the Law of Moses S. Paul saw God's 'promise,' a purpose of love by which the Law must be interpreted, and he appealed to the Law's own record of Abraham's saving faith in God. Thus he could quite truly say, 'We establish the Law' (Rom. iii. 31). He could say, 'In Christ Jesus neither circumcision availeth anything, nor uncircumcision; but faith working through love' (Gal. v. 6); and again, 'Circumcision is nothing, and uncircumcision is nothing, but the keeping of the commandments of God' (1 Cor. vii. 19). With him, as with His Master, love is the fulfilling of the Law. Jesus is shown in the Gospels to have revealed in His own character as well as in His teaching what kind of observance of the Law satisfies the heart of God. And having shown that true religion springs from trust and love, such love as led Him to the cross, He said to His disciples, 'Go ye therefore, and make disciples of all the nations, baptising them into the name of the Father, and of the Son, and of the Holy Ghost: teaching them to observe all things whatsoever I have commanded you' (Matt. xxviii. 19, 20).

§ 7. *Christ's Sayings on Eschatology.*

At the end of our second chapter we noticed the acute conflict which has lately been in progress between two different schools of semi-Christian and anti-Christian thought. The self-styled 'Liberal Protestants' have minimised important aspects of our

Lord's teaching about the end of the world. The Eschatological school, familiar to us in the writings of Schweitzer, Loisy, and Tyrrell, have taught that Christ steeped Himself in the eschatological doctrines of the Jews, and they have interpreted all Christianity by the key which those doctrines are supposed to furnish. A more searching and more temperate criticism than that of either school of thought will discover that the truth lies almost exactly half-way between the two. The teaching of our Lord with regard to the end of the world and His own office at the end can in a large measure be recovered, if indeed it has ever been lost.

In his very able essay at the end of *Studies in the Synoptic Problem*, Mr. Streeter has expounded the matter with such characteristic clearness that a few sentences will illustrate his view. He says, 'The Christian hope, first finding its expression in crude Apocalyptic like that of the Epistles to the Thessalonians, insensibly changes its emphasis, passes through the mysticism of the Epistles of the Captivity,[1] and culminates in the Johannine doctrines of the Spirit and Eternal Life. The critical recognition of the priority of Q to Mark and of Mark to Matthew makes it clear that there was taking place in other circles of the Church during the same period *an evolution in the contrary direction*. The Apocalyptic element in Mark has a precision and detail not found in Q; in Matthew is seen a still further development. The eschatological language of the Master becomes more and more conformed to the Apocalyptic picture which was cherished by the early Church.'[2] And again he says, 'In the series Q, Mark, Matthew, there is a steady development in the direction of emphasising, making more definite, and even creating, sayings of

[1] *I.e.* S. Paul's Epistles to Colossians, Philemon, Ephesians, Philippians.
[2] *Op. cit.* p. 425.

our Lord of the catastrophic Apocalyptic type, and of thrusting more and more into the background the sayings of a contrary turn.'[1] He justly remarks that this does not apply to Luke.[2]

The result of his investigation is that he holds that whereas Q may perhaps exaggerate the Apocalyptic element in our Lord's teaching, this most primitive and authentic record of our Lord's sayings still records very little of that nature. Its characteristic sayings are rather those which imply that the kingdom of God was already a spiritual force working in the world when Jesus was exercising His ministry. The kingdom is one that grows gradually like the mustard seed (Luke xiii. 18, 19 = Matt. xiii. 31, 32); it will slowly pervade society like leaven (Luke xiii. 20 = Matt. xiii. 33). It is already here, because he that is little in the kingdom of heaven *is* greater than the Baptist (Luke vii. 28 = Matt. xi. 11). At the same time there are passages in Q which represent our Lord as saying that He would come 'when ye think not' (Luke xii. 40 = Matt. xxiv. 44); appearing 'as the lightning' (Luke xvii. 24 = Matt. xxiv. 27); like the deluge in 'the days of Noah' (Luke xvii. 26 = Matt. xxiv. 37). Not till then would the kingdom of God be fully inaugurated, the twelve apostles sit on thrones (Luke xxii. 30 = Matt. xix. 28), a judgment take place in the presence of the angels of God (Luke xii. 9 = Matt. x. 33), and some be welcomed into and others rejected from the kingdom of God (Luke xiii. 28-30 = Matt. viii. 11, 12).

It is, in fact, by frankly recognising the presence of these two elements in our Lord's teaching about the kingdom of God that we save ourselves from the paradoxes and the pitfalls of the extreme critics on both sides. But it is only bare justice to the writers of the New Testament to add that the two elements

[1] *Loc. cit.* p. 433   [2] *Loc. cit.* p. 426.

THE GOSPEL ACCORDING TO S. MATTHEW 203

are present in the teaching of S. John and in the later teaching of S. Paul. S. John's Gospel, in spite of suggestions that have been made to the effect that such passages are later interpolations, distinctly teaches that Christ will come again, that there will be a future judgment and a future resurrection (John v. 29; vi. 39, 40, 44, 54; xi. 24; xiv. 3). Nor do such passages contradict those which teach that Christ's presence among men itself involved a judgment, and that eternal life may be enjoyed here and now. S. Paul, too, does not repeat in his existing Epistles the full description of the end of the world which he gives to the Thessalonians, and he seems to abandon the idea that Christ will return in his own lifetime. But he certainly does not abandon his belief in the return of Christ to execute judgment at the resurrection of the dead, and the future reward and punishment of mankind. There is no great distance between the teaching of S. John and S. Paul and that contained in Q. But we have to ask if Mark and Matthew did appreciably add to the genuine teaching of our Lord.

It is impossible for us to review every verse, but, broadly speaking, the question falls into two divisions. The first part is concerned with more or less isolated texts or groups of texts. The second depends upon the authenticity of our Lord's long discourse in Mark xiii., which has been copied with modifications in Matthew and Luke. The main facts under the first division are these: (1) according to *Matthew* (x. 23), Jesus said that He would come before His disciples had finished visiting the cities of Israel. (2) According to *Matthew*, some of the bystanders who heard our Lord would see the Son of Man coming in His kingdom; the other two Synoptists speak of this as a coming of the kingdom of God, though they, like Matthew, mention the visible return of the Son in the previous verse: Matt. xvi. 28; Mark ix. 1; Luke ix. 27. Note also that Matthew alone says that the Son of Man shall then 'render unto every man according to his deeds.' (3) In *Matthew* and *Mark* our Lord is described as telling the high priest that he would see the Son of Man 'sitting at the right hand of power and coming'; in *Luke* this statement merely appears as a description of the Son's glory in heaven: Mark xiv. 62; Matt. xxvi. 64; Luke xxii. 69. Matthew also shows an affection for certain apocalyptic phrases like 'the consummation of the age,' and in the parables of the tares and the drag-net shows a profound belief in a great catastrophe and judgment at the end of the world. We can therefore feel justified in saying that the author of Matthew took a special interest in apocalyptic and eschatological sayings, and that the vision in Daniel vii. may have led him to think that God's kingdom upon earth could not come without a visible return of the Son of Man in a comparatively near future. The other evangelists, including S. John, take a rather wider view, and hold that a longer increase of His kingdom and power will take place before He visibly returns.

But the most seriously debated passage is the discourse of our Lord in Mark xiii. Does it come from Q? And whether it comes from Q or from some wholly different source, does it correctly represent Christ's teaching? It has been plausibly maintained for many years that it is not authentic, but an interpolated 'fly-sheet' containing pointed references to the persecution of S. Paul before the Sanhedrin, the Synagogue, Felix and Festus, King Agrippa and the Emperor Nero. Certain other prophecies in this chapter are also said to be prophecies after the event. Among these some writers place even the prophecy of the fall of Jerusalem attributed to our Lord.

Now the above theory bristles with difficulties. It

cannot be proved that no form of Q contained the substance of this discourse. And, on the other hand, it can be proved that Q did contain at least some references to the sudden and visible return of Christ It cannot be proved that Christ did not make, or could not make, predictions with regard to the fortunes of His followers or the fate of Jerusalem. And it can be proved that this chapter was already in Mark when it was copied by the writer of Matthew as authentic. Since there is much in Matthew which implies that it was published rather before than after the fall of Jerusalem, it is exceedingly rash to hold that the prophecy in Mark was interpolated after Jerusalem was destroyed. When we say this we are not committing ourselves to the theory that all or any of the three Synoptic accounts of the end of the world can be considered to have been immune against the personal convictions of the writers. But we can affirm that the substance of the chapter shows no disagreement with the best primitive traditions of our Lord's teaching. The Christians of the second and third centuries were therefore in the right when they inserted in their creeds a record of their belief that Christ would return to judge the quick and the dead, and assumed at the same time that the kingdom of God is a divine force already present in the world.

CHAPTER VII

THE GOSPEL ACCORDING TO S. LUKE

§ 1. *General Characteristics.*

S. MARK wrote to show the Christian Church, most of all the Church in Rome, how Jesus lived, died, and rose again as the Son of God. The evangelist who combined S. Mark's Gospel with the sayings of our Lord collected by S. Matthew is a Jewish Christian who wishes above all to show that Jesus is the Messiah, that the Christian Church is the true Church, and Pharisaism a perversion of religion. S. Luke is a Gentile, who wishes to show that Jesus is indeed the Saviour of the world. He is writing in order that a certain Theophilus, apparently a convert of good social position, may be better informed and more deeply convinced. He arranges his material carefully, he puts aside everything which he considers unnecessary, discards sentences like the woes pronounced by Christ against the Pharisees, for a Greek would derive little profit from a denunciation of the sins which he did not commit. He omits the anointing of our Lord's feet by the woman of Bethany because he has a similar story concerning a sinful penitent woman who loved and was forgiven. He omits the long story about the daughter of Herodias and her dancing because he has to economise his space for the sake of showing how much Christ did for outcast men and women. He omits the story of the Syro-Phoenician woman in which a Gentile woman was willing to accept for all Gentiles the position of dogs beneath the Master's table. More than 'the beloved disciple' himself, S. Luke omits anything that would seem to imply that the Lord was ever weak or ever hard. He does not, like S. Mark, tell us that Jesus said that He was ignorant of the day of judgment, or record His cursing of the barren fig-tree. His words are sometimes stern, yet they are well indicated by the happy phrase in which S. Luke describes the Lord's address in the synagogue at Nazareth; 'words of grace' (iv. 22). He sets the faults of the twelve in a subdued light. He does not tell us that Christ once called S. Peter 'Satan,' or that Peter cursed and swore when he denied his Lord. He does not tell us, as S. Mark does, of the ambitious request of James and John that they might sit by the Messiah in His kingdom, or that all the disciples forsook Him and fled. Even when he speaks of the slumber of the disciples in Gethsemane, he says, perhaps very truly, that they were 'sleeping *for sorrow*' (xxii. 45).

He is a great artist. Mediaeval tradition ascribed to S. Luke some Byzantine pictures where the maid-mother, with grave wondering eyes,

> Sat smiling, babe in arm.

The legend that he was a painter is too late to be trusted, but it is an indication of the fact that long ago the Church was conscious of his artistic power. S. Mark gives us vignettes; S. Luke presents us with groups in harmonious surroundings. The scene of the *Nunc dimittis*, and the walk to Emmaus, are idyllic.

S. Luke's literary style shows real power of assimilation. In using Mark, he omits much in order to combine the rest with other materials. And yet in the parts of Mark which he retains he keeps their proper order and does not mix them much with other sources. He makes certain improvements in vocabulary and style, turning Mark into what we should call 'better Greek.' It runs smoothly. And yet, Gentile though he is, his style is deeply influenced by the Hebraic Greek of the Septuagint. The result is that his style, like his material, is a harmony well composed.

Side by side with the recent tendency to underline and even exaggerate the Pauline tendency in Mark, there has arisen a tendency to minimise the Pauline tendency in Luke. Thus Loisy says, 'if the third Gospel was written by Luke, a disciple of Paul, one has to recognise that this circumstance does not throw much light on its composition, its tendencies and its object.'[1] And Harnack, in his *Luke the Physician*, has drawn up a row of antitheses between the theology of the evangelist and the apostle, while fully defending the theory that one was the disciple of the other.[2] Now, it is comparatively seldom that we find a complete identity of ideas in a great teacher and an eminent disciple. The disciple would never rise to eminence if he had not a mind of his own. But the points of similarity between S. Paul and S. Luke are numerous. One is a theologian and the other is consciously a historian. But they fundamentally agree. Too much store is sometimes set upon mere words, for all religious controversies have shown that people may attribute very different meanings to exactly the same words—as disputes about the 'real presence' testify. But the fact remains that S. Luke's vocabulary is more Pauline than that of the other evangelists, and that among these words are some conspicuous in Pauline theology. Such are faith (eleven times), believe (nine times), grace (eight times), mercy (six times), forgiveness of sins (three times). He has phrases which are

[1] *Jésus et la Tradition Évangélique*, p. 17.
[2] *Op. cit.* pp. 140 ff. (English translation).

parallel with phrases in the important epistles of S. Paul.

No pains are spared to show that Jesus is the Saviour of the world, and no vestige of any Jewish particularism remains. It is sometimes urged that the Christology is rudimentary, and that S. Luke excludes any existence of the Son of God before He was born of Mary. S. Luke no doubt is giving expression to a simpler and less reflective faith than S. Paul, but he depicts the power of Christ and His relation to the Father in a manner which implies that He is in inseparable union with God. More often than the other Synoptists he gives to Jesus the favourite Pauline title of 'the Lord.' The Pauline principle that man is 'justified,' acquitted as righteous by God, in response to faith working through love, is perfectly exemplified in the story of the sinful woman whose love and faith are both commended by our Lord (vii. 47, 50). It is possible to draw a contrast between S. Luke's 'paradoxical love for sinners'[1] and S. Paul's stern denunciation of vice. But the paradox is not that of S. Luke so much as that of the omniscient and all-pitying Saviour. And he would be indeed a bold man who should say that S. Paul had no room in his heart for sinners after reading 2 Corinthians ii., vi. 11 and vii. When we make due allowance for the fact that S. Paul was always proud of being a Jew and never forgot his Pharisaic training, while S. Luke is more Greek in spirit than any other writer of the New Testament, we shall find that their attitude towards Judaism is very similar. S Luke at the beginning of his Gospel shows his interest in Jewish rites, S. Paul, on his last visit to Jerusalem, paid for four men who had taken a Nazarite vow (Acts xxi. 23 ff.). Both held that the inward meaning of the Law is permanently binding (Luke, xvi. 17; Rom. iii. 31). S. Paul thinks that the repulse

[1] Harnack, *loc. cit.*

of the Jews from the Kingdom of the Messiah was meant by God to lead to the inclusion of the Gentiles who would rouse the Jews to emulation (Rom. xi. 11, 12). S. Luke, in writing down the *Nunc dimittis* and the *Magnificat*, paid tribute to the peculiar spiritual glory of Israel, a glory not extinguished by 'the times of the Gentiles' following the destruction of the Holy City (Luke xxi. 24). It would be too much to say that S. Luke would have always put 'the Jew first' as S. Paul, himself a Jew, does steadily. But his writings prove that he would have supported S. Paul's noble statement of the prerogatives of Israel in Rom. ix. 4-5, and the respect which he shows towards the Christian mother Church of Jerusalem, in spite of her failings, is in full accord with S. Paul's own action. In his Catholicism S. Luke is Pauline, and in affection for Judaism he is as Pauline as a Gentile could be, short of becoming a Jew.

Thoroughly in accordance with the religious consciousness of S. Paul is the prominence given by S. Luke to the value of prayer and the power of the Holy Spirit. He shows that Christ insisted on the duty of prayer in two parables which no other evangelist records (xi. 5-13; xviii. 1-8). But above all, he shows how Christ prayed. On seven occasions S. Luke is alone in mentioning the prayers which our Lord offered at the crises of His life: at His baptism (iii. 21); before His first encounter with the Pharisees and scribes (v. 16); before choosing the Twelve (vi. 12); before the first prediction of His Passion (ix. 18); at the Transfiguration (ix. 29); before teaching the Lord's Prayer (xi. 1); and on the Cross (xxiii. 34, 46). And S. Luke alone records His declaration that He had made supplication for Peter, and His charge to the Twelve, 'Pray that ye enter not into temptation' (xxii. 32, 40).

The Holy Spirit operates alike in the birth, baptism

and ministry of our Lord. The 'Holy Spirit,' 'the power of the highest,' overshadows His virgin mother (i. 35). After His baptism He is 'full of the Holy Spirit,' and is 'led by the Spirit in the wilderness,' for the temptation (iv. 1). He returns to Galilee 'in the power of the Spirit' (iv. 14), and in beginning His ministry at Nazareth He applies to Himself the words of Isaiah, 'The Spirit of the Lord is upon me' (iv. 18). Jesus, in giving utterance to the great words in which He proclaims His unique knowledge of the Father, 'rejoiced in the Holy Spirit' (x. 21; note the parallel in Matt. xi. 25, where the Spirit is not mentioned). And as another instance of S. Luke's insight into the work of the Holy Spirit we may compare

Matt. vii. 11.	Luke xi. 13.
If ye then, being evil, know how to give good gifts unto your children, how much more shall your Father *which is in heaven* give *good things* to them that ask him?	If ye then, being evil, know how to give good gifts unto your children, how much more shall your *heavenly* Father give *the Holy Spirit* to them that ask Him?

Lastly, in xxiv. 49, the risen Lord describes the Holy Spirit as 'the promise of My Father,' and as 'power from on high.' The Book of Acts illustrates this truth continuously. The work of the Church is a continuation of Christ's own activity, its inspiring force is the Spirit who guided the human life of Jesus, and whom He has given to His Church from above. This is in harmony with both S. John's teaching and S. Paul's conception of the Church as the body of Christ.

§ 2. *Date of Luke.*

The date of S. Luke's Gospel is still in dispute. Sober criticism does not incline to the second century date which was favoured by those who considered Acts, which is of nearly the same date, to be necessarily later because it implies the existence of an organised Church.[1] The Gospel must have been well known in Rome early in the second century. Justin Martyr quotes it, and Marcion's Gospel was simply a mutilated version of it. Unlike the thorough Gnostics, Marcion did not issue forged Gospels and Epistles, but appealed to such as he and his Catholic opponents both acknowledged. Therefore he could hardly have issued his version of Luke about A.D. 144 unless the original had for a generation or so been acknowledged as authentic. Looking backwards into the first century, it is obvious to us that Luke was written later than Mark, which it combines with other materials. Therefore we must probably date it after A.D. 65. But as the writer shows no knowledge whatever of Matthew, it was probably written before Matthew or nearly simultaneously with it. The latter is the more probable view, because Matthew appears to show no knowledge whatever of Luke. Our first tentative conclusion is that Luke was written between A.D. 65 and A.D. 115, and our second is that like Matthew it was written within a few years of the destruction of Jerusalem in A.D. 70.

Against this latter view is the strongly advocated theory that it cannot have been written earlier than A.D. 95. Here we have to consider the relation of S. Luke's Gospel to Acts. It is generally admitted by critics of different tendencies and beliefs that the two books are by the same author, that Acts was, as it claims to be, written later than the Gospel, that both books contain older materials, and that Acts contains memoranda of S. Paul's travels written by S. Luke himself between A.D. 50 and A.D. 65. S. Luke accompanied S. Paul on these travels, as the memoranda, embodied in the 97 verses known as the 'we sections,' abundantly prove. In these sections the author uses

[1] Cf. Martineau, *Seat of Authority in Religion*, p 257.

the *first person plural*, implying that he was personally present on the occasions described. The style of the other sections of Acts makes it clear that the same person, S. Luke, wrote substantially the whole book, probably some years later than the memoranda. Could he have written Acts, and the Gospel, his 'former treatise,' as he calls it, as late as A.D. 95? It is not impossible, but it is hardly probable. We cannot reasonably place S. Paul's birth after A.D. 5 at the very latest; he calls himself 'aged' in writing to Philemon, A.D. 59-61. As S. Luke was his companion in A.D. 50, we might perhaps suppose that S. Luke was born about A.D. 25; but we have no reason for affirming that he was not much nearer S. Paul's own age. So, if he wrote his Gospel and Acts in or after A.D. 95, he would be at least seventy, and possibly much older. Only very clear evidence should be thought cogent enough to convince us that he postponed writing either of these fresh and vigorous books to an advanced old age, and that, writing at this date, he ignored the existence of S. Matthew's Gospel. What, then, is the alleged ground for this late date?

No real answer appears to be made with regard to his neglect of Matthew, except the very improbable conjecture that Matthew is equally late or later. And the only plausible reason for fixing Luke and Acts about A.D. 95 is that the Jewish historian Josephus published his *Antiquities* near that time, and S. Luke is said to show that he is undoubtedly acquainted with Josephus' work. Two important passages in S. Luke's writings are alleged to prove this. The allegation appears to me to be in one case disproved and in the other to be unproved. The first is in the Gospel where S. Luke connects the Baptist's ministry with the framework of contemporary history. 'In the fifteenth year of the reign of Tiberius Caesar, Pontius Pilate being governor of Judaea, and Herod being tetrarch of Galilee, and his brother Philip tetrarch of the region of Ituraea and Trachonitis, and *Lysanias tetrarch of Abilene*, in the high priesthood of Annas and Caiaphas, the word of God came to John' (iii. 1, 2). The year in question is probably A.D. 26-27.

This statement of S. Luke is said to have been derived from a careless recollection of a passage in Josephus.[1] Lysanias of Abila is known from a passage in Strabo to have been put to death by Mark Antony in B.C. 36. And Josephus says that in A.D. 53 Agrippa II. received the tetrarchy of Philip and Batanaea together with Trachonitis and Abila, adding that it 'had been the tetrarchy of Lysanias.' S. Luke is said to have read this passage, to have misunderstood it, and concluded that in the time of Tiberius the tetrarchy of Philip belonged to Philip—as it did—and the tetrarchy of Lysanias to Lysanias. If there was a second Lysanias there is no reason for supposing that S. Luke made any mistake, or had misunderstood or had read the passage in Josephus. And the existence of a second Lysanias was long ago practically proved. To say that it is 'at best conjectural,'[2] does not do justice to the facts. An ancient inscription shows that there was a 'tetrarch Lysanias' who was a contemporary of Tiberius, and another inscription is so worded as to make it probable that he was a descendant of the former Lysanias.[3] It is not even certain that Josephus, when he speaks of 'the tetrarchy of Lysanias,' is not referring to the later Lysanias. The original Lysanias probably bore a higher title. He was an independent ruler until his 'kingdom,' as Josephus elsewhere calls it,[4] and his life, were both taken away. Augustus, if he restored the territory to a submissive

[1] *Ant* xx. 7.
[2] Dr. James Moffatt, *Introduction to the Literature of the New Testament*, p. 30.
[3] See Godet, *Commentary on S. Luke*, p. 169 (English translation).
[4] *De Bello Judaico*, ii. 11.

descendant of its former ruler, would have been doing what he took a pleasure in doing. He did this very thing in the case of Iamblichus of Emesa and Archelaus of Cappadocia.

Therefore the mention of Lysanias by S. Luke does not prove that his Gospel was written after the publication of Josephus' *Antiquities* in A.D. 94.

The difficulty with regard to Acts is more serious. In Acts v. 34 ff. Gamaliel makes a speech in which he mentions two revolutionaries who headed seditious movements and were crushed by the government, 'For before these days rose up *Theudas*, giving himself out to be somebody; to whom a number of men about four hundred, joined themselves; who was slain; and all, as many as obeyed him, were dispersed and came to nought. After this man rose up *Judas of Galilee* in the days of the enrolment, and drew away some of the people after him: he also perished; and all, as many as obeyed him, were scattered about.' The alleged parallel to this is in Josephus, *Ant.* xx. 5. 1-2, where we are told that ' when Fadus was procurator of Judaea a certain charlatan named *Theudas* persuades a very great multitude . . . for he said that he was a prophet . . . Fadus sent a squadron of cavalry after them, which falling upon them unexpectedly, slew many of them and took many alive. Taking *Theudas* also alive, they cut off his head and carried it to Jerusalem.' A little later Josephus says that 'there were put to death the children of *Judas the Galilean*, who had stirred up the people to rebel against Rome when Quirinius assessed Judaea.' The former event would have been about A.D. 45, the latter about A.D. 47. The speech of Gamaliel in Acts is supposed to have been made some ten years before either of these took place.

The resemblances are obvious and the differences are remarkable. Each mentions two agitators, named respectively Theudas and Judas. S. Luke, while briefer than Josephus with regard to Theudas, adds that Theudas had about four hundred followers, and while S. Luke says Judas was put to death, Josephus says not that Judas, but his sons, met with this punishment. S. Luke says that Judas rose up 'after' Theudas, while Josephus implies that the sons of Judas were put to death after Theudas for the crime of their father forty years before!

Now, S. Luke may possibly have made a mistake in the details of Gamaliel's speech. Perhaps Theudas had not yet 'given himself out to be somebody,' and S. Luke's chronology must then be at fault. On the other hand, Josephus is not infallible, and he may have placed Theudas too late in spite of the many sources of information that he possessed. But what does seem unproved is that the passage in Acts is an inaccurate and distorted reflection of that in Josephus. The passage about the sons of Judas does not look like an interpolation in Josephus, but original, whether historically correct or not. But then S. Luke's 'recollection' has omitted its most striking feature, viz. that the sons were killed because their father had been seditious more than a generation ago. It appears to me that S. Luke had heard some stories about the Judas mentioned by Josephus, and about a Theudas who was an agitator, but not necessarily the charlatan described by Josephus. The name of Theudas was very common, and little insurrections were no novelty in the east end of the Roman Empire. S. Luke's importance as a saint and an evangelist would remain if he borrowed some of his history from the Jew, and even if his memory sometimes played him false. But the hypothesis of his having borrowed is not proved. If the coincidences between S. Luke and Josephus fail to prove that the Gospel and Acts were written between A.D. 95 and 100, an even worse failure has attended all efforts to show that the attitude of S. Luke's writings towards primitive Christianity betray a late date. They contain nothing which might not have been believed a generation earlier than Josephus' work. Against the critics who have assigned Luke and Acts to a time ranging from A.D. 95 onwards, we have now to set the fact that Harnack has very skilfully pleaded for a date between A.D. 60 and 70. Certain arguments which he has advanced in favour of this view are open to question and appear to me to be exaggerated and one-sided. Others are well collected and well marshalled. One of the simplest arguments for this early date is that Acts contains no account of the death of its great hero, S. Paul. The book ends very simply and impressively, leaving S. Paul in Rome, and the inference drawn from this ending is that S. Luke wrote no more because he had no more to write. This is not absolutely convincing. He might have intended to write a third volume. He might have omitted S. Paul's death because the structure of the book, as sketched in the first chapter, required room for the dawn of the Gospel in Rome and no more. It might truly be called *Acta Sanctorum*, but not in the sense that it is a collection of biographies and martyrdoms. The omission of S. Paul's martyrdom seems conceivable in a book written a few years after that death. If it is true, and it probably is true, that Q contained no account of our Lord's Passion, partly because the facts were still so fresh in the minds of the faithful, a similar reason may have weighed with the author of Acts. If S. Paul was executed in Rome, where the Christians were already numerous, there would be scores of people who knew how he perished. And the historian S. Luke hastened to record what very few knew and still fewer could write, viz. the story of the extension of the Church under the impulse of the Holy Spirit from Jerusalem through Judaea and Samaria to Rome, 'the world's mightiest.'

S. Luke's omission of S. Paul's death, therefore, seems to me to be compatible with a date either a little before or a few years later than that death, but not compatible with a date thirty or forty years later.

With the death of S. Paul we must connect his touching farewell speech at Miletus to the elders of Ephesus (Acts xx. 17 ff.). S. Luke after recording his speech says that they were 'sorrowing most of all for the words which he had spoken, that they should see his face no more.' Now S. Paul almost certainly did see them again, for he was released from his imprisonment at Rome and went to Asia Minor before his last and fatal journey to the capital. Until the Pastoral Epistles are proved to be wholly fictitious this visit to Asia Minor cannot be denied. And it is urged that if S. Luke wrote Acts after the apostle's death he would not have inserted in it S. Paul's words 'ye all shall see my face no more' (xx. 25), and thereby represented S. Paul as prophesying falsely. We can only say, 'Perhaps not.' But S. Luke, who did not remove all discrepancies from his book, may have had the desire simply to record what he believed to be true. And whether we regard him as an artist or as a historian, or as both, we may suppose that he left his account of the scene at Miletus as he had written it, with the full knowledge that S. Paul lived longer than he expected. But this is more likely to have been written when the elders of Ephesus were alive and able to bear testimony to S Luke than when most of them were gone to their reward.

Acts contains archaisms. Sunday is still called 'the first day of the week' (xx. 7) and not yet 'the Lord's day.' 'Christ,' when the name occurs alone, is still used as an official title meaning the Messiah. And though S. Luke informs us that the name 'Christians' (or Chrestians) first arose at Antioch, he knows that it was a nickname and himself calls the Christians 'the disciples.' The word 'Church' is applied to the separate Christian communities in Acts, but never to the whole Catholic Church except in xx. 28 in the report of the above speech of S. Paul. And on the other hand S. Luke, no doubt correctly, makes S. Paul refer to the Jewish nation as 'the people' (xxvi. 17, 23), in accordance with the practice of Greek-speaking Jews.

But all these seem possible in a writer who studied the past, who even revelled in it, though he had a clear and hopeful outlook into the future.

Apart from the practical certainty that Luke is largely based upon Mark, the Gospel contains but slight evidence as to its own date. But an important clue is perhaps to be found in the way in which S. Luke treats S. Mark's account of our Lord's prediction of the fall of Jerusalem. For this we must look at Luke xix. 43 f. and xxi. 20, 23, 24. The first passage contains a brief description of the siege of Jerusalem, the bank to be cast about it, the children to be dashed to the ground, not one stone being left upon another. In the next chapter we read that Jerusalem shall be compassed with armies, that there shall be 'wrath unto this people, and they shall fall by the edge of the sword, and shall be led captive into all the nations; and Jerusalem shall be trodden down of the Gentiles, until the times of the Gentiles be fulfilled.' These impressive sentences are not in the other Synoptic Gospels, and the last is similar in thought to Rom. xi. 25, where S. Paul holds that the Gentiles have an allotted time for their conversion before the restoration of the Jews to spiritual enlightenment. It might naturally be thought that S. Luke writes with the knowledge that Jerusalem has been destroyed, but the evidence is not conclusive until we reach xxi. 25. Here, though the alteration is very slight, we see that it is evident that S. Luke knew that 'the times of the Gentiles' are to intervene between the fall of Jerusalem and the end of the world. In Mark xiii. 24 and Matt. xxiv. 29 the perspective is different. The two earlier Gospels do not put this interval between the two events. But Luke xxi. 32 still retains the statement of Mark xiii. 30 that 'this generation shall not pass away till all these things be accomplished,' with the omission of the word *these*. Therefore if it be thought that there is adequate reason for dating Matthew shortly before A.D. 70, there is equal reason for dating Luke after, but not much after, A.D. 70. If we hold that Acts does not depend upon Josephus, there is no reason why it should not be quite as early as A.D. 75 or 80. I cannot regard the chronological question as closed, but the above theory leaves room for the utilisation of Mark by S. Luke, accounts for the fact that Luke and Matthew were written independently, allows for a slight change of style in Luke and Acts, and does not necessitate any improbable age in the author.

§ 3. *Asceticism in Luke.*

Side by side with S. Luke's poetry and his sense of proportion is his combined asceticism and reverence for womanhood. Here S. Luke seems to belong to the West rather than to the East, and to be in harmony with all that was best in the age of chivalry. His asceticism carries with it no suggestion of the self-torture which was sometimes encouraged among ancient hermits and later monks. The men who fed on grass or lived on pillars raised high above the earth could find no support in the pages of S. Luke. But real voluntary poverty and the 'daily' taking up of the cross, and a holy virginity such as S. Paul esteemed, were all dear to S. Luke.

The story of the incarnation and Mary praising God shows at once that the author realised the place of woman in the divine scheme of redemption. It has been asserted that by a very small alteration of the text of Luke we can do away with the virginity of our Lord's mother. It is true that if we omit in chap. i. verses 34 and 35 we can alter the story. But we may observe that if we do this, much of the artistic balance of this long and beautiful chapter is ruined. The chapter, as it stands in the universally accepted text, hints plainly at a similarity and a contrast between the birth of John the Forerunner and Jesus the Messiah. Like a true poet, S. Luke tells the story by a series of suggestive touches, gradually reaching the actual birth of Jesus. Now, John the Baptist is regarded as one born more or less out of the ordinary course of nature. His parents are 'well stricken in years' and he is to be 'filled with the Holy Ghost' (i. 15). Jesus, on the contrary, is to be born of a maiden who 'knows not a man,' and He is to be called the Son of God, being conceived by the direct action of the Holy Spirit. The contrast is completely ruined if we suppose that S. Luke meant that Jesus was the Child of a young man and a young woman, merely 'anointed' by the Holy Spirit at or after His birth.

Again we see at the Purification S. Luke's interest in Mary, and in a single life dedicated to God. There Simeon speaks of the sword that shall pierce Mary's soul (ii. 35), and thanks are given to God by 'one Anna, a prophetess, the daughter of Phanuel, of the tribe of Asher (she was of a great age, having lived with a husband seven years from her virginity, and she had been a widow even for four score and four years), which departed not from the temple, worshipping with fastings and supplications night and day.' This widow and prophetess is as interesting to S. Luke as the prophets and prophetesses whom he met when in the company of S. Paul. In A.D. 56 at Caesarea 'entering into the house of Philip the evangelist, who was one of the seven, we abode with him. Now this man had four daughters, virgins, which did prophesy' (Acts xxi. 9) We learn from Eusebius that they lived to a great age at Hierapolis in Asia,[1] and though the raving Montanist prophetesses of the second century brought the office into disrepute, the Western Church frequently recognised in women a gift akin to that known in the early Church as 'prophecy.' Modern theology has not always recognised the value which the first Christians attributed to virginity side by side with the entirely new honour which they gave to marriage. This esteem for virginity is partly, but not wholly, to be explained by the belief that the end of all things was at hand, and that marriage was therefore inadvisable. S. Luke's view is closely similar to that of S. Paul when he wrote to the Corinthians, 'He that is unmarried is careful for the things of the Lord, how he may please the Lord: but he that is married is careful for the things of the world, how he may please his wife.' . . . 'She that is unmarried is careful for the things of the Lord, that she may be holy both in body and in spirit: but she that is married is careful for the things of the world, how she may please her husband' (1 Cor. vii. 32-34). This is not the current Jewish doctrine, which treated marriage as a duty, and at the same time allowed divorce, and polygamy both simultaneous and consecutive. The doctrine of S. Paul in his Epistle to the Ephesians exalts marriage, comparing it with the union of Christ and His Church. And it is possible that when the promise of Christ's coming seemed to him to be less likely to have a speedy fulfilment, and

---

[1] *H. E.* III. 31.

when he saw the mischievous nastiness of the Gnostics who were 'forbidding to marry,' the apostle developed his original belief in the sanctity of Christian marriage. But the earlier conception was not therefore necessarily abandoned. And it is substantially that of S. John who speaks of the 'virgins' who 'follow the Lamb whithersoever he goeth,' and are 'the first-fruits unto God and unto the Lamb' (Rev. xiv. 4). The passages in this Gospel which deal with marriage deserve to be closely compared with the parallel passages in the other Synoptic Gospel. In quoting our Lord's stern teaching about adultery and divorce, Luke quotes it in its original rigour, unlike Matthew, but omits the statement (Matt. and Mark) of God's original intention with regard to the indissoluble nature of marriage.[1] He also omits the statement that 'there are eunuchs, which made themselves eunuchs for the kingdom of heaven's sake' (Matt. xix. 12). Later in the Gospel, when the Sadducees question Jesus about the resurrection, Luke differs from both. Matthew and Mark practically agree; so it will suffice to compare Mark and Luke.

Mark xii. 24.	Luke xx. 34 ff.
Jesus said unto them, *Is it not for this cause that ye err, that ye know not the scriptures, nor the power of God? For when they shall rise* from the dead, they neither marry, nor are given in marriage; but are as angels in heaven.	And Jesus said unto them, *The sons of this world marry, and are given in marriage: but they that are accounted worthy to attain to that world,* and the resurrection from the dead, neither marry, nor are given in marriage: *for neither can they die any more*: for they are *equal unto* the angels; *and are sons of God, being sons of the resurrection.*

Various interpretations can be put on the above

[1] Luke xvi. 18; Mark x. 2 ff.; Matt. xix. 1 ff.; v. 31 f.

divergences. If we were to suppose that he disliked and deliberately omitted the statement of our Lord that a man 'shall cleave to his wife, and the twain shall become one flesh,' we also might hold that he perverted our Lord's teaching about the risen life into a suggestion that only the unmarried can be raised from the dead to share the glories of God. But the former instance seems only to be part of his systematic abbreviation. And the latter is not patient of the above interpretation, because it would imply that Abraham, Isaac and Jacob would not be worthy of the resurrection, a conclusion which would destroy the whole argument directed by our Lord against the Sadducees. It cannot therefore be maintained with any plausibility that S. Luke intentionally meant to suggest that those who marry in this world will be unworthy of the next.

One very important fact emerges from the passages in which S. Luke calls attention to the truth that women have the same place in God's eyes as men, that with Him, as S. Paul says, 'there is neither male nor female.' The passages which are found only in his Gospel are familiar to all Christendom, the womanly touches in the story of Christ's birth, and of that of the Baptist, the story of the widow's son at Nain (vii. 11), the story of the sinful woman who anointed Christ's feet (vii. 36), the mention of the women who ministered to Him of their substance (viii. 3), 'the daughter of Abraham' who was healed (xiii. 16), the 'daughters of Jerusalem' weeping on the way of the Cross (xxiii. 28), the parable of the woman who lost one of her ten pieces of silver (xv. 8), and that of the importunate widow approaching the judge (xviii. 3). Some might ask if in assigning such a part to women, S. Luke has merely exercised his inventive and artistic faculty by developing a new aspect of the universalist mission which he assigns to Jesus Christ. But modern criticism enables us to reply to this question with an emphatic negative. For there are some stories about women which S. Luke has borrowed from Mark. There is the healing of Peter's mother (iv. 38; Mark i. 29), and the woman with an issue (viii. 43; Mark v. 25), and the account of the widow's mites (xxi. 2; Mark xii. 42). If S. Luke had embroidered these stories with new and important details, we should have a little less confidence in his other stories about women. But he gives them with no embellishment or addition. And we therefore can feel sure that the prominence which he assigns to women in other passages is founded upon historical fact, and that the interest which he shows in the sex which the Jews despised, was rooted in the action and the teaching of Christ.

S. Luke's teaching about voluntary poverty is also important. The deceitfulness of riches is nowhere denounced in a more uncompromising tone. S. Luke takes pleasure in recording sayings of our Lord which insist upon the renunciation of worldly goods and are not found in the other Gospels. This teaching is found in (a) the *Beatitudes* in Luke vi. 20 ff., where Christ says, 'Blessed are ye poor; for yours is the kingdom of God,' and denounces the rich as having received their consolation, whereas in Matthew the poor appear as 'the poor in spirit' and the rich are not denounced; (b) *commands to give up worldly goods*. In xii. 33, 34, the disciples are told to sell what they have and give alms, thereby making 'purses which wax not old,' *i.e.* treasure in heaven. In xiv. 33 it is said, 'Whosoever he be of you that renounceth not all that he hath, he cannot be my disciple'; (c) *various exhortations to almsgiving*. The most difficult is, perhaps, that in xi. 41, 'Give for alms those things which are within (or, which ye can); and behold, all things are clean unto you.' The meaning of the Greek being uncertain, we cannot say whether our Lord is here enjoining the giving of resources of inward pity, or of money. In xiv. 12-14 there is a command to entertain the poor at dinner, rather than kinsmen and rich neighbours. In xvi. 1-13 there is the parable of the Unjust Steward with its warning to 'make friends by means of the mammon of unrighteousness'; evidently these friends are the poor and needy; (*d*) *warnings against covetousness and callousness.* In xii. 13-21 there is our Lord's refusal to divide the inheritance of two brothers, the warning 'Keep yourselves from all covetousness; for a man's life consisteth not in the abundance of the things which he possesseth,' followed by the parable of the Rich Fool. And in xvi. 19-31 is the parable of Dives and Lazarus with its impressive 'Son, remember.'

No other part of the New Testament contains so many lessons on the right use of wealth, and very important questions naturally crop up as to the meaning of S. Luke and as to the mind of Christ towards wealth and self-denial. Since at least the time of Renan the evangelist has been accused of 'Ebionism,' but the word has not been happily chosen. Considerable obscurity exists with regard to the Ebionites, or semi-Christian Jews, whose name first occurs in the writings of S. Irenaeus about A.D. 185, but whose existence is first mentioned a generation earlier by S. Justin Martyr. They observed the Jewish Law, and regarded its observance as necessary to salvation for Jew and Gentile alike. They regarded Jesus as a human Messiah and not as divine. Their name means 'poor,' and had been used by some devout Jews to describe the pious nucleus of the nation who were filled with a sense of dependence upon God. Psalms ix., x., and xii. illustrate this meaning very clearly. Late in the fourth century S. Epiphanius shows that the Ebionites used their name to describe their apostolic and voluntary poverty, but it is not clear that they did this in the second century. The Jewish use of the word, and our Lord's blessing upon the poor in His beatitudes, may have seemed to them sufficient warrant for the title without any special reference to poverty being intended. It became as much a title as Friars 'Minor,' 'Minims,' 'Servites.' The most marked traits of the sect are peculiarly remote from S. Luke's convictions, for his attitude towards both the Law and the Person of Christ is essentially different. There is as much and as little sense in accusing him of Ebionism as there is in discovering Buddhism in his story of the sacred Infancy.

Further, the idea that this view of poverty must emanate from a period later than S. Luke's own age cannot be very seriously entertained. Voluntary poverty was practised by the Essenes, and Josephus speaks of them with the expectation of awakening sympathy among his readers, for there were both Jews and Gentiles who admired such an abnegation as philosophic. The primitive Church at Jerusalem is shown by S. Paul's writings to have been very poor, S. Luke believed it to have practised in its earlier days a voluntary communism, S. James assumes that his readers include the poor, who receive scant justice from the rich. Possibly some of the Christians of Jerusalem and even S. Luke himself may have gone further than the words of Jesus warranted in the direction of regarding riches as bad in themselves. The later Jewish theology attributed an extraordinary efficacy to almsgiving, and it is possible that generous almsgiving had an additional moral value in the case of a nation which gradually developed a unique capacity for amassing wealth. The view that alms are a means of erasing sins occurs in Ecclus. iii. 30, and is prominent in rabbinical Judaism. This seems to go beyond any reasonable interpretation even of Luke xi. 41, and on the whole we can feel justified in saying that S. Luke regarded the possession of wealth as hardly compatible with the highest type of Christian character, but not necessarily incompatible. Dives is not a sinner because he is rich, but because he has allowed his riches to act as an opiate making him oblivious to the voice of God and the needs of his neighbour.

The ascetic element in the teaching of our Lord cannot be minutely weighed so long as we remain a little uncertain about one or two of the above passages in S. Luke. But no serious doubts remain. Of recent years it has been alternately minimised and exaggerated. But something would be done in the cause of peace and truth if scholars, before discussing the question, would give some definition of the meaning that they attach to the word 'asceticism.' It has become ambiguous, though its origin is honourable. The Greek word *askēsis* means 'training' whether in athletics or learning, and such a training had a large share in Greek life. The Christians found the word congenial, and gave the name of 'athlete' to great monks who were recognised as masters of the spiritual life. Without denying that athleticism of this type, or of the modern type, has been marked by some follies and attended by some perils, one can see a great deal to recommend the name. The athlete knows that his training demands strictness even in the matter of the most legitimate enjoyments. His conduct does not always correspond with his environment but has sometimes to be inconsistent with it. It is consistent with the end that he sets before him.

Now, in some degree, Christ's moral teaching requires such asceticism of every man. The greater inwardness and intensity of His ethics demand a severer training than the Greek thought necessary. S. Paul's doctrine of the 'mortifying' or making dead of every sinful inclination, of 'crucifying' the lower nature with its voluntary or involuntary evil, is absolutely true to the whole spirit of the Sermon on the Mount. Our Lord requires of all men a struggle and a self-discipline for the conquest of mammon and of evil covetousness of every kind. This may truly be called asceticism, and seems quite as much implied in Matthew and Mark as in Luke. We may note that all the Synoptists relate our Lord's saying that His disciples will fast in the days when the bridegroom is taken away from them (Luke v. 35). And the appended words, which S. Luke calls 'a parable,' imply that the new religion will have new forms. Apparently the Church is to have the authority to make such 'fresh wine-skins' for herself and determine, not that fasting is useless, but what form fasting shall take. Our Lord's saying about the duty of fasting in secret, found in Matthew vi. 17, 18, is absent from S. Luke's Gospel, though it seems in harmony with his spirit. Both public and private fasting on the part of Christians is mentioned in Acts.

The question whether Christ taught asceticism for the personal benefit of the individual soul, as well as for the good of His kingdom, must be answered in the affirmative. It is not primarily for the extension of the Gospel, but for the good of the individual soul that the hand is to be cut off, and the eye plucked out, a severely ascetic demand which is also absent in Luke. But as our Lord's purpose is always directed towards the coming of His kingdom, He demands sacrifices for the good of the cause. Those who have made themselves better disciples of the despised Son of Man will be able to help others to be good. S. Luke shows how He went to eat and drink in a Pharisee's house and made himself at home in the household at Bethany. His enemies called Him 'a gluttonous man, and a wine-bibber,' and S. Luke does not hesitate to record the words of Jesus, also found in Matthew, 'The Son of Man is come eating and drinking' (Luke vii. 34). These facts are parallel to the story in John of His presence at the marriage feast at Cana, where He made the water wine. In thus mingling freely and joyfully with those whom He came to save, Jesus ever had before His eyes the fulfilment of the Father's will. For the sake of the same will of God He was hungry in the wilderness, and afterwards sometimes 'had not where to lay His head' (ix. 58). This should not be explained as a figurative description of the impossibility of adapting His sublime teaching to any of the existing forms of Jewish piety. It is a description of a wandering, homeless, and lonely life. Jesus calls some men to imitate this lonely life. When S. Peter said, 'Lo, we have left all and have followed thee' (Mark x. 28; Matt. xix. 27; Luke xviii. 28), he was not wrong in thinking that the Master had called them to leave all. But he may have been wrong in asking, 'What then shall we have?' (Matt. only). The service rendered to Jesus brings its own reward, and doubtless S. Thomas Aquinas was right when as a schoolboy he said, 'His servants shall serve Him' is the best thing that we know about heaven. The clue to the right interpretation of our Lord's severer demands is to be found in His own saying with regard to His teaching about celibacy, 'He that is able to receive it, let him receive it' (Matt. xix. 12). Unless He desired to subvert and destroy all civilisation, He could not have intended all His followers to live like monastic missionaries. The recent form of scepticism which represents Him as under the delusion that the Father would immediately establish a visible supernatural kingdom on earth in which all present human relationships would melt away, requires that His ethics should be ascetic in a very different sense. According to this theory, all His disciples were bound to live like the primitive Buddhist 'community,' regarding the present order of things as so transient and so inherently evil that they must needs extinguish every desire to remain in connection with it. None of the Gospels is disfigured by this bleak pessimism. Christ's continual recognition of the great worth of man, body and soul, is no excrescence on His teaching, inconsistent with His preaching of the second advent. And to lay up treasure in heaven is the correlative not of abstention from the duties of life, but of trading with the talents entrusted to our care.

§ 4. *S. Luke on The Passion.*

S. Luke's account of our Lord's Passion and Death is in many ways remarkable. We should notice before we come to the story of the Passion, that Luke is somewhat deficient in passages where the religious significance of the death of Christ is implied. Like the other Synoptists, S. Luke records his threefold prediction of the Passion (Luke ix. 22; ix. 43-45; xviii. 31-34). As S. Luke usually avoids repetition, we may be sure that he attached great importance both to the predictions and to the event predicted. But this is not the impression which we should gain from his treatment of certain other passages. Thus in Mark viii. 34, and Matt. xvi. 24, we have the saying of Jesus, 'If any man would come after Me, let him deny himself, and take up his cross, and follow Me.' In Luke ix. 23, this appears with the addition of *daily* after *his cross*. Whatever may be the origin of this word *daily*, it has the effect of slightly altering the lesson inculcated. In the two early Synoptists it comes immediately after the rebuke administered to S. Peter for his attempt to turn our Lord away from the thought of death. And it therefore suggests that for every true disciple of Christ there is a crisis, some culminating decision in which he must choose to do what Christ chose to do. S. Luke, with his usual tenderness towards the Twelve, omits the whole of the rebuke of S. Peter, and by representing the taking up of the cross as daily, implies that the cross is to be found in those vexations and humiliations which continually beset us. And this suggests that in S. Luke's mind all the life of Jesus was the bearing of the cross, and the believer's attention is less concentrated on the death itself.

Much more remarkable is S. Luke's total omission of the words 'The Son of man came not to be ministered unto, but to minister, and to give His life a ransom for many' (Matt. xx. 28; Mark x. 45). The recent sceptical school which has tried to make S. Paul the inventor of all specifically Christian doctrine, has denied this verse to be genuine, and treated it as a 'Pauline' interpolation. But the manuscripts are in its favour, and it is in harmony not only with the passage which it so grandly crowns, but also with the teaching of the Old Testament about an atoning ransom and with our Lord's entire plan of action. It agrees with the teaching of S. Peter as much as with that of S. Paul. S. Luke's omission of the anointing at Bethany in the house of Simon the leper is accounted for by his previous insertion of the story of the 'woman which was in the city, a sinner' (Luke vii. 37), but it has the result of leaving unrecorded in the third Gospel our Lord's touching reference to His burial, and His linking of the woman's generosity with the eternal Gospel. We must lastly notice that in the Lucan account of the Last Supper, a few important manuscripts have 'This is my body' without the words *which is given for you*, and also omit the whole of the next verse relating to the Eucharistic cup (xxii. 19*b*, 20). It is rather doubtful if the account of the Last Supper without these omitted words is what S. Luke originally wrote. It seems at least possible that the passage became corrupted and confused at a very early date by some scribe who was ignorant of the fact that the Jews drank several cups of wine at the Passover, and therefore altogether omitted the second, *i.e.* the Sacramental cup, while mentioning one of the others.

Whatever the text of this passage originally was, the late Professor Bruce went too far in saying that if the doubtful clauses in the evangelist's report of the Last Supper were omitted, 'Luke's Gospel would not contain a single word of Jesus that could be regarded as a contribution towards explaining the moral or theological significance of His death.'[1] The place of the death of Christ in the theology of the most primitive period of the Church's history is shown by the identification of Jesus the Messiah with the suffering servant of the Lord described in Isaiah. S. Luke in the Acts, which is a continuation of the Gospel, gives us abundant proof that the primitive Church did so regard Jesus. And in his Gospel he records the voice which was heard by our Lord at His baptism declaring that He was the One in whom the Father was well pleased (Isaiah xlii. 1 ff.),[2] and further says that Jesus applied to Himself the words 'he was reckoned with transgressors' (xxii. 37; Isaiah liii. 12). Both passages refer in Isaiah to the Servant who 'hath borne our griefs' and made his soul a 'guilt-offering,' a sacrificial reparation for sin. This is the true idea of what mediaeval writers describe as the 'satisfaction' paid by Jesus Christ to the Father. It is the reparation of perfect filial obedience for the heart-

---

[1] *With Open Face*, pp. 271-272.
[2] In some Western MSS. of Luke, the words heard at Christ's baptism are 'Thou art My beloved Son, this day have I begotten Thee.' It has been thought that this is original, and copied by S. Luke from Q. More probably it is the work of a scribe who wished to bring the words into closer conformity with Ps. ii. 7.

less sacrilege of our sins. And because death meant this for Jesus, He is described by S. Luke as saying earlier in His ministry, 'I have a baptism to be baptized with; and how am I straitened till it be accomplished' (Luke xii. 50). The baptism is the baptism which He mentions in His promise given to the sons of Zebedee after their request to sit on His right hand and on His left hand in glory (Mark x. 35 ff., omitted in Luke). It is the flood of death which is to carry Him away, a flood which He shrinks from, but which He desires, because when it is passed, the 'fire' which he has kindled will have free course.

S. Luke, then, both omits and adds in what he says about the theological significance of our Lord's death, and in his record of the actual Passion and dying of Jesus we find that he does the same. Sometimes he abbreviates the facts which are recorded by S. Mark. But he adds others which bear so plain a stamp of originality and probability that we cannot doubt that he had especially good means of learning the truth.

The Agony in the Garden as told by Luke in chap. xxii. shows so much abbreviation, that if it was based on the story in Mark, it must be said to alter it greatly. Here again there is a serious difficulty with regard to the text: verses 43 and 44 are:—

And there appeared unto Him an angel from heaven, strengthening Him. And being in an agony He prayed more earnestly · and His sweat became as it were great drops of blood falling down upon the ground.

Here we have described an awful struggle and an aid sent down from heaven. But the manuscripts leave us uncertain as to the origin of these verses. They are probably not genuine, and were inserted in order to supply what the undoubtedly Lucan record conspicuously lacks. For the other verses represent our Lord going 'as His custom was,' with His disciples, and kneeling in prayer without any mention of a terrible distress. S. Luke neither says that only the three favourite disciples were taken apart from the others, nor that they were commanded twice to 'watch,' nor that Jesus said that His soul was exceeding sorrowful, even unto death, nor that He fell on the ground. Jesus makes one act of prayer and then returns to find them sleeping 'for sorrow.' S. Luke spares the disciples somewhat, but appears to give us an infinitely less pathetic picture of our Lord's distress. Continuing to abbreviate, he omits in xxii. 47 to say that the multitude came 'with swords and staves' to take Jesus, and also leaves out the actual capture, though the fact that 'they seized Him' is stated just afterwards in *v*. 54. He also leaves out the stern words in Mark that the disciples 'all left Him, and fled.' We may notice that like the Fourth Gospel Luke attributes the work of Judas to the suggestion of Satan (xxii. 3; John xiii. 2).

The account of our Lord's trial before Caiaphas and then before the Council, and finally Pilate, is most significant. The account in Matthew and Mark implies beyond any doubt that immediately Jesus was arrested, he was taken to Caiaphas the high-priest, and that the whole Sanhedrin was met together and that Jesus was accused before them of saying that He would destroy the temple. When adjured by the high priest, He declares that He is the Son of God and speaks of His second advent. He is then condemned to death, and His face is covered (Mark) and He is smitten by the officials of the high-priest. Then in Mark xv. 1 the same authorities hold a consultation in the morning, apparently as to how they should enlist the support of Pilate, to whom Jesus is taken. In Matthew it is said that they took counsel *against Jesus to put Him to death*, and then delivered Him to Pilate the governor. In Mark nothing is said as to the nature of the consultation, but we are told that they 'bound' Jesus, and carried Him away, and delivered Him up to Pilate.

From this S. Luke diverges rather widely. He says nothing of any trial during the night, and he places in the morning the solemn meeting of the Sanhedrin at which Jesus confesses that He is the Son of Man and the Son of God, although he does not make the circumstances identical. He says nothing of the high priest rending his clothes to show that he regarded the claim of Jesus as blasphemy, nor does he even mention that the assembly condemned Jesus to death. The fact that he makes these omissions leaves it conceivable that like S. Mark he held that there were two meetings of the Sanhedrin, and was merely abbreviating. This view is slightly strengthened by his arrangement of the story of S. Peter's fall. Like the other evangelists he places S. Peter's denials during the night. But, unlike them all, he does not divide the story but gives it consecutively (xxii. 54-62: cf. Mark xiv. 54, 66-72; John xviii. 15-18, 25-27). This is probably for the sake of brevity. But can we say the same of his view that the chief part of the examination of our Lord took place in the morning?

S. John's narrative appears rather to favour that of S. Luke. In John xviii. 12 Jesus is led by 'the band and the chief captain, and the officers of the Jews,' to Annas, the father-in-law of Caiaphas. He is sharply interrogated, but no meeting of the Sanhedrin is mentioned. Then in John xviii. 24 Annas sends Jesus bound to Caiaphas, and S. John continues the story of Peter. He says nothing of what happened to Jesus when he was with Caiaphas, the narrative distinctly creating the impression that the writer was not near Jesus but near Peter at the time in question. From Caiaphas Jesus was led to Pilate. Complete certainty seems impossible of attainment. But the narrative of Luke seems to be far from improbable, especially as S. John supports the theory that the Sanhedrin had not met together at the time of the arrest. They might have met that night without infringing any law, for S. Mark's Gospel testifies against itself by showing that the night of the arrest was not the Passover night. But so long as they could finish the trial and execution before their sacred hour began, the Sanhedrin would naturally prefer to postpone the public trial until the morning. Our Lord was detained in custody until they were ready. Then, as Professor Burkitt says, ' A prisoner, and deserted by His followers, He is naturally exposed to the vulgar insults of the Temple police who had arrested Him (xxii. 63-65); in point of fact, they have nothing else to do. Meanwhile Peter slinks into a corner of the great court; we are even told that he showed his face in the light of the fire (v. 56). He denies his Master, as we know, during the hours that slowly pass by. All the action takes place in the court: in one corner is the Prisoner, in another is Peter and the group of servants. I can very well believe that the one group was visible to the other, and that the Lord really did turn and look upon Peter (v. 61). At last the day breaks and the elders of the people gather together, chief priests and scribes; they give their Prisoner a hasty trial (vv. 66-71) and as soon as He is condemned they bring Him at once before Pilate (xxiii. 1 ff).'[1]

The succeeding narrative is marked by the same distinctive notes. We find that Luke omits the fact that at the Passover the governor was in the habit of releasing a prisoner (Mark xv. 6), though the omission renders less intelligible the cry of the populace that Barabbas should be released (Luke xxiii. 18). On the other hand we find in Luke xxiii. 2 that the accusation which the Sanhedrin brought against Jesus to secure His condemnation by Pilate was that He had been guilty of 'forbidding to give tribute to Caesar, saying that He Himself is *the King Messiah*.' This technical

[1] *The Gospel History and its Transmission*, p. 137.

Jewish phrase is found neither in Matthew nor Mark. And the false charge with regard to the tribute shows how cleverly some of the Jews, after opposing Him for not taking up the rôle of a temporal potentate, secured His condemnation on the ground that He had claimed to be a King and to control the tribute, as the false Messiah Bar-Cochba did in A.D. 134. And just as Luke gives a specially clear account of the answers given by Jesus to the Sanhedrin, so the scene between our Lord and Pilate is represented with some special additions. From Mark and Matthew we gather that Pilate was really convinced of the innocence of the Prisoner, but in Luke Pilate three times pronounces Him to be innocent (*vv.* 4, 14, 22). In the Fourth Gospel we find the same threefold assertion of our Lord's innocence (John xviii. 38; xix. 4, 6). Luke and John also agree with regard to the scourging of our Lord. In Mark and Matthew the flagellation appears as a preliminary to the crucifixion, as part of the punishment and that only. A far more subtle significance attaches to it in Luke and John, and one which is in harmony with the whole picture of Pilate. Twice, in Luke xxiii. 16 and 22, Pilate says, 'I will therefore chastise Him and release Him.' He meant to appeal to the pity of the mob, thinking that they might be satisfied if they saw the weak and crushed form of Him whom they pursued with such unreasoning hatred. So in John xix. 5 he says, 'Behold the man!' He hoped that the sight of the bleeding thorn-crowned Jesus would make them sure that there was nothing that deserved either their fear or their cruelty. And Pilate, who yielded a step to the Jews at the beginning, found retreat impossible. The mob knew their man, and howled to him that he should crucify the criminal whom he had already scourged. The story in Luke seems to me to carry conviction.

After the scourging, the three other Gospels represent Jesus as mocked by the Roman soldiers. The story, which appeals to the heart of all Christendom, looks pitifully true, and it is hard to think that S. Luke omitted it because he thought it to be unhistorical or because he deliberately tried, as is sometimes suggested, to exculpate the Romans and throw the whole blame on the Jews. It is Matthew, the Jewish Gospel, which paints Jewish guilt most darkly in the cry of the people, 'His blood be on us, and on our children.' And though the Roman soldiers are not definitely mentioned by S. Luke as having taken Christ to Calvary (Luke xxiii. 26), they are said to have mocked Him while on the Cross ($v.$ 36). S. Luke tells us how Jesus was mocked by Herod Antipas and his soldiers, and the whole passage which describes Jesus before Herod (xxiii. 7-12) is peculiar to his Gospel. Not only is it intrinsically probable that He was sent to Herod, but it again fits the character of Pilate, who dodges his conscience and tries at one stroke to conciliate Herod and avoid the responsibility of putting Jesus to death. Having narrated the first mocking, S. Luke probably omitted the second for the sake of brevity. The fact that he omits to mention that the Sanhedrin condemned Jesus to death would alone be sufficient to show that he does not wish to treat the Jews as the only persons guilty of the world's greatest crime.

The scene of Jesus before Herod seems to give us a clue which is well worth following:

Herod and Pilate became friends with each other that very day: for before they were at enmity between themselves.

It is not easy to regard these words as a mere embellishment inserted by the author between his pictures of the stations of the Passion. Herod Antipas, as we saw in speaking of Mark, was an important external factor in our Lord's ministry. And Herod is mentioned in a passage peculiar to this evangelist in xiii. 31 ff., where the Pharisees tell Jesus 'Herod would fain kill Thee.' Also in ix. 7 ff., where S. Luke records that Herod was perplexed when he heard of Jesus, fearing that John the Baptist was risen from the dead, he alone adds that Herod *sought to see him*, words which prepare us for this incident in the Passion. In Acts iv. 27 the disciples are represented as mentioning in prayer 'Herod and Pontius Pilate' as together conspiring against Jesus. We naturally ask, were there any persons who would give S. Luke any special information about Herod? The answer is 'yes.' In viii. 3 we are told that Joanna, the wife of Chuza the steward of Herod, was one of the women who followed Jesus and ministered to Him, a statement not found in the other Gospels. And in Acts xiii. 1, Manaen, 'the foster brother of Herod the tetrarch,' appears not only as a Christian but actually as an official of the Church at Antioch, a place with which S. Luke always displays a special acquaintance. Further, in Luke xxiv. 10, Joanna is mentioned as one of the women who were with the disciples at the time of the resurrection. Lastly, from Acts i. 14, we gather that the women who had been with Jesus remained at first with His mother and with the apostles. It is therefore quite possible that S. Luke, who himself visited Jerusalem in A.D. 56, may have learned facts connected with our Lord's infancy and His Passion from some member of this group of holy women. And it is equally possible that he derived some of his knowledge from Manaen.

In the story of the Crucifixion Luke mentions only one of the two draughts offered to our Lord, that of the vinegar (xxiii. 36). There is a fuller account of the conduct of the malefactors with the promise 'Today shalt thou be with Me in Paradise.' The words, 'My God, My God, why hast Thou forsaken Me,' are omitted and also the rending of the temple veil. On the other hand, we find only in Luke the dying words 'Father, into Thy hands I commend My spirit.' It has been thought that the cry of desolation in which Jesus gave expression to a sense of the whole calamity of man's sin as though that calamity was personally His own, was purposely omitted by S. Luke as impossible on the lips of one whom he believed to be the Son of God. Whether he thought the words would prove a stone of stumbling we cannot really decide. But if so, it is strange that the testimony of the centurion to the true character of Jesus appears in a much weaker form than in the other Synoptists. In both Mark and Matthew the centurion calls Him 'the Son of God.' In Luke he says, 'Certainly this was a righteous man' (xxiii. 47).

§ 5. *S. Luke and S. John.*

It is not only in the story of the Passion that we find approximations between S. Luke's Gospel and S. John's. They have other historical traits in common. Matthew follows Mark in representing the ministry of our Lord as not beginning until John the Baptist had been arrested (Mark i. 14-15; Matt. iv. 12). S. Luke avoids this. He mentions the arrest before he mentions the baptism of our Lord (iii. 18 ff.) because it is in logical connection with the Baptist's preaching. He does not mention it at the time of the return of Jesus into Galilee like Matthew and Mark. What S. Luke does not deny S. John deliberately asserts, showing that the ministry of the Baptist and that of our Lord actually overlapped, 'for John was not yet cast into prison' (John iii. 24 ff., cf. iv. 1, 2). Both S. Luke and S. John show that some men wondered whether the Baptist was the Messiah (iii. 15; John

i. 19 f.). Both show the interest taken by our Lord in the Samaritans, and in Mary and Martha (x. 38 ; John xi. 1). It is also important to notice the connection between S. Luke's narrative of the appearance of our Lord to the disciples on the evening of Easter Day and the similar narrative given by S. John, who adds to it an account of the doubt of S. Thomas (xxiv. 36-43 ; John xx. 19-25). This appearance is omitted in Matthew, and in Mark the story is merely taken from Luke and is not original, being part of the unauthentic ending of Mark (see above, p. 138).

In matters more directly doctrinal we notice that in both these Gospels Jesus is very frequently called 'Lord.' He is also called 'Saviour,' and the blessing that He brings is 'salvation' (Luke ii. 11 ; John iv. 42 ; Luke ii. 30 ; John iv. 22). In both there is less stress on the apocalyptic outward return of Jesus Christ to judge the world than we find in Mark and Matthew. In both we have the same prominence given to the work of the Holy Spirit, and the deep interest shown throughout Acts in the unity of the Church reflects the spirit of our Lord's prayer in John xvii.

CHAPTER VIII

THE FOURTH GOSPEL AND THE SYNOPTISTS

§ 1. *Some Marks of Style.*

THAT the Fourth Gospel had a profound influence upon the early Church, and the Church of all subsequent ages, is unquestioned. It was regarded as a document of the highest worth from at least A.D. 160 onwards. Even if we grant that the writings earlier than this date only show a familiarity with a Johannine atmosphere, and not a familiarity with the Johannine Gospel, none of us can deny that the whole Christian Church became imbued with its teaching. S. Irenaeus and Origen, S. Athanasius and S. Hilary of Poictiers, S. Ambrose and S. Augustine, all drank from this deep cool well. It was as much prized in the practical West as in the mystical East. In the later Middle Ages the figures of S. Mary and S. John stood in our English churches, as they stand in the Fourth Gospel, by the figure of the Crucified. In the Roman liturgy the first fourteen verses of the Gospel came to be recited at the end of every Eucharist. The Reformation left S. John's Gospel on the altar or the lectern. Luther extolled it, even some of the earlier Rationalists delighted in it. But what is it worth for us? A book which makes such a claim must be examined with the strictest scrutiny. It is a dishonour to Truth to decline to ask if the book is historically true, just as it

THE GOSPELS

is to assume that it is a fiction because it teaches that Jesus is essentially divine.

In considering the relation of the Synoptic Gospels to each other we noted that the two later evangelists prove conclusively the very great value which they attached to the written materials which were in their hands. They valued the record of S. Mark so much that they reproduced almost the whole of it. And the collections of our Lord's sayings which they possessed were prized as highly as Mark. But here we have a Gospel which seems at first sight to manifest an almost equal indifference to Mark and the sayings embodied in Matthew and Luke.

First, the form of the teaching is distinctive. The short pregnant sayings, the brilliant similes in the discourses of Christ, have nearly, though not wholly, disappeared in the Fourth Gospel. He speaks of Himself, His relation to the Father in heaven, His coming into the world, the absolute necessity of believing in Him, His own relation to the Jews, and His present and future relation to His disciples. The style is the same throughout. It is almost impossible to say in some cases where the Speaker ceases and the writer begins. Thus in the third chapter there occurs the well-known verse, 'God so loved the world that He gave His only begotten Son, that whosoever believeth on Him should not perish, but have eternal life.' But it is not certain whether this verse is a reflection by the evangelist or a statement made by our Lord to Nicodemus. In other cases also we find that Jesus speaks of Himself in the third person, as in chapter v. 19-23, where He begins by saying, 'Verily, verily, I say unto you, The Son can do nothing of Himself, but what He seeth the Father doing.' Then in verse 24 we have the first person, and in the next verse the third person is resumed; we have first 'My word,' then 'Me,' and then 'the Son of God.' Such passages have given rise to the criticism that the evangelist 'betrays himself,' and speaks through the lips of Jesus. But we must at least weigh the probability that he was generally quite conscious of what he was doing, and that after all Jesus may have spoken of Himself in the third person. Few critics accuse the Synoptists of 'betraying themselves' when they represent Jesus as describing Himself by the title of 'the Son of Man.' In fact the use of the name 'the Son of Man,' and of the third person is more common on our Lord's lips in the Synoptists than His use of the pronoun 'I.' Another fact which has aroused a strong hostile criticism against the discourses in the Fourth Gospel, is that the evangelist represents Jesus as misunderstood by so many of His hearers. Nicodemus, the Samaritan woman, the disciples and the Jews, misunderstand Him, and they do so because He uses phrases which have a double meaning; they seize upon the outward significance of His words, they miss the inner. For instance, our Lord says to Nicodemus, 'Except a man be born anew, he cannot see the kingdom of God' (iii. 3). And Nicodemus immediately asks how it is possible for a man to enter the second time into his mother's womb, and be born? To the Samaritan woman He says that He would have given her 'living water' (iv. 10). She replies that He has nothing to draw with and the well is deep. Again, in the sixth chapter, which is typically Johannine, the Jews question how Jesus can give them His flesh to eat; and instead of giving any full explanation of His words, our Lord adds to the mystery by saying, 'Except ye eat the flesh of the Son of Man, and drink His blood, ye have not life in yourselves' (vi. 53). The antagonists of the Gospel say that these and other discourses are entirely the creation of the writer. They declare that they are not a record of Christ speaking to His hearers, but instances of a writer talking to his readers. They say that the second century readers of the Gospel, familiar with baptism, with the extension of the Church outside the bounds of Judaism, and with the Eucharist, would understand what the writer wished them to believe, they would be encouraged to think more highly of the Church as they knew it, and to feel a deeper, if somewhat misplaced, affection for its Founder.

This criticism seems to assume that there is a wider difference between the Synoptists and the Fourth Gospel than really exists. Christ is always greater than His hearers and greater than His critics. It would be a gross exaggeration to represent Him as talking down to the level of His audience in the Synoptic Gospels, and as always talking above their heads in the Fourth Gospel. The Synoptists testify that He was not always understood, even by His nearest disciples. It is S. Mark, the most primitive of the three, who gives the most outspoken evidence to their slowness of heart and difficulty in understanding their Master. And he emphasises it most in the case of the leader of the apostles, S. Peter. If we pass from the apostles to the populace, we find the same phenomenon. They do not understand Christ's parables. Corn and sowing and digging are words which are perfectly intelligible to them. But both in Mark and Matthew we find that the mysteries of the kingdom of God are not mysteries to the crowd. Their hearts are too hard, their eyes too dim to see what is hidden beneath the outward sign. The crowd did not realise the principles which underlie the spread of God's reign in the world any more than the disciples understood Christ's prophecies of His death and resurrection. Another fact which strikes us in this connection is significant of the whole trend of recent Rationalism. It is the tendency to appeal to the Synoptists as giving us the real key to the ministry of Jesus whenever they seem to contradict the fourth evangelist, and then, having made them serve this purpose, to reject their evidence. If a conservative critic asks why the sayings of Jesus in John are to be regarded as no better than the speeches in Homer, he is told that the Synoptists show that Jesus did not and could not speak in such an obscure manner, or meet the density of His hearers with renewed assertions of His divine origin. If in answer it be pointed out that the Synoptists also represent Him as misunderstood, the rationalist replies that even Mark wrote for 'edification,' and endeavoured to give a plausible reason for the failure of Jesus among the Jews, by representing Him as deliberately saying what they could not understand!

2. *Our Lord and the Jews.*

The attitude of Jesus towards the whole Jewish people, as depicted in the Fourth Gospel, is often declared to be fictitious. It is said to be so stiff and harsh that the Christ of the Fourth Gospel could never, like the Christ of S. Luke, have wept over Jerusalem (Luke xix. 41). Is not this another paradox? The fourth evangelist represents Jesus as weeping by the grave of one Jew whom He loved, and it shows a strange kind of psychological insight to say that this Jesus could not have wept over the city which contained His Father's house. Only from John do we learn how often He was in Jerusalem, and that in that place 'many believed on His name' (ii. 32, cf. vii. 40). It is therefore evident that the evangelist does not represent our Lord as condemning the whole nation as hopelessly hardened and lost. The Jews who are condemned are mainly 'the chief priests and the Pharisees' (vii. 32), and the official party in Jerusalem. It cannot even be said that the Fourth Gospel represents Jesus as from the first hostile to this official party. What is said of His relation to the men with whom He came in contact on His first visit to Jerusalem is that 'Jesus did not trust Himself unto them, for that He knew all men' (ii. 24). He was cautious from the beginning. 'The Jews' became hostile when He set aside their ridiculous regulations about the observance of the Sabbath (v. 10 ff.). S. Mark, no doubt correctly, assigns exactly the same reason, though not the same occasion, for this hostility. In reading some of the most recent criticisms of S. John's Gospel, one would suppose that the evangelist represented Jesus as denouncing the Jews from the first because they did not and would not immediately recognise Him as the Messiah and Son of God who came down from heaven.[1] And this is contrasted with His denunciation of the scribes and Pharisees recorded in the Synoptic Gospels. The former is represented as a dogmatic anathema, the latter as a moral protest against their parade of outward piety. But Christ in the Fourth Gospel does not call His Jewish antagonists children of the devil, the first murderer, until they seek to kill Him (v. 18; viii. 37, 44). The opposition is gradual, and it began on their side, not on His. Both in Mark and in John He defends His action on the Sabbath by an appeal to His unique authority. In Mark, when the Pharisees complained that His disciples broke the Sabbath by plucking corn, He says, 'the Son of man is lord even of the Sabbath' (Mark ii. 28). In John, after healing the impotent man at the pool of Bethesda, He says, 'My Father worketh even until now, and I work' (v. 17). He co-operates with God, who from creation has preserved life on the Sabbath day as on other days, and He does so in virtue of His nature and His office. The Fourth Gospel is not copying Mark, but their testimony agrees. It seems to me to be intelligible. But

[1] W. Heitmuller, *Das Johannes-Evangelium*, p. 165 (*Die Schriften des Neuen Testaments*, Lfg. 10).

it will be difficult to convince the people who have persuaded themselves that the whole account of the healing at the pool of Bethesda is an 'allegory,' and that its five porches are only the five books of the Pentateuch in which the Jewish Church lay impotent.

The mention of the Jews as 'Jews,' of the passover as 'a feast of the Jews,' of 'the Jews' feast, the feast of tabernacles,' is surely natural enough. They show that the Gospel was written among Gentiles, and for Gentiles. And no one need deny that the word 'Jews' sometimes carries with it an unfriendly flavour. The author looks upon himself as apart from them; he has severed his connection with them. Why should this be regarded as a proof that he was not a Jew by birth, and not a personal attendant of Christ? The Apocalypse is by far the most Jewish book in the New Testament. But the author speaks of 'them who say they are Jews, and they are not, but are a synagogue of Satan' (Rev. ii. 9), with a bitterness exceeding the bitterness of the Fourth Gospel. And S. Paul, who remained proud of his Jewish origin, speaks exactly like the Fourth Gospel. Writing to Gentiles at Thessalonica, many years before the Fourth Gospel was written, he says, 'Ye also suffered the same things of your own countrymen, even as they (the Churches in Judaea) did of the Jews' (1 Thess. ii. 14). If an apostle, writing about A.D. 51, could thus contrast the Christians and the non-Christian Jews, why should it be impossible for another apostle to do this thirty years later? In spite of the evangelist's dislike of unbelieving Judaism, he never takes up the attitude of the second-century anti-Semite. The acute hatred of Judaism as a religion, which was a symptom of some semi-Christian heresies of that period, is not discoverable in this Gospel. It was commonly held by the Gnostic sects that the God of the Jews was an evil God or demi-god, that the world He made was inherently evil, and that the Jewish religion was a diabolical invention. But our evangelist puts on the lips of Jesus Himself the words 'salvation is from the Jews' (iv. 22). He not only quotes the Jewish Scriptures, but even shows an unmistakable acquaintance with the Hebrew original.[1] And at the very beginning of the Gospel he speaks of Jesus coming to Palestine as 'His own home' and to the Jews as 'His own people' (i. 11). Our Lord's attitude towards Judaism in the Fourth Gospel agrees with that in Matthew, where Jesus says, 'The kingdom of God shall be taken away from you, and shall be given to a nation bringing forth the fruits thereof' (Matt. xxi. 43). It is therefore a perversion of the facts to speak of the Fourth Gospel as if one of the main objects with which it was written was to preach a crusade against the Jews, or to represent it as so hostile to Judaism that it could not have been written by one who was born a Jew.

3. *The Baptist in the Fourth Gospel.*

The accusation that it was intended to push the memory of S. John the Baptist into the background and to humiliate his admirers is even more unfounded. He is mentioned several times, in i. 6-8, 15, 19 ff.; iii. 22 ff.; v. 33 ff.; x. 41. Not one of these passages can fairly be interpreted as depreciating the greatness of the Baptist. He is the friend of the bridegroom, Jesus. He is said by our Lord to have been 'the lamp that burneth and shineth.' He is regarded by Him as eminently a witness to the truth, and a speaker of truth. It is a weak criticism to say that in the Fourth Gospel the Baptist has no independent position, no importance except as the forerunner and witness to the Messiah. We have no evidence to show that the Baptist claimed

[1] Especially in xiii. 18, and xix. 37.

to be anything else. In his preaching of repentance, which the Synoptists place in high relief, he was preparing for the Messianic kingdom, as those writers tell us. He was 'a voice,' calling on men to make ready for the era of salvation. This is taught by all the evangelists. The fourth evangelist, in accordance with his usual plan of citing witnesses to Jesus, lays most stress upon this part of the Baptist's work. He does not mention that John baptised our Lord, taking for granted that his readers would know this. But he does refer to John's work of baptising in a way which is likely to give the student a prejudice in favour of his accuracy in other particulars. In iii. 22 ff. we read, 'After these things came Jesus and His disciples into the land of Judaea; and there he tarried with them, and baptised. And John also was baptising in Ænon near to Salim, because there was much water there: and they came, and were baptised. For John was not yet cast into prison.' Then in iv. 3 we read that Jesus 'left Judaea, and departed again into Galilee.' This word 'again' is important, and must be taken in connection with the statement that John was not yet imprisoned. They are a quiet correction of the impression conveyed by Matthew and Mark, where the first and the second journey of Jesus to Galilee are confused, and Jesus does not go to Galilee till John is in prison. This error is avoided by Luke and corrected by John i. 43, iii. 24 and iv. 3. And we can conceive no motive for this correction, except the simple desire for historical accuracy. It is an unworthy insinuation to suggest that it is a falsehood written to emphasise the contrast between the Baptist and our Lord (see below, p. 254). The mention of Ænon near Salim is another point in the evangelist's favour. The word Ænon is a Semitic word, meaning springs or wells, and even Renan ridiculed the idea of such a name being invented by a Greek. The place has been identified, and the identification has been aided by the survival of the name Salem. From fourth-century writers we know that the Christians long regarded the spot as sacred. Like so many other sacred sites, it was annexed by a later religion. The Moslems took it as they took the tombs of the patriarchs at Hebron and the supposed house of John Mark at Jerusalem. They have erected a building there, and have consecrated it by dubbing it the tomb of a Sheikh named Salim [1]

As the Fourth Gospel shows signs of a special knowledge of the time and place of the Baptist's work, we may think it probable that the writer knew something of the Baptist's character. The more sceptical modern critics, such as Schmiedel, insist that Matthew is correct in saying that the Baptist doubted whether Jesus was the Messiah (xi. 2 f.), and insist that the statement in the same Gospel that in his reverence for Christ he hesitated to baptise Him is 'a later trait.' In the opinion of these writers there was no such distinction between John the Baptist and our Lord as would justify such a hesitation. They hold that the Fourth Gospel exalts the latter over the former in a most unhistorical fashion, and that when we find in Luke and Matthew any traces of the same tendency to exalt Jesus so far above the Baptist, we are necessarily in the presence of 'later traits.' In their eyes the really important fact about the Baptist's relation to Christ is that he had religious doubts. Matthew records how the Baptist sent disciples to Jesus to ask, 'Art thou He that cometh, or look we for another'—was He the Messiah, or not? It seems possible that the Baptist sent his disciples to ask this question for their own instruction rather than on account of doubts in his own heart. And yet it is surely quite probable that he felt such doubts. In prison and despondent, learning that the Messiah had not established any external kingdom

---

[1] Dr. W. Sanday, *Sacred Sites of the Gospel*, p 35.

such as even the apostles expected, may he not have
doubted? But this doubt is now brought forward as
a convincing proof that the Fourth Gospel is a
romance. It is said to be impossible that he could
have doubted if he had at the beginning of Christ's
entrance into public life recognised Him as the Saviour
who should die for the world (i. 27, 29), and as having
existed with God in heaven before His work began on
earth (i. 15, 30)

The above objection seems to imply that a sincere
and fervent belief makes subsequent doubt, even in a
time of special distress, absolutely impossible. The
experience of many generations of Christians tells us a
very different tale. It has been the sorrow of the
saints that they have had to pass through doubts and
desolations which seem to deny what they really believe.
And why should not John the Baptist have believed
more about the Messiah than was believed by the
lower type of Jew? Why should he not have thought
that Jesus would be the Saviour, and that He had been
with God in heaven? If he was the greatest of those
who represented Old Testament piety, and the words
of Jesus imply this (Matt. xi. 11), we may presume
that he studied the Old Testament prophets. Why
should he not have seen in Jesus a strength and meekness which recalled to him Isaiah's picture of the suffering Servant of the Lord whose soul became an offering
for sin? He had also read in Isaiah that the Messiah
would be 'God with us' (vii. 14) and the 'everlasting
Father' (ix. 6), in Micah that 'his goings forth are
from of old, from everlasting' (v. 2). Why should he
not have thought that the Messiah had some specially
close relation to God, and even that He existed in
heaven with God before He came on earth? The
belief was not confined to Isaiah and Micah. It actually formed part of contemporary Jewish belief, so far
as can now be determined. The idea that the Messiah

existed with God, hidden with God, and would mysteriously be revealed at the right moment, was held by some of the Jews of the first century of our era.[1] The Fourth Gospel contains an allusion to this idea. In vii. 42 we have mention of the popular belief that the Messiah should come from Bethlehem. But in vii. 31 there is a reference to the other view. Some of the Jerusalem Jews, familiar with rabbinical traditions, say, 'When Christ cometh, no man knoweth whence He is.' Only a writer who was a born Jew would have introduced this allusion to the hidden existence of the Messiah in this passing but effective manner. And it shows us how slow we ought to be in deciding that the Baptist necessarily held precisely the same views about the Messiah as those who expected Him to be merely a Hebrew 'Grand Monarch.'

A further question has to be asked with regard to the representation of John the Baptist in the Fourth Gospel. If those critics are correct who say that this book was written long after the apostolic age was over, what need was there to depreciate the Baptist? Why should a writer of A.D. 100 or 140 want to give a false picture of the Baptist? The motive assigned to him is said to have been supplied by the existence of a sect which venerated John the Baptist more than Jesus, or so highly as to menace the honour which a second-century Christian considered to be due to Jesus. Now, the existence of this sect is purely hypothetical. We have not a shred of proof that in the second century there was any such sect, either Jewish or Christian. The sceptical critics know this well enough. But to show us that such a sect might have existed, they appeal to Acts xix. 1-5. Here we find that S. Paul, when he arrived at Ephesus about A.D. 54, found certain disciples who had only been baptised 'unto

[1] Emil Schurer, *History of the Jewish People in the time of Jesus Christ*, Division II., vol. II. p. 163 (English translation).

THE FOURTH GOSPEL AND THE SYNOPTISTS 255

John's baptism.' We may be fairly sure that they were men of Jewish birth who had heard the Baptist's call to repentance, received baptism at his hands, and then became disciples under the Christian preacher Apollos. S. Luke represents S. Paul as using words which exactly corroborate the assertion of the Fourth Gospel that the Baptist bore special witness to Jesus as the Messiah. These disciples, who only numbered 'about twelve,' then received Christian baptism. So the pseudo-critical argument reduces itself to this syllogism :

1. In A.D. 54, twelve Christians at Ephesus had been disciples of John the Baptist.
2. The Fourth Gospel, which was probably written at Ephesus between A.D. 100 and 140, represents the Baptist as saying that he was much inferior to Christ.
3. Therefore the author of the Fourth Gospel perverted history in order to oppose a sect which preferred the Baptist to Christ.

To sum up the attitude of the Fourth Gospel towards the Jews and S. John the Baptist, it is a religious rather than a controversial attitude. There is no teaching to the effect that Judaism as such is an evil thing. Nor is there any preference for Gentiles as such. The prologue shows that the divine Word 'lighteth every man,' whether Jew or Gentile. The record of the touching incident of the Greeks at Jerusalem who came to Philip saying, 'Sir, we would see Jesus' (xii. 21), shows the writer's sympathy, but no more. This is not what we should expect from a romancer of the second century. A modern prophetess of theosophy asserts that Jesus, after he had reached manhood, went to Egypt. Philostratus tells his readers how Apollonius of Tyana visited kingdoms of the mysterious East. And a second-century forger would probably have represented Jesus as floating from

Jerusalem to Athens and disputing with the philosophers or contending with magicians. The fragments of heretical literature which have survived from early times also show what the romancer of the period could do, and what his readers enjoyed. The atmosphere of these romances resembles that of the Fourth Gospel as much as a scene from a melodrama resembles a stately cathedral. As for the alleged depreciation of S. John the Baptist, there is no such depreciation. It is quite true that the Fourth Gospel contradicts two of the Synoptists with regard to the time of the Baptist's imprisonment. But it is ludicrous to say that the author gives the Baptist a fictitious freedom, leaving him out of prison until he has had the opportunity of sending his disciples to Jesus. For Matthew expressly tells us that when John was 'in prison' (Matt. xi. 2), he was able to send disciples to Jesus. If all that the author desired was an emphatic testimony of an inferior to his Superior, he could have invented this testimony without being so foolish as to lay himself open to the charge of contradicting the Gospel which was most widely known to the early Church.

§ 4. *Time and Scene of Christ's Ministry.*

In considering the time of the Baptist's imprisonment, we have already entered on the vexed question of chronology. With this is intimately connected the question of the scene of Christ's ministry. According to the Fourth Gospel, the ministry of our Lord lasted rather more than two years. Three Passovers are mentioned. The first when Jesus went to Jerusalem and drove the money-changers out of the Temple (ii. 13). A little before the second Passover, He miraculously fed the five thousand in Galilee near the Sea of Gennesaret (vi. 4). At the third Passover He

THE FOURTH GOSPEL AND THE SYNOPTISTS 257

was put to death (xi. 55; xii. 1; xiii. 1). Between these three Passovers, three other feasts are mentioned. The first is merely called 'a feast of the Jews'—it was probably Pentecost (v. 1). The second is the feast of Tabernacles in October (vii. 2). The third is the feast of the Dedication of the Temple in December (x. 22). Passover fell, roughly speaking, in our month of March. The Synoptists on the other hand, give us very few indications of time. They directly mention no Passover, except the one when Jesus was put to death. Consequently some writers now try to cramp the ministry recorded in the Synoptists within the space of one year, some even within the space of a few months. There is a similar difference as to the districts where Jesus 'went about doing good.' These districts were, roundly speaking, four. There was Galilee in the north, Judaea with its chief city Jerusalem in the south. Between them lay Samaria. And eastward beyond the river Jordan was Peraea, through which Jesus perhaps made part of His last journey to Jerusalem (see p. 150). It is possible that some of the sections in the middle of S. Luke's Gospel are to be connected with Peraea. And the same district is referred to in John x. 40 as 'beyond Jordan.' The difficulty is that in the Synoptists the scene of our Lord's ministry is Galilee, near the shores of Lake Gennesaret, though He made excursions to the district of Tyre and Sidon (Mark vii. 24, 31), and also to the neighbourhood of Caesarea Philippi (Mark viii. 27). The Synoptists describe no visit of Jesus to Jerusalem except the visit which occasioned His death. On the other hand, we find little in John about His work in Galilee, and very much about his work in Judaea and Jerusalem. Most of the Gospel is connected with His visits to the city. We also find in John clear mention of Christ visiting Samaria with His disciples (iv. 4 ff.). It is urged by the 'radical' critics that this is completely unhistorical, that Jesus never went to Samaria, and never visited Jerusalem before the Passover at which He died. The Fourth Gospel is therefore declared to be false as to both the duration and the scene of our Lord's ministry.

As to the length of Christ's ministry, the notes of time in the Fourth Gospel are quite consistent with themselves. They are also consistent with probability. On any reasonable hypothesis, we must allow time for the development of both faith in Christ and opposition. A space of somewhat more than two years is not too long to account for the training of the little band of faithful disciples, the changed attitude of the populace towards the Messiah and the calculated hostility of the Pharisees and Sadducees. The mere fact that two parties so hostile to each other as the Pharisees and Sadducees did combine to crush the new Teacher, powerfully suggests that His work had not been confined within a few months, or even a year. And the evidence that they did combine is decisive. Further, there are one or two small indications in the Synoptists that Christ's ministry was not so short as it first appears. We can here merely note that in Mark, where we have a particularly accurate account of the earlier part of our Lord's ministry, the mention of ripe corn in ii. 23, and green grass in vi. 39, implies two spring times before the last Passover.

With regard to the scene of our Lord's ministry, the 'radical' critics are in a much greater difficulty than they are inclined to confess. S. Luke definitely asserts that Jesus came into contact with Samaritans and journeyed through Samaria (Luke ix. 52; xvii. 11). Schmiedel, in his anxiety to deny the historical accuracy of the Fourth Gospel, declares that what S. Luke says about this journey is unworthy of credit.[1] We can be content with the fact that S. Luke thought

[1] *Das 4. Evangelium gegenuber den 3 ersten*, p. 8.

otherwise, especially as this evangelist, who is usually so tender towards the faults of the apostles, connects the beginning of this journey with a rebuke administered by Christ to James and John. This rebuke is by itself sufficient to give the hall-mark of veracity to the narrative in Luke ix. 51 ff. With regard to Galilee, it is true that Christ's visits to that region appear in John rather as important episodes than anything more (ii. 1-12; iv. 43-54; vi. 1-vii. 10). This may quite well be accounted for by the theory that the evangelist did not wish to record much of what he knew was already in his readers' hands and minds. He may have known a great deal about the work of Christ in Galilee which he does not tell us. There is one suggestive verse which should here be mentioned. We are told that when Jesus left Samaria, ' He went forth from thence into Galilee. For Jesus Himself testified, that a prophet hath no honour in his own country ' (iv. 43, 44). This ' country ' is evidently intended by the evangelist to be Judaea, where Matthew and Luke say that Christ was born. He cannot have imagined that Christ by birth or education belonged to Samaria. Now the words here quoted in John are said by S. Luke to have been spoken by Jesus at Nazareth in Galilee (Luke iv. 24), that is, in Luke they referred to Galilee, or a district of Galilee. And the fourth evangelist, though he is speaking of Judaea, to which country they applied with even greater force, apparently quotes them to lay stress on the deliberate intention of Christ to work in Galilee.

Just as this Gospel shows a knowledge of the ministry exercised by Christ in Galilee, so Matthew and Luke show a knowledge of the fact that He was more than once in Jerusalem. In Matt. xxiii. 37, and Luke xiii. 34, we have unequivocal testimony to our Lord's lament over the repeated disregard which His message experienced in Jerusalem.

O Jerusalem, Jerusalem, which killeth the prophets, and stoneth them that are sent unto her! *how often would I have gathered thy children together,* even as a hen gathereth her chickens under her wings, and ye would not! Behold, your house is left unto you desolate. For I say unto you, Ye shall not see Me henceforth, till ye shall say, Blessed is He that cometh in the name of the Lord.

This saying, whether uttered more than once by our Lord or not, is very strongly attested. It must have been in the collections of sayings used by the first and third evangelists. It points to an inference directly opposite to the wishes of the critics who deny the historical character of the Fourth Gospel. Consequently we find elaborate attempts to explain it away. Wellhausen tries to discredit the passage by treating the prophecy about the destruction of Jerusalem as a prophecy after the event. He says 'the destruction of the city is not something in the future, it is already destroyed and is to remain in ruins.' There is, however, no reason why this expression should not be what is called a 'prophetic future,' such as is common enough in Hebrew writings, and Harnack very properly treats it as such.[1] Schmiedel falls foul of the words which have been printed above in italics. He suggests that in the documents employed by our evangelists, the words about the hen and her chickens were attributed not to Jesus, but to 'the wisdom of God.' This wisdom is mentioned in Luke xi. 49, as sending prophets and apostles to Jerusalem, and since prophets and men sent with God's message are also mentioned in Luke xiii. 34, where Christ laments over Jerusalem, Schmiedel says that to apply the words to Jesus is a complete mistake.[2] It was only God's 'wisdom,' which some unknown book or other, written by a pious Jew, described as showing this maternal solicitude for Jerusalem. This book was then quoted

[1] *The Sayings of Jesus,* p. 30 (English translation).
[2] *Op. cit.* p. 45.

by the early collectors of Christ's sayings, and finally put into His mouth. Anything more tortuous than this argument it would be hard to invent. It cannot be reasonably considered to disprove the accuracy of John in recording the visits of Christ to Judaea and Jerusalem. There is nothing to make us think it unlikely that Jesus would visit the place which was the centre of the religion which He came to fulfil. To believe that He made such visits causes one to do no real violence to the obviously imperfect record in Mark. And it has the support not only of John and Matthew, but of at least three passages in Luke, and one in Acts. In Luke iv. 44 (see margin of the Revised Version), we find Christ preaching in the synagogues of Judaea. In Luke v. 17, the presence in Galilee of Pharisees from *Jerusalem* is a testimony to the impression which Christ had made in the holy city. Luke xiii. 34 has been noticed above. In Acts x. 37 the gospel is said to have been 'published throughout all Judaea, beginning from Galilee, after the baptism which John preached.' This last passage is very simple and natural, and there is nothing to make us think that S. Luke is inventing the facts. We have, therefore, no ground whatever for saying that the Synoptic evangelists, or the documents which they used, prove that the visits of our Lord to Judaea and Jerusalem recorded in John are fictitious.

Lastly, if He paid several visits to Jerusalem, it seems quite possible that He drove the money-changers out of the temple early in His ministry, as recorded in John ii. 14. This is not in the least excluded, as many critics assert, by the cleansing of the temple at the time of His final visit in Mark xi. 15.

§ 5. *The Personal Claims of Christ.*

Another charge against the Fourth Gospel is that it

contradicts the other Gospels with regard to the personal claims made by our Lord. It is said that in the Synoptists there is a gradual development in His claims to the Messiahship and divine Sonship, and that this development has been ignored or obliterated by the author of the Fourth Gospel. As a simple specimen of the manner in which this accusation is sometimes made, I will quote Heitmüller. 'From the older Gospels we definitely recognise that Jesus only spoke of His Messianic dignity, the secret of His life, very seldom, and first towards the end of His activity; He exercised, as we can understand, a modest reserve with regard to this most delicate and intimate fact of His most inward life. In John Jesus manifests Himself from the beginning as the Messiah (i. 50, etc.). From the Synoptists we further gather that even the disciples at a rather late period, first in the celebrated scene at Caesarea Philippi (Mark viii. 27 ff.), arrived at the belief that their Master was the Messiah of Israel. According to the Gospel of John they are on the contrary convinced of it from the commencement; they only become the disciples of Jesus because they have recognised Him as the Messiah (i. 41 ff.).'[1]

Criticisms of this kind are frequently made. But they can never injure the reputation of the evangelist until it can be shown that the Synoptists prove that the thought of Jesus with regard to His Messiahship developed after the commencement of His ministry, and that the Johannine portrait of Jesus is inconsistent with a modest reserve in the statement of His claims. For the first point we may consult Schmiedel's article on the Gospels in the *Encyclopaedia Biblica*.[2] He says 'it would be quite out of place to look in the Gospels for direct statements as to any development in Jesus during the period of his public activity. The latest date at which reverence for him would have

[1] *Op. cit.* p 165.   [2] Vol. ii. col. 1888.

allowed a conception of anything of the kind to be assigned is that of his temptation before his ministry began.' In spite of this, Schmiedel 'ventures to conjecture some development in Jesus during his public life' with regard to His idea of His Messiahship. He points out that in all the Synoptists Christ commands His disciples to keep secret the substance of S. Peter's confession of His dignity. He also says that in Mark, unlike Matthew, Christ only twice calls Himself by the Messianic title 'Son of Man' before S. Peter called Him 'the Christ.' The inference to be drawn from the above criticisms, and indeed from the Synoptists themselves, is obvious. It is that all the documents we possess affirm that Jesus was conscious of His dignity throughout His ministry. We can go further back than this, for the remarkable saying which S. Luke attributes to the boy Jesus when He was found by His parents in the Temple, shows that S. Luke believed that in His boyhood He was fully conscious of His divine Sonship, though still 'growing in wisdom and stature.' But the Synoptists do prove that our Lord showed a very careful reserve in teaching His Messiahship. In Mark this is very evident. He would not have every one proclaim what He himself knew. That would have meant disaster before His disciples were sufficiently trained to face it. And the Fourth Gospel not only shows that Christ taught gradually and cautiously, but even records the fact that the Jews reproached Him for so doing. At quite a late period in His ministry the Jews 'came round about Him, and said unto Him, How long dost Thou hold us in suspense? if Thou art the Christ, tell us plainly' (x. 24). The whole passage deserves the most careful study. It represents Christ as in no way forcing His hearers to believe, but as meeting His opponents on their own ground and then refusing to retreat from His position. The earlier chapters of the Gospel do not militate against this view. The Baptist, who in all the Gospels appears as a great prophet, in the first chapter of John greets Christ 'as the Lamb of God which taketh away the sin of the world.' And to His chosen disciples He reveals Himself as the Messiah. This does not render S. Peter's later confession otiose. It was one thing to follow Him as Messiah in the lower Jewish sense of the word when His disciples thought that He would command as well as deserve success. It was a different thing to confess Him when they had begun to understand that His office as Messiah depended upon a mysterious and unique sonship, and that in spite of this close relation to God, His ministry was to involve His death (Mark viii. 31). At first they probably only thought that He was Son of God in the very inferior sense of being God's chosen representative. This is what a Jew would ordinarily have thought about the Messiah. And the Fourth Gospel in a most interesting manner throws light on the first view of Jesus held by His disciples in the exclamation with which Nathanael hails Him. He says, 'Rabbi, thou art the Son of God; Thou art King of Israel' (i. 49). Apparently the one title is here used as the equivalent of the other. Philip, before bringing Nathanael to Jesus, had convinced himself that 'the son of Joseph' was indeed the Messiah, and his trust in our Lord corresponded with that conviction. But the very evening of Christ's betrayal, he says to Jesus, 'Lord, shew us the Father' (xiv. 8). Even then he hardly knew what the divine Sonship was, though the title probably did not seem to him extravagant when he first heard it uttered. There is in fact development in the Fourth Gospel, not in our Lord's belief concerning Himself, but in His revelation of His own dignity, and in the belief or unbelief with which that revelation was received.[1]

---

[1] It would be impossible to discuss at length in this book the evangelist's doctrine of Christ's Person. For this the reader should

§ 6. *The Raising of Lazarus.*

The raising of Lazarus and the date given by the Fourth Gospel to the death of Jesus Christ have been for many years the objects of special adverse criticism. The two events are closely connected in the author's mind. The raising of Lazarus, which is the greatest of the miracles of Jesus, prepares for the coming catastrophe. It provokes a definite resolution on the part of the Jewish Sanhedrin, and this resolution takes effect. For our Lord, having shown that He is Master of life and death, is ready to die. His death is voluntary and is the gate to His own risen life and ascent to the Father. He dies too as 'the Lamb of God' sacrificing Himself on man's behalf, and dies on the very day and near the very moment when the Passover lambs were sacrificed by the Jews in memory of their deliverance from the land of bondage.

That Jesus died upon the Cross is almost undisputed, except by the few men who deny that He ever existed, or those who think that He was scarcely half dead when put into the grave, and therefore able to come out of the grave after three days of repose. At present neither of these two views is sufficiently popular to need a closer examination. But it is still sometimes asserted that the Fourth Gospel assigns a false date to His death, placing it a day too early in order to create an artificial symmetry between that death and the slaying of the Passover lambs. It is also asserted that the raising of Lazarus is devoid of any historical foun-

consult Liddon's *Bampton Lectures*, and Dr R L. Ottley, *The Doctrine of the Incarnation.* We may just notice that the doctrine of the author's prologue (i. 1-14) consistently agrees with his record of the acts and words of Jesus. He has found in Jesus the Logos, the perfect Word or Expression of an active loving God. But with the possible exception of a hint in x. 35 he never represents our Lord as calling Himself the Word.

dation, being constructed out of the stories of the raising of the daughter of Jairus and the widow's son of Nain, with various ingredients from other sources. The raising of Lazarus is said to be excluded by the silence of the Synoptists, and John's date of the crucifixion is said to be incompatible with their evidence.

To estimate the value of the criticisms passed on the story of Lazarus, it is well to gain some knowledge of the manner in which the different critics have criticised each other. The story itself is detailed and dramatic. The figures are no mere silhouettes. The women are sketched in firm and delicate lines. The Jews, to whom this evangelist is said to be so severe, appear as at least sympathetic towards the family which Jesus loved, and Jesus when most divine appears most human. No one can deny that the story has a persuasive charm. And it admirably fits into the chain of events. The manner in which its reality has been explained away has greatly varied, and has illustrated to perfection the different phases through which non-Christian and semi-Christian thought have passed during the last hundred years. But it leaves upon our minds the impression of being not an explanation, but an expedient. It does not prove to us that the story is incompatible with the estimate of Christ formed by the men who knew Him. It only tells us how one who never knew Jesus in the flesh might conceivably have invented a miraculous story in order to glorify his Hero. The older form of rationalism, that of Paulus, Schweitzer, and others, declared that Lazarus never really died, and that when Jesus arrived at the sepulchre He called upon a Lazarus who was already reviving amid the cool air and spices of his tomb. The second stage of modern rationalism, that of Strauss and Baur, poured ridicule on this theory, but its two great exponents disagreed as to the real origin of the story. Strauss held that it was a Christian legend which arose under the influence of similar legends in the Old Testament. Baur acutely criticised the theory of Strauss, and declared the story to be a piece of speculation, a picture invented to illustrate the words of Jesus, 'I am the resurrection and the life.'[1] That it was really intended as such an illustration is more than probable. The author of the Gospel does give concrete instances of the power of Jesus, and does it in order that his readers may believe that Jesus is the Messiah, the Son of God, and that believing they may have life in His name (xx. 31). But it does not follow that the story is only a symbolic representation of a religious truth. Loisy adheres in the main to the explanation of Baur. Renan, on the contrary, saw that the miracle forms such a natural link in the development of the last days of the Son of Man, that he held that Jesus was guilty of a pious fraud, and condescended to perform a burlesque resurrection which imposed upon the bystanders.

More recent rationalism usually favours another line of interpretation. The story is said by Holtzmann, Schmiedel, Heitmüller and others to have taken its start from the parable of Dives and Lazarus in Luke xvi. There Lazarus is not allowed to leave his rest in the unseen world to warn the unrepentant brothers of Dives. But the author of the Fourth Gospel is said to have selected his name—not an uncommon Jewish name even nowadays—and then improved upon the parable of Jesus. The new Lazarus is allowed to leave the regions of the dead. In spite of his resurrection, the Jews remain unconverted, just as Abraham said that the brothers of Dives would not repent though one rose from the dead to warn them. Such is Heitmüller's explanation.[2] But he is once more too much

---

[1] A good brief summary of the older rationalistic theories about Lazarus can be found in Godet, *L'Évangile de St. Jean*, vol. iii. p. 257 (3rd edition).   [2] *Op. cit.* pp. 268-9.

dominated by the idea that the Fourth Gospel is a direct polemic against the Jews. For our evangelist, instead of using the story of Lazarus as a mere demonstration of the power of Christ, and of the hardened stupidity of the Jews, expressly says that the result of the miracle was that many of the Jews believed on Jesus (xi. 45). It is worth noticing that the third Gospel is now accused of the same aberrations as the fourth. For Johannes Weiss, the author of the commentary on Luke, in the same series as that for which Heitmüller has written, confidently asserts that the parable has been influenced by the fact that the Jews remained unbelieving though Christ rose from the dead. It is a perversion of the original teaching of Jesus, and the name of Lazarus possibly was taken into the third Gospel from the fourth![1]

Of all the explanations which have been proposed there is none which is sufficiently natural or probable to make us abandon the literal story. If we are willing to believe that Jesus could raise the dead, the story presents no serious difficulty. The fact that Jesus died and rose from the dead was, as we see in Acts, the central fact in the earliest preaching of the Gospel. It overshadowed everything else, even His miracles of raising the daughter of Jairus, the widow's son, and Lazarus. Luke has taken the story of the raising of the widow's son from an unknown source; and the story of the daughter of Jairus is borrowed by Matthew and Luke from Mark. We are reduced to one authority for each of the three miracles, and the authority may still be good. What is more remarkable is that the most important appearance of the risen Jesus, that which S. Paul mentions as having been made to above five hundred brethren at once, is not mentioned in a single Gospel. S. Paul is sure that it

[1] *Das Lukas-Evangelium*, p. 453 (*Die Schriften des Neuen Testaments*, Lfg. 7).

took place, and the epistle in which he mentions it is certainly genuine. The author of the Fourth Gospel may have been equally sure that Lazarus was raised from the dead, and the silence of the Synoptists does not prove that either S. Paul or S. John were wrong.

§ 7. *The Date of Christ's Death.*

The date of the death of Jesus is the last difficulty to be discussed in this chapter. The controversy about the day on which Jesus died has been one of the most important theological controversies of the last eighty years. Baur and his followers claimed that they had gained a clear and decisive victory over their orthodox opponents at a point of the greatest strategical importance. They contended that while the Synoptic Gospels make Christ die on Nisan 15th, the author of the Fourth Gospel 'deliberately shifted' the date of the Last Supper from Nisan 14th to the 13th, in order to make it appear that Christ died on the 14th, at the time when the Passover lambs were sacrificed. But, they urged, the Asiatic Churches which claimed to have been founded by S. John observed their Paschal festival when the Jews observed it; that is, they kept as sacred the evening which closed the 14th day of the month Nisan, and believed that Jesus died on the 15th. They therefore agreed with the Synoptic Gospels and disagreed with the Fourth Gospel. The period at which the Asiatic Churches are known to have defended their practice was between A.D. 140 and A.D. 200. The conclusion of Baur was that S. John could not have been the author of a Gospel which (i) differs from all the Synoptic Gospels with regard to the date of Christ's death, and (ii) differs from the Churches of the second century which claimed to have preserved S. John's teaching and practice.

For the sake of additional clearness the following table is appended. The crucifixion of our Lord is marked by †.

The Synoptists.	Days of the Month.	The Fourth Gospel.
Wednesday.	13th.	Thursday, Last Supper.
Thursday, Last Supper.	14th, Jews' Passover in evening	† Friday.
Friday †.	15th.	Saturday.

The difference is glaring. We have only to ask if the Synoptists do differ in this way from the Fourth Gospel, and if the Asiatic Churches sided with them. The answer seems perfectly plain. The present form of the Synoptic narrative on the whole favours the above scheme attributed to it, but contains several traces of having originally agreed with the Fourth Gospel; and the Asiatic Churches unequivocally support the latter. Baur's argument appeared at first to be so simple and effective that it was adopted by unorthodox and anti-Christian writers with enthusiasm. It is very greatly to the credit of a few men like Reuss and Dr. Drummond that they threw away an argument which the 'man in the street' considered to be advantageous to their general position. But it is continually reappearing, and less conscientious men are using it with effrontery.

As a preliminary, it has to be observed that there are, independently of the Gospels, some means provided by the New Testament and the earliest Church traditions, of determining the year of our Lord's death. They are sufficient to give ground for believing that the year was A.D. 29, our popular chronology for the beginning of the Christian era being certainly corrupt. In that year the Friday at the beginning of the Passover season was Nisan 14th, as the Fourth Gospel implies. Also the early, though apocryphal, Gospel of Peter supports the same view by representing the crucifixion as not on, but before, the first day of unleavened bread. This agrees with John xviii. 28, where the Jews refuse to go into the Roman praetorium in the early morning before the crucifixion lest they should be defiled, and so unable to eat the Passover. Further, the Jewish Talmud itself asserts that Jesus was executed on the eve of the Passover, which was the eve of the Sabbath. It is very improbable that the Jews would have invented this date or extracted it from the Gospels.

As for the Synoptic Gospels, it must be admitted that Mark, followed by Matthew and Luke, makes our Lord keep the Last Supper on the evening when the Jews kept their Passover. At least this is the most probable meaning of the words 'on the first day of unleavened bread, when they sacrificed the passover' (Mark xiv. 12; cf. Matt. xxvi. 17, Luke xxii. 7). But, in disagreement with the above words, the Synoptic Gospels mention a number of facts which really favour the Fourth Gospel and imply that our Lord did not eat the Jewish Passover but died on the 14th. They make the Sanhedrin say that they will not arrest Jesus 'on the feast day.' They represent the guards, and one of the disciples, as carrying arms, an unlawful act on that day (Mark xiv. 47); they tell us that Jesus was tried by the Sanhedrin between His arrest and His trial before Pilate. They tell us of a man coming on the day of the crucifixion 'from the field,' *i.e.* from work in the field (Mark xv. 21), Joseph of Arimathaea buys a linen cloth to wrap round the body of Jesus (Mark xv. 46), and the holy women prepare spices for the same purpose (Luke xxiii. 56). All this testifies that our Lord was not arrested and crucified on the feast day, and therefore corroborates the statement of the fourth evangelist. It is also to be noted that though the Synoptists show that our Lord observed certain Paschal ceremonies at the meal which He made with His disciples, there is no mention of His eating the Passover lamb.

The last fact was observed by church writers at a very early date. It of course supports the theory that our Lord died on the 14th, before the lambs were ready to be eaten. In spite of Baur and his followers, this was firmly rooted in the belief of the early Christians, not only in the Asiatic Churches, but elsewhere. It is taught by Clement, the first great writer of the Church of Alexandria, and S. Hippolytus, the leading writer of the Roman Church in the first half of the third century. In Asia Minor it is known that Melito, bishop of Sardis, and Apollinarius of Hierapolis, both observed the 14th day as holy.

It is urged by the opponents of the authenticity of the Fourth Gospel that the so-called 'Quartodeciman controversy' in A.D. 190 between Victor, bishop of Rome, and Polycrates, bishop of Ephesus, a controversy which can be traced back to its birth in A.D. 154, favours the view of Baur. It really annihilates it. For the dispute between the Church of Ephesus and the Church of Rome was a dispute as to whether the Christian Passover should be kept on the 14th day of the *month*, whatever day of the week it might fall, or on the first day of the *week* at the same season. The former was the practice at Ephesus, the latter at

Rome. This fact alone is sufficient to prove that the rationalistic theory is wrong. For if the dispute had been specially concerned with the commemoration of the Last Supper, the disputants would have discussed whether it should be commemorated on the 13th day of the month (according to the Fourth Gospel) or on the 14th day of the month (according to the general interpretation of the Synoptic Gospels). Further, it is quite unproved that Melito and Apollinarius, or any Asiatic Christians, kept the 14th as holy in honour of the institution of the Eucharist. As a matter of fact, both in Rome and in Ephesus 'to keep the Passover' among the Christians did not mean to keep the anniversary of the Last Supper, but that of the death and resurrection of our Lord, the true Paschal Lamb. It was a feast, preceded by a fast. In this joyful feast a commemoration of the Passion was included. The Eucharist was certainly celebrated, but it must not be supposed that the significance of the Christian Passover was exhausted by this celebration. There is a large mass of early evidence which supports the author of the *Paschal Chronicle* of the seventh century, who says that Christ, the true Lamb, was sacrificed at the feast of the Jewish Passover, and rose the third day, when the Jewish priest was required to offer the sheaf. He ends a long discussion with the words 'Christ our Passover was sacrificed and rose for us, and we call the death and the resurrection of the Lord *Passover*.'[1]

Quite correctly the ancient writer just quoted sees that S. Paul is on the side of S. John's Gospel. His first epistle to the Corinthians, written from Ephesus itself, at or near the Christian Paschal festival, proves the primitive antiquity of the Johannine view and the less primitive character of the view that the Last Supper

[1] See Dr. J. Drummond, *The Character and Authorship of the Fourth Gospel*, p. 475; and my *History of Early Christianity*, p. 92.

coincided in time with the Jewish Passover. S. Paul declares that the Christian Passover is the sacrifice of Christ (1 Cor. v. 7, 8), and implies that the Christian festival of the Firstfruits is His resurrection 'on the third day' (xv. 4, 20). So much is this idea of Christ as our Firstfruits in the thoughts of the apostle that it influences much, if not all, of his magnificent chapter on the resurrection. Christ is the first of a great harvest of souls redeemed from death; He is the buried Wheat which emerges as a Sheaf to be offered to God like the sheaf offered by the Jews on Nisan 16th. This day, according to the Hebrew reckoning, was three days after Nisan 14th, each part of a period of twenty-four hours being reckoned as a day. If even the apostle of the Gentiles so greatly valued a Christian Passover celebrated on the 14th, the older apostles with their more conservative instincts in all probability held it in no less esteem. The Johannine and Ephesian usage is therefore much more likely to be apostolic than any other.

To sum up. There is overwhelming evidence to show that the main body of orthodox Christians, whether in Rome, Asia, or Alexandria, kept the feast which they called Passover in united honour of the death and resurrection of Christ the Paschal Lamb. It was a feast terminating a fast. There is no hint that the Asiatics merely commemorated the Last Supper, and their opponents never seem to have charged them with so doing. The Asiatic Quartodecimans kept the 14th day, believing that *Christ died* on that day. They therefore agreed with the Fourth Gospel, and it is granted on all sides that they appealed to the authority of John, the disciple of the Lord. Polycrates, bishop of Ephesus, the bishop most concerned in the controversy, says so. In view of all the above facts, the argument that the Fourth Gospel cannot be by an apostle, because it deliberately falsifies the date of

Christ's death in its love of symbolism, appears to be futile.[1]

---

[1] Dr. Charles Bigg, in his *Origins of Christianity*, p. 201, upheld the view that S. Polycrates appealed to S. John's example and not to his Gospel. Dr. Bigg relied upon the opinion that Apollinarius, bishop of Hierapolis in Asia, was an opponent of Quartodecimanism. In this opinion he differs from such distinguished scholars as Lightfoot, Hefele, Mgr. Duchesne, and Dr. Drummond. The view that Apollinarius opposed Quartodecimanism seems to me to be quite inconsistent with his glorification of 'the fourteenth day.'

CHAPTER IX

THE AUTHOR OF THE FOURTH GOSPEL

§ 1. *Some Primitive Testimony.*

It is frequently said that the external evidence to the genuineness of the Fourth Gospel is indecisive. But it is at any rate so strong as to guide us a long way towards an affirmative decision, and the internal evidence finishes the work which the external testimony begins. It cannot be denied that when the Church emerges into the clear daylight of the latter part of the second century, the Fourth Gospel was one of its most revered books. In all the great centres of Christian life it held the same position.

(*a*) In *Carthage* about A.D. 200, Tertullian uses it and ascribes it to S. John.

(*b*) In *Alexandria*, about A.D. 200, Clement, the most influential Christian of that great city, uses it in the same way.

(*c*) In *Ephesus*, about A.D. 190, Polycrates, the bishop, quotes it.

(*d*) In *Gaul*, about A.D. 185, S. Irenaeus, who was in touch with Roman and Asiatic Christianity as well as that of Gaul, is wholly convinced of its genuineness. And about A.D. 175 the letter of the Churches of Vienne and Lyons quotes it.

(*e*) In *Rome*, rather before A.D. 160, Tatian quotes it in his Discourse to the Greeks, and a few years later embodied it in his *Diatessaron* or Harmony of the

THE AUTHOR OF THE FOURTH GOSPEL

Gospels. It is also quoted at an earlier date by his teacher, S. Justin Martyr.

(*f*) At *Antioch*, about A.D. 175, it is quoted by Theophilus, the bishop.

(*g*) What is perhaps equally important, the Gospel is treated as Scripture by two important sects on the extreme right and extreme left of the Catholic Church respectively, the Montanists and the Gnostics. The Montanist sect, which spread from Asia to the West, arose about A.D. 158, and based its teaching about the new advent of the Paraclete on the discourses of our Lord in the Fourth Gospel. The Gnostics, who repudiated both the distinctive teaching and the austere discipline of the Montanists, held the Gospel in the same reverence before that date. And about A.D. 170, Heracleon, a leader of the Italian Gnostics, wrote a commentary upon it. The unity of Catholics, Montanists, and Gnostics on this subject is one of the most important facts in the evidence for the authenticity of the book. No book about which serious doubts were felt by thoughtful men could have won so undisputed a rank at such an early date.

It has recently been said that 'the Church consented slowly, and not without misgiving, to accept it as the work of S. John.'[1] The truth is that the only known 'misgiving' was that of a small insignificant group of Asiatic origin, we hardly know that it was even a sect, the so-called *Alogoi* or *Irrationalists*. They attributed it to Cerinthus, a contemporary of S. John, who lived at Ephesus. They were therefore grotesquely ignorant, for the teaching of Cerinthus differed more widely from that of the Fourth Gospel than the teaching of John Knox differed from that of the Jesuits.[2] It

---

[1] Dr. Ernest F. Scott, *The Historical and Religious Value of the Fourth Gospel*, p. 14.

[2] For Cerinthus, see Dr. R. L. Ottley, *Doctrine of the Incarnation*, vol. 1. p. 171.

is necessary to recall this fact, because these people are sometimes quoted to show that the early Church felt serious doubts about the value and authorship of the book.

Among the writers who bear testimony to the reverence in which the Fourth Gospel was held, S. Irenaeus is the most important. His writings are by no means the sole key to the Johannine problem. But his evidence is the most weighty external evidence that we have. Clear, explicit, and inherently probable as the words of Clement are as to the origin of the Fourth Gospel, S. Irenaeus is earlier and closer to the heart of Christian tradition. Let us very briefly review the main points in his testimony.

1. He travelled widely and read widely, and was acquainted with Christian thought in Asia Minor, Rome, and Gaul. If he had been mistaken as to the Gospel, no one would have been in a better position to correct his own mistakes.

2. He attributes the Gospel to the apostle John and quotes it freely and repeatedly as one of the only four authentic Gospels. He says that John 'published the Gospel in Ephesus.'

3. He declares that he perfectly remembers S. Polycarp, bishop of Smyrna, and his conversations about John and others who had known the Lord. As Polycarp died in A.D. 155, when Irenaeus was probably about twenty-five years of age, we have no reason to doubt his statement. Further, Irenaeus says that S. John survived till the time of Trajan, *i.e.* about A.D. 98, and Polycarp just before his death said that he had been a Christian eighty-six years. Having therefore been born not later than A.D. 69 or 70, Polycarp might well remember the apostle if nearly thirty years old when the apostle died.

4. It is admitted by critics of all schools of thought that Irenaeus believed that Polycarp knew John the

apostle. In his letter to Florinus, he reckons Polycarp among the elders who had known the apostles, and says this with special reference to John.

It is, of course, vital to the theory which opposes the apostolic origin of the Fourth Gospel, that the evidence of S. Irenaeus should be explained away, and we find that continuous attempts are made to do this. 'If,' as Dr. Moffat says, 'Irenaeus is correct, his testimony to John the apostle is of first-rate importance.'[1] No real argument against his testimony is forthcoming, and therefore Dr. Moffat says that 'he must be held to have mistaken what Polykarp said, and to have confused John the presbyter with John the apostle.' It would surely be a more reasonable thing to say that Irenaeus must be held to be correct unless there is a still better testimony to prove that he is wrong. The only possible testimony that can be so employed will be discussed below on p. 301. The argument that something 'must have been' is a very ancient, and one might have hoped extinct, method of substituting some cherished conjecture for rational proof. Another wellworn method in dealing with Irenaeus is that of blackening his testimony to S. John by mentioning mistakes that he made in other matters with which he was less well acquainted. No writer, however honest and well-informed, and Irenaeus was both, would stand so unjust a trial, and his critics would sometimes stand it less successfully than himself.

Before the time when S. Irenaeus wrote, and even before the time when Tatian wrote, we have indisputable evidence for at least the existence of a body of theology substantially the same as that which we find in the Fourth Gospel. This fact, like the fact that in and after the time of Tatian S. John the apostle was regarded as its author, is admitted even by critics who adopt a very sceptical attitude towards the apostolic

[1] *Introduction to the Literature of the New Testament*, p. 609.

origin of the book. But they do not always do justice to the nature of the evidence which this theology affords. It may be quite fair when they describe the evidence as consisting of 'echoes' or traces of the influence of the Gospel, or a theology resembling that of the Gospel. But it is not fair to describe them as 'trembling away' as we approach their supposed origin 'instead of becoming clearer and more unmistakable.'[1] There is no generation in which the echoes of at least the Johannine theology are not clear. If we divide the second century into three generations of the average length, viz. A.D. 100 to 133, A.D. 134 to 166, A.D. 167 to 199, we shall find that in proportion to the amount of Christian literature which has survived from each of these three generations the Johannine influence is as strong in the second, and even in the first, generation as in the last.

To the second generation we assign the works of Tatian and his teacher Justin, who was probably born about A.D. 100. Justin describes the author of the Apocalypse as 'a man of the name of John, one of the apostles of Christ,'[2] and as he was acquainted with Ephesus where the Apocalypse was written, this evidence is of great importance. He does not mention by name the author of the Fourth Gospel, but his writings show numerous points of contact with it and include a statement plainly based on John iii. 3-5. The connection between Justin's writings and the Fourth Gospel is too clear to be ignored. And in spite of the distinct superiority and greater originality of the latter it has been perversely argued that its author borrowed from Justin.

Near the border line between the first and the second generation we find that the great Gnostics

---

[1] Dr. B. W. Bacon, *The Fourth Gospel in Research and Debate*, p. 32.   [2] *Adv. Tryph.* 81.

Basilides and Valentinus (A.D. 125-150) almost certainly made a free use of the Fourth Gospel. This has been disputed, mainly on the alleged ground that S. Hippolytus, when he refers to these two heresiarchs, is really speaking not of their own views, but those of their followers. But Tertullian, whose evidence is earlier than that of Hippolytus, and quite as good, represents Valentinus as using the Fourth Gospel, and it is at least certain that soon after the time of Valentinus his followers used it. As for Basilides, Hippolytus evidently means that he employed this Gospel, and so unorthodox a critic as Matthew Arnold trenchantly defended this view. The fact that the Fourth Gospel contains much which can only be reconciled with Gnosticism by violent and fantastic explanations, disposes of the idea that the Gnostics liked it because they knew it to be of Gnostic origin. If we pass into the company of the men who were in their prime during the first generation of the second century, the Johannine 'echoes' are plain and loud. In Papias, who probably collected his materials near A.D. 100 and wrote his books later, we find a clear use of the First Epistle of S. John, and a probable use of the Gospel. He knew and accepted the Apocalypse as the work of S. John. S. Polycarp in his one remaining Epistle (near A.D. 110), quotes the First Epistle of S. John. The Epistles of S. Ignatius of Antioch (about A.D. 110) are much more important. For though he does not mention the apostle by name, and cannot be absolutely proved to have used the Fourth Gospel, his theology and language are so intensely Johannine that they are far more easily explained by the hypothesis that he knew the Gospel than by any other theory. In the little Church manual known as the *Didaché*, which is probably some years older than the letters of Ignatius, there are phrases which appear to be genuine echoes, especially the phrase 'make perfect in love' (cf. John

xvii. 23). But S. Ignatius has much more than this. His letters are not coloured but saturated with the leading doctrines of S. John, so much so that we are inevitably led to the conclusion that he was either familiar with the Fourth Gospel or had been taught in early life by some great master, whether the apostle or not the apostle, whose teaching is represented by the Fourth Gospel and whose principles he had enthusiastically imbibed. The theory that he had been brought up in an environment where there had been simply a natural development of S. Paul's theology in a Johannine direction does not meet the case. The coincidences between the spirit of S. Paul's Epistles and that of the Fourth Gospel are sometimes striking. But the coincidences between the Fourth Gospel and the letters of Ignatius are coincidences of spirit and letter alike. Nor must we overlook the fact that Ignatius takes for granted that the Churches to which he writes are in sympathy with this Johannine theology. The phenomena presented to us in the letters of Ignatius are all the more remarkable inasmuch as the later tendency of Antiochene theology was not in this direction. It is the old Antiochene theology, that of Ignatius and Theophilus, which finds Johannine thought entirely congenial.

Against the above evidence as to the existence of the Fourth Gospel, it is often urged that some of the earliest references to the author of the Fourth Gospel found in the literature of the Church, though they describe him as *John*, do not call him the 'apostle' or 'son of Zebedee.' Thus Polycrates, bishop of Ephesus, in his famous letter written to Victor, bishop of Rome, in A.D. 190, calls the John who lived at Ephesus, 'John who lay upon the breast of the Lord.' He therefore is sure that he is the beloved disciple mentioned in the Gospel, but he does not call him an 'apostle.' The *Muratorian Canon*, probably written in Italy about

THE AUTHOR OF THE FOURTH GOSPEL

A.D. 180, calls the author of the Fourth Gospel 'one of the disciples' only, while it calls S. Andrew 'one of the apostles.' It nevertheless speaks of them as if they were equals, and asserts that this disciple was an eye-witness of the acts of Christ. That the word 'disciple' might be used synonymously with the word 'apostle' in the second century as in our day is shown by S. Irenaeus. He usually describes S. John as 'the disciple of the Lord,' and when he mentions the origin of the Gospel he says, 'Then John, the disciple of the Lord, who also leant upon His breast, and himself published the Gospel while dwelling at Ephesus in Asia.'[1] Now, he includes this John among the apostles. For after calling John 'the disciple of the Lord,' he says that some of the elders in Asia 'not only saw John, but also other apostles.'[2] We have already noticed that S. Justin Martyr calls the author of the Apocalypse 'John, one of the apostles of Christ,' and if the author of the Apocalypse and that of the Gospel are identical, this bears intimately upon the question now under discussion.[3] The first book in which we find this Gospel attributed to a man named John is in the apology for Christianity addressed by Theophilus, bishop of Antioch, to a pagan named Autolycus, written about A.D. 170, or 175. He quotes the beginning of the Gospel as by 'John,' whom he numbers among 'men inspired.' This, like the statement of Polycrates, does not absolutely prove that the writer held the evangelist to have been an apostle. But it is favourable to that view and in harmony with the reverence felt for the apostles in the

---

[1] *Adv. Haer.* iii. 1.
[2] *Op. cit.* ii. 22. § 5. Dr. W. Sanday, *Criticism of the Fourth Gospel*, p. 105, says that Irenaeus 'does perhaps hint at this title,' and he refers to Eus. *H. E.* iii. 23-4. But the words which I have quoted seem more than a hint, though it is just possible that Irenaeus meant, not 'other apostles,' but 'apostles as well.'
[3] See below, p. 303.

second half of the second century. And it is not only possible, but probable, that writers who mentioned John, while knowing him to have been an apostle, preferred to call him 'disciple,' for they would, if they read the Gospel, almost unconsciously fall into the habit of so doing. In this Gospel the apostles are usually described by the earlier title 'disciple,' which is one of the proofs of its genuineness. And we do not find the phrase 'the apostle whom Jesus loved,' but 'the disciple whom Jesus loved.' The disciples in S. John's Gospel are the apostles.

It therefore seems to be a well founded opinion that throughout the second century the Fourth Gospel together with the Apocalypse and First Epistle was known in Eastern Christendom, and its use by Justin Martyr favours the view that it was already current in Rome when he was there. It is more sparingly quoted than the other Gospels, but this can be accounted for by the fact that the other Gospels got a good start, probably a start of more than twenty years. And its claim to be by the apostle John is so much less evident than its claim to be by an eye-witness of Christ's ministry that it is not very surprising that in the scanty evidence that has come down to us from the period A.D. 100 to 170, the name of John is not mentioned in direct connection with the Gospel, though it is mentioned in connection with the Apocalypse. The phenomena can be explained if it was not made public until near the time of the author's death, as the conclusion of the last chapter suggests. So soon as an author is ascribed to it, he is named John, and, as we shall see later, his name is most clearly heard among the men connected with the neighbourhood in which the Gospel is admitted to have had its origin.

The above account is merely an impartial summary. The real value of it can only be judged by a careful consideration of the passages in detail, such as is given by Ezra Abbot, Dr. Drummond, and Dr. Stanton.

These passages must also be considered in the light of the formation of the fourfold Canon of the Gospels, which has been briefly dealt with in our first chapter.

§ 2. *Does the Gospel claim an apostolic origin?*

We must now turn to consider what the Fourth Gospel itself says about its own author. Occasionally its claims are merely ignored, or elaborately explained to mean something quite different from the natural impression which common sense would derive from them. Now, common sense is a very excellent handmaid of criticism, and she is quite able to see that, for good or evil, the author of the Gospel claims to be an eye-witness of Christ.

He claims it first in John i. 14: 'the Word became flesh, and dwelt among us (and we beheld His glory, glory as of the only begotten from the Father), full of grace and truth.' The glory, in correspondence with a Hebrew metaphor, means the manifested attributes of God, and the passage refers to these attributes as manifested when the Word came to dwell or 'tabernacle' on earth like the divine Presence in the tabernacle of Moses. It seems to be from modesty that the writer says 'we' and not 'I.' He does not wish to push himself forward, or to claim that he saw more than the other immediate disciples of Jesus. But he does speak of himself as one of those so peculiarly privileged.

This is corroborated by the First Epistle bearing the name of S. John. It is very difficult, and the difficulty is fully realised in recent rationalistic literature, to separate the authorship of the Gospel from that of this beautiful epistle. The theology and circle of ideas are substantially the same, the language and the development of those ideas are slightly different. In maintaining the ancient tradition that they come from the same writer, one possibly exposes oneself to the sneer that similarity is taken to prove identity of authorship, and dissimilarity to corroborate it. But the sneer is not worth much. In this case the dissimilarity is of the kind which an imitator of the Gospel would probably have avoided. It shows reflection, it applies a lesson already learnt. And from a critical point of view, it is much harder to think that neither the Gospel nor the Epistle are by a disciple of Christ, than to think that the Gospel records what Christ said, and the Epistle what his disciple thought.

Now this Epistle begins with the words:

> That which was from the beginning, that which we have heard, that which we have seen with our eyes, that which we beheld, and our hands handled, concerning the Word of life (and the life was manifested, and we have seen, and bear witness, and declare unto you the life, the eternal *life*, which was with the Father, and was manifested unto us); that which we have seen and heard declare we unto you also, that ye also may have fellowship with us: yea, and our fellowship is with the Father, and with His Son Jesus Christ.

It would be difficult to frame a stronger statement than this. In exact agreement with the beginning of the Fourth Gospel, it asserts that the writer saw and touched that Being who is eternally the living Word or Expression of the Father, and is also His Son. To tone down this obvious meaning, it has been suggested by some living critics that the word 'beheld' refers to a spiritual inward vision, and not an outward vision. This is not only an open defiance of the meaning which the Greek word bears throughout the New Testament, but it also forces us to ask if the word 'hands' signifies some 'mystical' inward organ. With this question we may leave the verses to be understood as best they may; confident that whenever words are interpreted to mean exactly what they were apparently intended to exclude, biblical criticism will command more ridicule than respect.

Another important but less unambiguous passage is in John xix. 35. The writer here, in telling the story of the crucifixion, speaks of the thrust of the lance into our Saviour's side and the issue of blood and water, a phenomenon explained by modern medical science. He adds:

And he that hath seen hath borne witness, and his witness is true: and he (ἐκεῖνος) knoweth that he saith true, that ye also may believe.

Simple as these words are, they have been interpreted in very different ways. Is the writer merely declaring that he saw the lance thrust, and asserting that he is speaking the truth? Or is the writer, while declaring that he saw the lance thrust, appealing to Him whose side was pierced as knowing that he is saying what is true? Either of these two explanations is possible. And if it be urged that according to neither of these interpretations the Greek can be considered classical, we can fairly reply that the Greek of this Gospel is never classical. The other interpretations which imply that the Gospel was not by an eye-witness require us to believe that the writer is distinct from the man who 'hath borne witness,' and one of such interpretations further demands that the writer is also distinct from the man who 'knoweth that he saith true.' According to this last theory, the information given as to the thrust of the lance is not even second hand, but third hand. When we remember that the author of the Gospel always speaks of himself in the third person, it is far easier to think that the writer either truly or falsely claims to be identical with the man who stood by the pierced side of Christ.

The connection which exists between the First and Third Epistles of S. John and the 'he knoweth that he saith true' in John xix. 35 has not escaped the vigilance of one of the strongest recent opponents of the apostolic authorship of the Gospel, Dr. Bacon of Yale. He has to introduce that obliging 'deus ex machina,' the imaginary 'editor' or 'redactor.' This redactor held that the apostle did really witness 'the phenomenon of the blood and water.' He 'will not say in so many words, "This was the 'disciple whom Jesus loved';" still less, "This was John the son of Zebedee," but he makes it impossible to think of any one else.'[1] Further, this editor also identified the disciple whom Jesus loved with him 'who, in the Epistles, whose language he borrows, had laid such stress upon the "water and blood," declaring this to be a "witness of the Spirit" in some sense present and eternal.' Dr. Bacon significantly adds that the standpoint of the redactor 'is identically that of subsequent tradition, except that instead of plain statement he shelters himself behind purposed ambiguity.' In other words, this learned critic asks us to believe that a second century editor took certain Epistles which the apostle did not really write (according to his theory) and inserted from these Epistles phrases which made it appear that the beloved disciple was S. John and the original author of the Gospel. The view which Dr. Bacon holds concerning other methods of this redactor is illuminated by his theory that he cancelled 'references which seemed to present obstacles to his own theory of the authorship.'[2] By this means Dr. Bacon endeavours to dispose of the cogent argument that the

[1] *Op. cit.* p. 309.   [2] *Op. cit.* p. 202.

THE AUTHOR OF THE FOURTH GOSPEL

Gospel mentions by name neither of the two sons of Zebedee, James and John, a fact which is hardly explicable if the writer of the Gospel was not one of the two.

The last passage is xxi. 24. Almost at the very end of the Gospel come the words:

> This is the disciple which beareth witness of these things, and wrote these things; and we know that his witness is true.

This verse directly asserts that the disciple who was with S. Peter in our Lord's company immediately after the resurrection, wrote the account of what then happened. This is not a verse which commends itself to certain schools of critics. Even Professor Burkitt, in the chapter on the Fourth Gospel in his book *The Gospel History and its Transmission*, ignores it. It is one of the most suggestive passages which bear upon the transmission of the Gospel, but it does not support his idea that the Fourth Gospel was written between A.D. 100 and 110. A disciple who was one of the foremost disciples and a companion of S. Peter in A.D. 29 is not a very likely person to have written a Gospel between seventy and eighty years later. Other critics, such as Renan, Réville, Harnack, and Bacon, are less restrained than Professor Burkitt. As Dr. Bacon does not scatter statements which he does not endeavour to support, let us consider what he has to say about the writer of this last chapter of the Fourth Gospel. Once again he takes refuge in a charge of fraud.

'For the sake of securing to the "spiritual" Gospel the standing which in his age it could not have unless declared to be "apostolic," he has cautiously and by veiled suggestion, yet unmistakably, introduced his own interpretation, cancelling, it would seem, a few traits which offered obstacles in the body of the work, and attaching at least the direct declaration in xix. 35, perhaps other and longer passages. The enigmatic figure, he believes, was John the son of Zebedee, next to Peter in prominence in apostolic story. John was suited to the rôle as author of a Gospel of Ephesian provenance by the currently accepted representation that he had written the Asiatic book of Revelation.'[1] Having selected John, this editor set aside the tradition that S. John had followed Christ in martyrdom even before the death of S. Peter (the nature of this alleged 'tradition' will be noticed later, p. 301). He then made use of a local tradition about some witness to the Messiah who would abide until the return of Christ (Mark ix. 1), or about John the Elder mentioned by Papias, and adjusted it to his own theory. He did this by 'suggesting' in John xxi. that John the apostle might abide till the return of Christ, though he really meant that not the apostle, but the Gospel, would remain as a permanent witness to Christ. After completing this strange device, the 'editor' himself finally guaranteed this witness to be 'true.'

Dr. Bacon, in fact, and he is not alone, accuses the editor of a deliberate imposture. He is said to have cancelled and to have added what he liked. He is said to have attached to the writer a tradition about another man, thereby starting a false legend with the intention of creating an apostolic halo round the book. This is the kind of accusation which should not be made apart from convincing evidence. But whether the editor, who calls himself ' we,' was scrupulous or unscrupulous in his methods, how did he come to believe that ' the enigmatic figure was John the son of Zebedee'? Why should the belief have been a delusion?

The editors of the Gospel who say so plainly that it was written by the disciple who plays such an important part in the book, were probably the presbyters

[1] *Op. cit.* p. 326.

of the Church in whose midst S. John died. That this Gospel was first circulated in Asia Minor, and more particularly in the neighbourhood of Ephesus, has lately been almost undisputed. We need not discuss the theory of Baur and Keim that it was composed at Alexandria, any more than the theory of Resch that it was written in the Decapolis. The most adverse critics now agree with S. Irenaeus that it was written at Ephesus, or near it. So far as we can penetrate into the second century, we are fully justified in saying that in this region, more even than in Rome, primitive Christian tradition and life were vigorous. Polycrates, bishop of Ephesus, says, 'throughout Asia, great luminaries have gone to their rest, which will rise on the day of the Lord's coming.'[1] It was this Roman province of 'Asia' which was, in the language of Isaiah, a 'hearth of God' after Jerusalem was destroyed. Here, Polycrates says, 'Philip, one of the twelve apostles, sleeps at Hierapolis.' Possibly the *Muratorian Canon* is correct in saying that Andrew, the apostle, was with S. John when his Gospel was written. It has even been conjectured that the editors who certified that the author of the Fourth Gospel is the disciple who was so intimate with the Lord, were none other than S. Philip and S. Andrew. This theory is hardly credible. For unless the Gospel was published soon after the Synoptic Gospels, that is, unless it was made known to the Church near A.D. 80, it is improbable that it could have had this double attestation. Let us rather keep to the safest line of inquiry; let us suppose that the editors, who might have forged apostolic signatures if they had wished to do so, but added no names to the sacred page, were only presbyters of Ephesus and its neighbourhood. Why should we accuse them of fraud? What had they to gain in testifying to a writing which they had not written, a

[1] Eus. *H.E.* v. 24.

writing, moreover, which does not mention the office of presbyter, which does not use the word 'Church,' and emphasises the subjective element in Christian experience? It is really time that the eighteenth century ideal of a 'designing priesthood,' creating Christianity by frauds more bold than those of a disreputable dealer in antiques, was for ever left in peace. Rightly or wrongly, the editors honestly believed the Gospel to be by an eye-witness. And the Gospel itself claims, modestly but distinctly, truly or untruly, to be by an eye-witness. It is also admitted even by those who handle it most roughly, that it was written in or near Ephesus.

§ 3. *Indirect Internal Evidence.*

We have already shown (i) that the Gospel claims directly to have been written by an eye-witness of our Lord's ministry, and also (ii) that the John of Ephesus to whom early tradition attributed the Gospel was probably the apostle. It is now necessary to interrogate the Gospel itself to find whether the indirect testimony which it contains joins together these two separate links. The author never mentions his own name. Perhaps he gives a suggestion by describing John the Baptist as 'John' without the title added by the Synoptists. Unlike the forgers who made the most of the apostolic names which they used as passports for their wares, he hides himself under the names 'the other disciple, whom Jesus loved,' 'the other disciple' (xx. 2-3). He thinks so little of posing or imposing that he never calls himself 'the son of Zebedee' or 'John the disciple,' or 'John the apostle.' The very silence is a suggestion, but it is no more. What we have to ask is whether there is evidence to show

THE AUTHOR OF THE FOURTH GOSPEL 293

that the eye-witness of the Gospel is the apostle of tradition.

A series of passages provides us with evidence of this kind, showing that the author belonged to the inner and higher circle of the apostles. Again and again we have descriptions which are most naturally explained as coming from within that group. Why in the second half of the first chapter is one of the two disciples of the Baptist who followed Jesus named and the other not named? The first is Andrew. Others are immediately mentioned, but this one still remains unrevealed. May not he be the one who first told the story? Why in iii. 22-25 should we be told of the distinction between the disciples of Jesus and the disciples of John the Baptist and the dispute of the latter with a Jew? To one of the immediate disciples of Jesus or of the Baptist this would be of some importance. But Christians of the second century would think it more probable that the disciples of Jesus, and not those of John, would dispute with a Jew about purifying, and a writer of fiction would have accommodated himself to their ideas. There are touches in chapter v. with its story of the woman of Samaria, and certainly in the close of chapter vi., which tells us of the desertion of many of those who had hitherto walked with Jesus, which are not likely to be the work of any one but an eye-witness. We have no right to take it for granted that no disciple of Jesus was near the well where He sat weary, or that Jesus never was heard to utter those pathetic words, 'Will ye also go away?'

Let us consider the story of the Samaritan woman. Is it artificial, or suggestively real? The critics who tell us that the Christ of the Fourth Gospel is not truly human but only a mythical god wandering on the earth, are here confronted with the picture of Jesus sitting 'weary' by the side of a well. He is met by a woman of bad character who has had 'five husbands.' These critics tell us that this is an allegory, she is really the Gentile world and her 'husbands' signify the five different nationalities from which the population of Samaria was recruited. The topographical details in the story are perfect. There is Sychar, the modern Al 'Askar; the deep well to which the woman comes to draw water, probably for human use, distinct from the inferior well nearer to the town; above the speakers rises 'this mountain' of Gerizim crowned by the temple of which vestiges still exist, where the Samaritans 'said men ought to worship.' It was winter as we reckon it, four months yet to the harvest, but the fields of human souls were nearly ripe. The evangelist knows the road and knows the well, and the social barrier between Jews and Samaritans. He tells us how the woman, when her conscience begins to be uneasy, tries to divert the conversation to points of theological controversy, how Christ leads her to spiritual truth. And he tells us how His own disciples came back and were shocked to find their Teacher transgressing the rabbinical maxim that a man must not speak with a woman in public.

The picture is convincing because it is never overdone. To attribute it to an Asiatic writer of the second century seems worse than paradox. Let any unprejudiced reader of the Greek language compare it with a scene from the life of Apollonius of Tyana written by Philostratus. Apollonius was the pagan rival of Christ about A.D. 200. His story was perhaps not written in conscious opposition to the Gospels, though it is not always easy to escape the idea that it was written with that intention. Philostratus represents him as a lover and teacher of virtue, not without considerable dignity, and with astonishing miraculous powers. But the book limps lamely and bungles crudely. It is uncritical, absurd. Yet it enjoyed considerable vogue. It offered men a Saviour of the kind that was acceptable in kings' houses. The Graeco-Roman world read it with relish. Put it by the side of our Fourth Gospel with its unobtrusive allusions to real geography and genuine customs, and its natural representations of the character of men and women. We pass from lay figures in Greek drapery to living people moving in their mother country. And there is therefore no real difficulty in believing that a young disciple lingering near his Master while his comrades had gone into the city of Samaria to buy food did hear the substance of the dialogue unfolded in this narrative.

The allusions to places, customs, beliefs, and ceremonies, which are so frequent in this Gospel, show that the author was a Jew who had been acquainted with Jerusalem when its old life and worship were still in vigour. But what we are now considering is the evidence as to personal feelings and actions which can most naturally be explained as coming from an apostle, and cannot be naturally explained as serving the purpose of a writer of fiction, even of the highest allegorical fiction. The discussion between our Lord and His still unbelieving brethren (vii. 3-8) is valuable as throwing a side-light on the inmost life of Jesus and His disciples. But it is quite worthless if the Christ of the Fourth Gospel is not the Christ of history. For it serves no allegorical purpose. It is a fragment of history, quite out of harmony with the later tendency to idealise the family of our Lord. If Nicodemus is typical of a class of men who are interested in Jesus Christ, he is no mere allegorical figure. The part assigned to him by the evangelist in the burial of our Lord shows that his portrait was meant to be the portrait of a real person. The Greeks who wish to see Jesus are typical of another class, but it does not therefore follow that they never existed and are

mere literary symbols of the Gentile world. All
Christendom has regarded the scepticism of S. Thomas
as typical of the attitude of those who say 'seeing is
believing.' It does not therefore follow that there
was no Thomas or that he never doubted. The evangelist introduces Mary and Martha on two separate
occasions, and throughout draws a delicate and consistent contrast between the two characters. Yet he
does not call our attention to this contrast, but
relates his story with simplicity as an eye-witness
might write it. To call it the invention of a later
generation seems extraordinarily difficult when one
considers the writings which are known to have been
written between A.D. 100 and 150. For instance,
the *Shepherd of Hermas* is an allegorical Christian
book composed within this latter period. It was very
highly esteemed by the early Church, so much so that
it seems to have been nearer than any other non-
canonical book to inclusion within the canon of the
New Testament. But the difference between the
Gospel according to S. John and the *Shepherd* is like
the difference between York minster and an effort in
'Churchwarden Gothic.'

Let us now pass to the Last Supper. If the Fourth
Gospel had been meant to be history pure and simple,
its account of the Last Supper, and of many other
things, might fitly be called misleading. But it is a
Gospel, not a biography, and it selects certain incidents
and certain discourses with a special purpose. Just as
Mark so often omits what was extant in Q, so the
Fourth Gospel omits what was to be found in the
Synoptists. It takes for granted that its readers
are acquainted with the Eucharist, a rite already
recorded in three Gospels and in S. Paul's Epistle to
the Corinthians, a rite repeated continually in the
Church. Now, any Jew accustomed to the religious
practices of his nation would be acquainted with the

arrangement of the table at the Passover. He would know that the ritual required that the celebrant should recline on a particular seat. But he would scarcely have been able to make the actions of our Lord and Judas, S. John and S. Peter, fit certain places at the table with such perfection. The author says nothing about the places which the disciples actually occupied. But the beloved disciple who 'was at the table reclining in Jesus' bosom' and then 'leant back on Jesus' breast' (xiii. 23, 25) was on our Lord's right hand. Judas took the position of principal guest on our Lord's left, so that he could receive the 'sop' of bitter herbs and bread, and be addressed by Jesus in words which only the beloved disciple could hear (xiii. 27-29). According to this explanation, which is that given by the learned Jewish Christian scholar, Dr. Edersheim,[1] S. Peter was opposite S. John on the other side of the table, having impetuously taken this, the lowest place. This is at least probable, and agrees with his 'beckoning' to the beloved disciple. Once more, we can only say that this chapter has not the air of fiction. It is natural, simple, and unaffected, and the very fact that the beloved disciple does not occupy the place of honour is a telling point on the side of its genuineness.

The above instances can be fortified by other passages in the Gospel. They give us at least a strong presumption in favour of the truthfulness of the verses in which it is directly claimed that the writer saw what he narrates. They give an almost equally strong presumption in favour of his being an apostle, and of this apostle being John the son of Zebedee. In xxi. 2 it is mentioned that 'the sons of Zebedee' were among the disciples near the sea of Tiberias when our Lord showed Himself there after His resurrection. The narrative does not make it clear that 'the disciple whom Jesus loved' (xxi. 7) was one of these sons, for

[1] *Life and Times of Jesus the Messiah*, vol. ii. p. 494.

there are two other disciples whose names are unspecified. But his association with Simon Peter is notable. For in the Synoptic Gospels Peter is named in close connection with two other apostles, and these two are the sons of Zebedee. These three men formed the inner circle of the twelve apostles. And Mark v. 37, the early chapters of Acts, and Galatians ii. 9, show that S. Mark, S. Luke and S. Paul, all regarded John the son of Zebedee as a close friend and ally of S. Peter. James, the other son of Zebedee, need not detain us. Acts xii. 2 shows that he was put to death about A.D. 44, and no one dreams of identifying him with the author of the Gospel which bears such strong marks of being the latest Gospel of the four. And no one attributes the Fourth Gospel to S. Peter, who was doubtless loved by Christ, but is most clearly distinguished in this Gospel from the beloved disciple, his friend.

Only John remains.

§ 4. *Did John the Apostle live at Ephesus?*

It is the hope of the hostile critics to prove that S. John died early and never went to Ephesus at all. For if he died early he could not have written a Gospel which supplements and corrects the Synoptists, and if he never went to Ephesus, it is improbable that he wrote a Gospel which appears to have been first given recognition in the neighbourhood of that city. Let it be stated provisionally that whereas there is some early evidence to the effect that S. John suffered martyrdom, there is no known evidence to the effect that he died early or that he died elsewhere than in Asia Minor. It is therefore highly disingenuous to make use of the evidence for his martyrdom as though it supported either of the two latter inferences. The evidence for his martyrdom is contained in (i) a prophecy of our Lord concerning the sons of Zebedee preserved in Mark x. 39 = Matt. xx. 23, and (ii.) a quotation from Papias, preserved in a corrupted form in certain later writers.

Mark.	*Matthew.*
And Jesus said unto them, The cup *that I drink* ye shall drink ; *and with the baptism that I am baptised withal shall ye be baptised* : but to sit on My right hand, or on My left hand is not Mine to give : but it is for them for whom it hath been prepared.	He saith unto them, *My* cup *indeed* ye shall drink : but to sit on My right hand, or on My left hand is not Mine to give, but it is for them for whom it hath been prepared *of my Father*.

In these words our Lord foretold that James and John would suffer deeply for His sake. Perhaps He meant to foretell their death, for He Himself elsewhere refers to His own sufferings as a baptism (Luke xii. 50) and as 'the cup' which the Father gave Him to drink (Mark xiv. 36). But there is no justification whatever for saying, as is sometimes said, that the evangelist would not have recorded these words of Jesus if he had not known that James and John had been put to death before he wrote his Gospel. S. Mark may have simply written down what he had heard S. Peter say, in the belief that somehow the prophecy would be fulfilled in the case of S. John as it had been already fulfilled in the case of his brother. It is worth noting that S. Luke omits this prophecy of Jesus. It is possible that he omitted it, not only because the ambitious request which preceded it reflected little honour on the apostles, but also because John was not yet dead when he wrote. Such an action would accord with his tendency to leave out facts which would perplex his readers. S. Luke in Acts also records the death of S. James and not that of S. John. This omission therefore on the part of S. Luke is more intelligible on the hypothesis that S. John lived to be an old man than on the hypothesis that he died young.

Next there is the quotation from Papias. It ought to be considered in connection with the familiar passage quoted by Eusebius (*H. E.* iii. 39) in which Papias speaks of the manner in which he gained information from the Christians of a past generation, the men who had known the 'elders,' or had known the apostles whom Papias perhaps included among the elders. This information was apparently gathered about A.D. 100. Papias ends the passage by saying :—

Furthermore, if any one chanced to arrive who had been an actual follower of the elders, I would inquire as to the sayings of the elders—as to what Andrew or Peter said, or Philip, or Thomas, or James, or John, or Matthew, or any other of the Lord's disciples, also as to what Aristion and the presbyter John, the Lord's disciples, say. For I supposed that things out of books would not profit me so much as the utterance of a living voice which was yet with us.

The whole passage is of importance as showing how tradition was for a long time preferred to a written book of the Lord's commandments. It is also of importance in considering the Johannine question. It proves that when Papias made his inquiries John and Matthew were dead, while Aristion and John the presbyter were alive. He contrasts the 'said' of the two former with the 'say' of the two latter. There is no chronological difficulty with regard to his meaning. If Aristion and John the presbyter were born about A.D. 10 or 15, they may have personally come into contact with our Lord before His death, and may have survived till A.D. 100 or later. I have myself conversed with three men whose powers of recollection remained vivid and trustworthy when they were over ninety years of age. Papias clearly puts John the apostle at an earlier stage than John the presbyter. Probably no one who believes in the existence of the two Johns would dispute this. But the passage proves no more than an interval, of few years or many, between the death of the apostle and that of the presbyter. It has no bearing upon the residence of the apostle at Ephesus, nor does it make the date of his death more probable in the fifth or sixth decade of the first century than in the ninth.

The second fragment of Papias which refers to the apostle has been said by a recent critic to corroborate the first 'by proving not only that he did not survive to a late age, but that he died early as a martyr.'[1] We have seen that all that this first passage proves is that John the apostle was dead by about A.D. 100. The second passage in no way corroborates it in the manner alleged, for it contains no allusion whatever, direct or indirect, to the date, whether early or late, of S. John's death. It is to be found in a reference made about A.D. 430 by Philip of Side in his Church History. He says that Papias in his second book says that 'John the divine and his brother James were put to death by the Jews.'[2] And the same statement is made by George Hamartolos in his Chronicle written in the ninth century, in which the testimony of Papias is again quoted, either from Papias or more probably from the history of Philip of Side. Now it is fairly evident that Papias has been slightly misunderstood by Philip and George. For if he actually said that John was 'put to death' by the Jews it is practically certain that Eusebius, who made use of Papias for his own Church History, would have told us so, and it is equally certain that S. Irenaeus would have known the fact. A very probable explanation is that Papias

---

[1] Dr. J. Moffatt, *op. cit.* p. 601.
[2] Ἰωάννης ὁ θεολόγος καὶ Ἰάκωβος ὁ ἀδελφὸς αὐτοῦ ὑπὸ Ἰουδαίων ἀνῃρέθησαν. See *Texte u. Untersuchungen*, v. 2.

said that those two apostles 'became *martyrs*[1] through the action of the Jews.' The writers who copied him understood by a 'martyr' one who died for the name of Christ, according to the ordinary meaning of the word 'martyr' in their time. But in earlier Christian times this name of martyr or 'witness' was applied to those who suffered for the cause of Christ, whether they were actually put to death or not. In this sense S. John may very well have endured martyrdom. Exile in the dismal island of Patmos would be 'martyrdom.' The Jews in Asia Minor were busy in stirring up the pagans against the Christians. And it may have been at their instigation that S. John was persecuted and exiled, for they were active enough when S. Polycarp was put to death. That this is no fanciful interpretation of the passage can be proved from Origen, who regards the banishment of S. John to Patmos as a martyrdom which fulfilled Christ's prophecy of his sufferings.

But even if Papias said and said correctly that S. John was put to death, we have no ground for thinking that he said that S. John died in Judaea: George Hamartolos says that he died at Ephesus. There is therefore no evidence to be drawn from Papias which can for a moment be set against either the evidence of the New Testament or the general tradition of the Church with regard to the apostle. The evidence of the New Testament is, so far as it goes, perfectly plain, and adverse to the modern argument drawn from Papias. We have first our Lord's declaration that the sons of Zebedee would drink of His cup, and be baptised with His baptism. We have the statement of S. Luke that S. James, one of these brothers, was put to death by Herod at a date which is about A.D. 44, and we have the equally good testimony of S. Paul to the effect that John was with Peter at Jerusalem when he visited

[1] ἐμαρτύρησαν.

that city about A.D. 49 (Gal. ii. 9). If the apostle was put to death by the Jews, it may have been forty or fifty years later than the death of his brother James, and more probably at Ephesus than anywhere else. And whether he died in Ephesus or not it is still quite conceivable that he wrote the Fourth Gospel before he died. The prophecy of our Lord may have been fulfilled in the most literal sense, and nevertheless John the son of Zebedee may have been the last survivor of the apostolic band, living to a late period of the first century. As S. Peter glorified God (John xxi. 19) by his death, so may John the son of Zebedee have done at a subsequent period.

Let us now turn to the Apocalypse. In its present form the book almost certainly belongs to the reign of Domitian, about A.D. 93, though it very probably includes passages of an earlier date. We know that the book was attributed to John the apostle by Justin Martyr about A.D. 155, and know that Justin was acquainted with Ephesus. These facts are important; all the more important because Justin must have been aware that the Apocalypse issued from Ephesus, the Church of which city is addressed in the first chapter of the book before the other Churches of the same region. Whether the Revelation was written by the apostle or not, it affords us positive proof that at the close of the first century an eminent servant of Jesus Christ named John was believed to have worked, or to be still working, at Ephesus. It also cannot be disputed that from the time of Justin onwards the book was believed to be by the apostle until Dionysius of Alexandria, about A.D. 255, suggested that it was the work of another John. This belief, and the internal evidence of the Apocalypse, so strongly support the theory that the apostle was the author of the book, that Dr. Bacon is compelled once more to call in the help of an unknown unscrupulous primitive editor. He says, 'the tone of authority assumed in the prologue and epilogue, the simple "John to the seven churches of Asia," the utter non-existence of any other John who could be thought of as thus addressing the seven churches of Asia, should be conclusive as to who is here meant.'[1] It is the apostle. And the writer 'ventured' to attribute it to the apostle, because the apostle was dead! The prologue and epilogue are therefore forged. But the book still contains in chap. xi. 7-12 a passage which the critic values very highly. It speaks of 'two witnesses' of Christ, whose lineaments are unmistakably derived from those of Moses and Elijah, and who are put to death in the city where ' the Lord was crucified.' It is possible that the passage contains a reference to the martyrdom of James the Lord's brother, *not* the son of Zebedee, and of one or more of ' some others' whom Josephus in *Ant.* xx. ix. 1 shows to have been put to death by Ananus the high priest, about A.D. 62. Dr. Bacon conjectures that one witness was James the Lord's brother, and the other John the apostle, the son of Zebedee. And yet thirty years later, not only were the death of this prominent disciple, and the meaning of the passage in which it was recorded, totally forgotten, but important circular letters and an appended revelation were issued in one of the principal centres of Christendom claiming to be from the pen of that apostle! Let it be remarked that the prologue with these letters deals with the actual state of the Church, not in the time of Nero, but in the time of Domitian, and yet claims to be the work of a man supposed, on this theory, to be dead thirty years before. We are asked to believe that the early Christian forger was always either diabolically clever or inconceivably silly.

A further appeal is sometimes made to a Syrian Martyrology. This is a Calendar of the Church of

[1] *Op. cit.* p. 176.

Edessa, dated A.D. 411. In the month of December it has

'On the 26th, the first martyr, at Jerusalem, Stephen the apostle, the head of the martyrs.

'On the 27th, John and James, the apostles, at Jerusalem.'

This Calendar has been quoted as definitely proving that the Church commemorated as martyrs two brothers who died at the same place and time. But a closer investigation would show that this Arian Calendar neither proves that the writer held that S. John was put to death, nor that he died at Jerusalem. For under June 6th we find the entry:

'At Alexandria, Arius the presbyter.'[1]

Now Arius the presbyter, who lived at Alexandria, and was no doubt commemorated there by his followers, was not put to death, nor did he die at Alexandria, but at Constantinople. So the copyist of this Calendar might have been well aware that John the brother of James, who once lived at Jerusalem and was there commemorated, died at Ephesus. The same list includes the notorious Arian bishop Eusebius of Nicomedia, a man who, so far from dying as a martyr, died after reaching the very summit of his ambition, the episcopal throne of Constantinople. As for the idea that the commemoration of the two sons of Zebedee on the same day implies that they died on the same day, and that this idea is corroborated by the double commemoration of S. Peter and S. Paul on the same festival in the Roman Calendar, the analogy suggests nothing of the kind. S. Peter and S. Paul probably died on

[1] For this Martyrology, see Dom. Butler, *Journal of Theological Studies*, 11. 447 ff. It is unfortunate that in quoting this Calendar in support of 'the statement ascribed to Papias,' Professor Burkitt, *op. cit.* p. 254, has overlooked this illuminating commemoration of Arius.

different days, and their festival, on June 29th, shows nothing to the contrary. For it commemorates, not their death, but the removal of their relics from the catacombs where they were placed when the Christians were persecuted by the Emperor Valerian in A.D. 258.

The Syrian Church of Edessa had, so far as is known, no tradition to the effect that S. John died at or near Jerusalem. The *Doctrine of Addai*, an important Syriac work of about A.D. 400, says that the Book of Acts was sent to Edessa from Ephesus by John the son of Zebedee. Whether this is correct, or not, the Christians of Edessa appear to have been as ignorant as the Christians of Rome about any early martyrdom of S. John.

The desire to commemorate the two sons of Zebedee on or near the same day in certain Martyrologies arose quite naturally from the fact that they were closely associated by their brotherhood, by their devotion to our Lord, and by their association in the New Testament. A clear illustration of such a desire is found in some of the early service-books of Spain. The oldest known Mozarabic service-book, the *Orationale Gothicum*, commemorates S. John on December 29, but has no commemoration on the day before or the day after. But at some time between the seventh century and the eleventh the blanks were filled and we find:

December 28th. S. James the Lord's brother.
,, 29th. S. John the evangelist.
,, 30th. S. James the brother of John.

We must be prepared to hear before long that this is a proof from an orthodox source that S. John died the day before S. James. In the meantime we can be content to know that the residence of S. John at Ephesus has not been disproved.

§ 5. *Rival Theories of Authorship.*

Against the tradition that the apostle John while at Ephesus wrote our Fourth Gospel, three rival theories are advanced. They are:

(*a*) The author was an unknown Christian of the second century, who may have composed almost all the Gospel, or may have been an editor who used some older materials both written and oral. The critics are sharply divided on this question. They are also sharply divided as to the date, placing it in various decades up to A.D. 140.

(*b*) The author was the younger John, the presbyter described by Papias, an eye-witness of our Lord's ministry, younger than the apostles, and one who lived at Ephesus till the close of the first century.

(*c*) The author was John the presbyter, but he was much younger than the apostles, and did not know Christ.

The critics who support these three theories, and the subdivisions of these theories, are united in no single matter of importance, except in their denial that the apostle John was the writer of the Gospel. They are opposed to one another in principle and in detail. They include every conceivable view from the conclusion that the Gospel is historically worthless, but spiritually valuable at the present day, to the conclusion that its history is sometimes correct, but its theology a delusion of the second century. The theory that the evangelist was neither the apostle John nor any other eye-witness is widely held, more widely by far than the second of the two theories just noted. It has to struggle with a large amount of internal evidence, some of which we have considered. It has also to reject all the evidence of the early Church, including that of S. Irenaeus, as to the venerated John of Ephesus (whether apostle or younger disciple) having seen Christ. Further, it has to deal with the question of fraud. Did the author or authors of the last chapter, or of the conclusion of that chapter, attribute to an eye-witness chapters i.-xx., knowing that they were not the work of an eye-witness? Were there removed from the body of the Gospel passages which contradicted the view for which they were trying to gain acceptance? It is not a question of 'uncritical piety' but of unblushing imposture. And if no imposture was intended, and the editors believed the Gospel to have been written by an eye-witness, how could such a mistake have been made at so early a date, a date when men like Polycarp were still alive? And if the Gospel was partly fraudulent or perverted the true story of Christ's ministry, how did it come to be numbered among the elect Gospels by a Church which had the acumen to reject all the other false Gospels? The mere fact that it is so unlike the three earlier orthodox Gospels would have been a serious obstacle to its acceptance by the Church, unless it had an imprimatur which was above suspicion.

More reasonable than the theory that the author was an unknown Christian, is the theory that he was John the presbyter. From a chronological point of view this is not impossible. The passage quoted above (p. 300) from Papias shows that John the presbyter was one of those venerable persons whose opinions he had collected at a former time. If I understand Dr. Sanday correctly, he dates the extracts from Papias preserved in Eusebius about A.D. 100.[1] I agree with this opinion if it means that Papias collected these materials about that time, and wrote of them a good many years later. But it is not possible without the use of some fanciful arithmetic to date the work of Papias, as Harnack has done, about A.D. 145-

[1] *The Criticism of the Fourth Gospel*, p. 251.

160. S. Irenaeus, who was living at this later date, gives the name of 'ancient' (ἀρχαῖος—*Adv. Haer.* v. 33) to Papias and Polycarp alone among the elders. He could hardly have given such a name to any one who was not greatly his senior. Polycarp was such a senior, having been born at latest about A.D. 70. Probably Papias was born near the same time. His words suggest that when he had reached manhood, John the presbyter was one of the last of a passing generation. If he died about A.D. 105, and wrote a Gospel about A.D. 90, the dates would cause no difficulty.

It has indeed been denied that John the presbyter ever lived in Asia Minor. This is excessive scepticism. There is more testimony in early Christian literature to the residence of John the apostle in Asia Minor than to the residence of the presbyter in the same region. But there is not the least reason for setting aside the statement of Dionysius of Alexandria, a man of sense and culture, to the effect that his tomb existed at Ephesus. This statement may perfectly well be true, whether we follow Dionysius or not in attributing the Apocalypse to this John.

The question is whether this John the presbyter wrote the Fourth Gospel, whether he knew the Lord, and whether, if he wrote the Gospel, he wrote what is historically true.

Those who hold that he knew the Lord can appeal to the fact that Papias calls him, like Aristion, a 'disciple' of the Lord. The Greek reading is not quite certain at this point, but for the present we may give the supporters of this view the full benefit of the doubt. The same critics are impressed by the first-hand knowledge which the Gospel shows. They have made much of the statement that the beloved disciple 'was known unto the high priest' (xviii. 15), that he knew the name of the high priest's servant Malchus, that he had special knowledge of Nicodemus, that he gives details about the action of Annas the high priest, possesses an intimate acquaintance with Jerusalem, and finally had himself in Jerusalem a 'home' to which he took the mother of our Lord after the crucifixion (xix. 27). They note, too, that the Gospel is concerned much more with Jerusalem than with Galilee.

Such points as these have been thought to show that the beloved disciple was not John the son of Zebedee, but an aristocratic Jerusalem Jew, probably a Sadducee, who afterwards lived at Ephesus. It has been observed also that Polycrates, bishop of Ephesus, speaks of the John 'who leaned on the bosom of the Lord,' as having become 'a priest who wore the priestly mitre' ($\pi \acute{\epsilon} \tau a \lambda o \nu$).[1] This passage might suggest that the beloved disciple belonged to the priestly order in Jerusalem.

The attention which these points deserve is important. And it has done something at least to dispose of the theory that the author of the Fourth Gospel was an imaginative Gentile of the second century, or even a Jew of that period. But when it is assumed that the son of Zebedee, the Galilean fisherman, could not have known the high priest, or been familiar with the holy city, or worn a mitre, we must demur. We are once more in the presence of that mischievous hobgoblin, the False Antithesis. It is a spirit which is always appearing unexpectedly to turn good milk sour, and disturb domestic harmony. Zebedee was not a poor man; he had hired servants, and his wife was one of the women who gave of their substance to support our Lord and His disciples. It was possible a few years ago, and may still be possible, to find in parts of Great Britain men very well to do and fairly well educated in a position analogous to that which we believe to have been occupied by Zebedee and his

[1] Eus. *H. E.* iii. 31, 3; v. 24, 2.

family. When critics assume that because S. Peter spoke Aramaic he could not learn to write Greek, and that because S. John was a Galilean he could not acquire a good knowledge of Jerusalem, or be acquainted with leading Sadducees, they are building on a foundation which may be only sand and refuse. In some countries and at certain periods a sharp line has been drawn between those who are engaged in trade, and those who consider themselves superior to such methods of gaining their livelihood. That line did not exist among the Jews, just as for many centuries it did not exist in England, or was habitually crossed. We therefore are doing no violence to the Fourth Gospel, or those analogies with which history furnishes us, when we suppose that the son of Zebedee may have known the topography of Jerusalem, have known the Jewish high priest, and in his old age at Ephesus worn, as Polycrates says, the high priest's mitre as a sign that he was an apostle of the new 'Israel of God.'

If it were at all clear that the Jews had put to death, or had been the means of putting to death, John the son of Zebedee at any time near the death of his brother, we might be obliged with little or no hesitation to assign the Fourth Gospel to the younger John, the Ephesian presbyter. And it is not impossible that some disciple deeply attached to his divine Master may have been admitted to share the Last Supper in the upper room, though this is to put a very unnatural interpretation on the narrative of the evangelists (Mark xiv. 17; Matthew xxvi. 20; Luke xxii. 14). Again it is possible that there were two Johns among the more intimate followers of our Lord. Personal names in Palestine were far fewer in number than they are in modern Europe, and we find that the list of the apostles includes beyond all doubt two men of the name of James and two of the name of Simon.

But there is no proved reference to such a younger John in parts of the New Testament where we should expect to find it. We may take it almost as an axiom of criticism that Acts and the Epistle to the Galatians were written independently and that the authors were unacquainted with the Fourth Gospel. Now, the only Johns in the two former books and in the Synoptic Gospels are the Baptist, and John Mark, and the John who appears in Acts iv. 6, as an unconverted kinsman of the high priest, and the son of Zebedee, who is found occupying just that degree of prominence which befits the beloved disciple of the Fourth Gospel. And, as we have already noted, he is in the same close association with S. Peter. Why is there no mention of the younger John, and how can we reconcile this absence of mention with the theory that he was alive, was a companion of our Lord, and a 'supernumerary apostle'? This is only an argument from silence. And arguments from silence have been laboured and belaboured in recent criticism. We have ample reason for not regarding such an argument as infallible. But the critics who have laid such stress upon the argument from silence which they derived from the writers of the second century, ought in fairness to pay equal attention to the silence of certain writers of the first century. We have been repeatedly told that genuine writings of the second century, or at least of the first half of that century, say little or nothing that indicates their belief that S. John died at Ephesus or wrote the Fourth Gospel. And in reply we would ask such critics to explain why S. Mark, S. Luke, and S. Paul, writers of the second half of the first century, all of whom were alive during Christ's ministry, never mention the younger John. Or rather, we prefer to say that these silences are not conclusive, but far the more conclusive of the two is this silence with regard to the younger John. For the writings to which we have referred are

THE AUTHOR OF THE FOURTH GOSPEL 313

concerned with those who knew and bore testimony to Jesus (Acts i. 21). It is hardly conceivable that, by a conspiracy of jealousy, the authors omitted to mention the younger John. Assuming that he existed, they left out his name because they either did not know him, or regarded him as of little importance. Certainly they cannot have known him as 'the beloved disciple.'

It is not therefore probable that the Gospel was written by a John who knew our Lord, but was not the apostle.

But whenever we have to deal with the theory that John the presbyter wrote the Gospel, it has to be borne in mind that the really vital point is not whether the author was the son of Zebedee, but whether he wrote the truth. It is logically possible, though in fact very uncommon, for an acute critic such as Dr. Drummond to hold that the author was John the son of Zebedee, but that a variety of causes led him to transform the history and character of his Master. How far a true affection for that Master, and a deep religious instinct, could permit this flattering travesty, it is hardly necessary to inquire. A pagan might represent his intercourse with a venerated friend as intercourse with a divine Being. But it is, to put the matter mildly, very improbable that a sincere monotheist would perform an intellectual feat of so immoral a character. And no wide acceptance has been won for the theory that an apostle and beloved friend of Christ was guilty of this pious fraud of transubstantiating a human Master.

More probable than the theory of Dr. Drummond is the view already discussed, that the Fourth Gospel is the work of a younger John who knew our Lord and in later life at Ephesus wrote a true account of his Master's life and claims. Such a work would be entitled to an authority only just short of apostolic authority. Indeed, since none of the Synoptic Gospels, not even S. Matthew's Gospel in its present form, was written by one who lived in our Lord's company, the Fourth Gospel might still be of supreme value if composed by a younger John who knew Him. This theory, unlike the last, contains nothing that is morally objectionable. But I am unable to reconcile it with the New Testament.

The theory which we have numbered (c), viz.: that the author was John the presbyter, but that he was much younger than the apostles and did not know Christ during His life on earth, escapes from the necessity of having to discover room for a supernumerary apostle unknown to the Synoptists and S. Paul. But it has to contend with the internal evidence which points to a knowledge of the origin of Christianity such as no one but an apostle would be likely to possess. And like the criticism which attributes the Gospel to an unknown writer of the second century, it is apt to be dominated by a want of sympathy and even by hostility towards the fundamental teaching of the Gospel. It is futile to ignore the fact that the hostile criticism directed against the authenticity of this Gospel has in the great majority of cases been associated with, and stimulated by, a repudiation of the evangelist's conception of Jesus Christ and His relation to God the Father. The arguments attributing it to a 'great unknown' have been almost entirely supplied from non-Christian and anti-Christian sources, though they have occasionally been borrowed by Christian theologians. In our chapter on the 'Criticism of the Gospels' it was noticed in outline that the criticism which denies the historical truth of the Fourth Gospel has been connected with a theological plan of campaign. Even comparatively temperate writers like Weizsäcker and Jülicher have quite frankly shown that they object to the evangelist's 'deification' of Jesus. They assume that he was not divine. They have to reject not only the teaching of the Fourth Gospel concerning Christ, but also that of the great Epistles of S. Paul, of the Epistle to the Hebrews, and of the Apocalypse, all of which can be proved to demonstration to be works of the first Christian century. Traces, by no means obscure, of the influence of such prejudices can be found in other critics who hesitate to break so openly with Christian history. The evangelist is regarded as possessed by a 'theological conception,' the idea of the Logos. It is granted that 'ever and again the remembrance of the living Person breaks altogether through the theological conception.'[1] But not only is this conception treated as having largely lost its value for modern Christianity; it is also said that 'for much of the fruitless controversy of the succeeding centuries the fourth evangelist must be held responsible.'[2]

The so-called 'fruitless controversy' which the Christian Church had to wage against those heresies which either denied all the human experiences of Jesus, like Gnosticism, or reduced Him to a demi-god, like Arianism, or regarded Him as a hybrid, like some later errors, was regarded by the early Church as a matter of life or death. The worship, the creeds, the experience, of Christianity were based upon the belief that God, without ceasing to be God, became man, and shared our griefs. The Fourth Gospel powerfully upheld this belief, though it did not originate it. According to this belief, we do not adequately understand what Deity is until we realise it in the personality of Jesus Christ, and we cannot understand His human life with its mysterious vicissitudes and tragic close unless we find its explanation in His 'hidden Deity.' This Deity in the background of the human life of Jesus, and inseparably united with it, the fourth evangelist calls the 'Logos,' the Word who has been

[1] Dr. Ernest F. Scott, *The Historical and Religious value of the Fourth Gospel*, p. 47.   [2] *Op. cit.* p. 87.

uttered from eternity by the Father. He is the 'only-begotten' Son, whose generation is like a pulse of divine life which can never cease to beat. The other conception of Christianity finds much to reverence in Christ.[1] But it does not believe that He possessed and revealed the divine life in its fulness, or that He is able to impart this life to His disciples. And this latter conception the early Church consistently repudiated whenever it found expression, for the sufficient reason that she had 'not so learned Christ.'

[1] This of course refers merely to the more sober and moderate type of semi-Christianity, and not to the more unscrupulous and offensive type which is equally common.

INDEX

Abbot, Ezra, 285.
Abilene, 214.
Abrahams, Mr. Israel, on Matt., 195.
Achamoth, Gnostic deity, 6.
Acts of the Apostles—
  archaisms in, 218.
  author is the diarist, S. Luke, 212.
  date of, 217.
  Josephus not used, 215.
Addai, Doctrine of, 306
Alexander and Rufus, 139.
Allegory, 5, 249.
Allen, Ven. W. C., references to, 64, 138, 178.
Alogoi, repudiated Fourth Gospel, 277.
Antioch, Matt. written near, 188; S. Luke knows, 240.
Antiochene theology, 282.
Apocalypse of S. John, 283, 303, 309.
Apocalypses, Jewish, 142.
Apocalyptic 'fly-sheet,' so-called, 204.
Apocalyptic sayings, 119, 200.
Apollonius of Tyana, 255, 294.
Aramaic, language of Christ, 106; original of Gospels, 41, 138.
Arian Calendar, on S. John and S. James, 305.
Aristion (Ariston), probable author of conclusion of Mark, 140; in Papias, 300.
Asceticism in Luke, 220.
Augustine, S., on Manichean view of Gospels, 3.

Bacon, Prof. B. W.—
  on John, 280, 288, 290, 304.
  on Mark, 158, 160.

Baptism of Christ, 113, 126, 166, 210.
—— of Christians, 60, 184, 246.
Bar-Cochba, 238.
Barnabas, Epistle of, 180.
Bartlet, Dr. J. V., on Luke, 82.
Basilides, the Gnostic, 22, 281.
Baur, F. C., 45, 291.
Beatitudes, 113, 225.
Besant, Mrs. A., her esoteric Christianity, 22.
Bethany, our Lord at, 155.
Bethesda, miracle at, 249.
Bigg, Dr. C., on Quartodecimanism, 275.
Bruce, Prof. A. B., 233.
Burkitt, Prof. F. C.—
  on date of Fourth Gospel, 289.
  on death of S. John, 305 n.
  on geography of Mark, 146.
  on trial of Christ, 237.
  on Virgin birth, 93
Butler, Dom E. C, on Arian martyrology, 305.

Caesarea Philippi, 147, 150.
Calendars, Church, 305.
Cambridge Biblical Essays, 195.
Canon, New Testament, 1.
Capernaum, 98, 149.
Carpenter, Dr. J. E, on Matt., 183.
Centurion's servant, healing of, 117.
Cerinthus, 18, 277.
Chapman, Dom J., on Harnack, 132.
Chazars, Tartar proselytes to Judaism, 186.
Christology, of Q, 126; of Mark, 162, 168; of Matt., 169; of Luke, 209; of John, 261, 314.

THE GOSPELS

Church, nature of, 57, 183.
Clement of Alexandria, on order of Gospels, 65; on origin of Mark, 134; testimony to John, 276.
Clement of Rome, S., First Epistle of, 11; so-called Second Epistle, 4, 7.
Clementine literature, apocryphal, 157, 185.
Conybeare, Mr. F. C., on origin of conclusion of Mark, 140.
Criticism of the Gospels, 32.
Cross, Christ's bearing of, in John, 17; our bearing of, in Luke, 231.

DALMANUTHA, 150.
Decapolis, 148, 150, 291.
Diatessaron of Tatian, 7, 8.
Didaché, 4, 99, 281.
Diognetus, Epistle to, 4.
Dionysius of Alexandria, 303, 309.
Disciplina Arcani, 22.
Dives and Lazarus, 226, 267.
Divorce, 190, 223.
Docetic heresy, 15.
Documents, Two, the sources of the Synoptic Gospels, 54, 89.
Domitian, 303.
Doublets in the Gospels, 86.
Drummond, Dr. J., on Paschal controversy, 273; on author of Fourth Gospel, 313.

EBIONITES, rejected Virgin birth, 92; S. Luke not influenced by, 226.
Edersheim, Dr. A., on Last Supper, 297.
Edessa, Church of, 306.
Encyclopaedia Biblica, 262.
Enoch, Book of, 165.
Epiphanius, S., on Ebonites, 226.
Eschatology, 58, 200.
Eusebius, *H. E.*, 7, 10, 65, 104, 105, 106, 291, 310.
Evangelists, their accuracy tested, 96, 122, 157.
Expository Times, 79, 178.

FASTING, Christian, 229.
Feasts, Jewish, in John, 256.
Feeding of four thousand, 87.
Fig-tree, the barren, 163.

Florinus, S. Irenaeus' *Epistle to*, 279.
Fourth Gospel. *See* John.
Francis, S., of Assisi, Lives of, 97.

GALILEE, our Lord in, 149, 257.
Gamaliel, 215.
Gennesaret, 149, 257.
George Hamartolos, on S. John, 301.
Gethsemane, Christ's prayer in, 235.
Gieseler, J. K. L., his theory of origin of the Gospels, 42.
Glaucias, pretended interpreter of S. Peter, 22.
Gnosticism, 20, 280.
Godet, F., on John, 53, 267; on Luke, 214.
Gore, Bishop, on prophecy, 29.
Gospel, meaning of term, 4, 103, 174.
Gospels, apocryphal, 6, 8.
—— canon of, 1; dates of, 134, 178, 211, 284, 291.

HARNACK, Prof. A., 54.—
on Christ's lament over Jerusalem, 260.
on Christology of Q, 131; of Mark, 168.
on date of Matt., 94; of Luke, 94, 217.
on Virgin birth of Christ, 94, 95.
Hawkins, Canon Sir J C.—
on sayings of our Lord, 113.
on Synoptic Problem, 64, 79, 85, 160.
Hebrews, Gospel according to the, 6.
Hegesippus, 6.
Heitmüller, W., on John, 248, 267.
Herod Antipas, 147, 240.
Herodians, 99, 149.
High priest, our Lord before, 235.
Horae Synopticae. *See* Hawkins.

IDOLS, eating meat offered to, 194.
Ignatius, S., of Antioch, knows Matt., 181; relation to fourth Gospel, 19, 281; testimony to primitive Christianity, 18.
Infancy of our Lord, stories of, apocryphal, 8; canonical, 89.

INDEX

Interpolation, the great, so-called, in Mark, 73
Irenaeus, S., on canon of Gospels, 31; on order of Gospels, 65; on date of Mark, 134; on appointment of Linus, 185; testimony to John, 278.

JAIRUS' daughter, 144, 162.
James and John, ambitious request of, 71, 207; martyrdom of, 301.
Jesus Christ, our Lord—
  attitude towards Jewish law, 188.
  baptism of, 113, 126, 166.
  birth of, 89.
  claims in Q, 127; in Fourth Gospel, 261.
  date of His death, 269.
  doctrine of His Person, in Mark, 164; in Matt., 169; in Luke, 69, 242; in John, 37, 263, 313.
  Founder of the Church, 183.
  human nature of, 16, 163, 266, 293.
  Messiah, 126, 169, 237.
  miracles of, 35.
  rationalistic accounts of, 40, 125, 131, 158, 168, 261.
  resurrection of, 34, 159.
  Sayings of, 102.
  scene of ministry, 39, 149, 256.
  second coming of, 202.
  silences enjoined by, 143.
  teaching misunderstood by hearers, 145, 245.
  temptation of, 113, 133.
  training of disciples, 140.
  trial of, 235.
  universalist teaching of, 124, 200.
John the Elder or Presbyter, Papias on, 300; was he the author of the Fourth Gospel? 307.
John, S., the Baptist, death of, in Mark, 71; preaching of, in Q, 113; relation to Christ in Q, 127; miraculous birth in Luke, 95, 221; attitude of Fourth Gospel towards, 250.
John, S., the Evangelist, alleged residence in Asia, 269, 298; author of Apocalypse, 280, 283, 303; author of Fourth Gospel, 276, 307.
John, S., Gospel according to—
  agreement with Luke, 241; with Matt., 250.
  authorship of, 276.
  canonical early, 9.
  date, 284, 289, 291.
  discourses of Christ in, 37, 244.
  Docetism opposed in, 17.
  doctrine of Christ's Person in, 37, 261, 314.
  eschatology of, 203
  external evidence of use, 276.
  Holy Spirit in, 211, 277.
  internal evidence of genuineness, 285, 292.
  Jews in, 247.
  John the Baptist in, 250.
  Last Supper in, 135, 270, 296.
  Lazarus, 265.
  local colour in, 97, 294.
  Logos or Word in, 265, 315.
  Mark resembles, 161, 165.
  rationalistic treatment of, 43, 47, 51, 56, 247, 255.
  time of Christ's ministry in, 39, 256.
Josephus, alleged use of his works by S. Luke, 213.
Judaeo-German scepticism, 43, 62.
Judgment, the, Christ's teaching on, 202.
Jülicher, A., on Fourth Gospel, 57, 314.
Justification, in S. Luke and S. Paul, 209.
Justin Martyr, S.—
  four Gospels in, 4, 24.
  Gospel of Peter in, 8.
  names for the Gospels, 4, 24.
  quotes Fourth Gospel, 280; Sermon on the Mount, 109.
  Revelation ascribed to S. John, 280
  worship of Christians described, 26.

KEIM, Th., on life of Christ, 51.
Kingdom of God, 57, 59, 176.
  its relation to the Church, 183.

Knowling, Dr. R. J., on Virgin birth, 93.

LAST SUPPER, day of, in Synoptists, 136, 271; in John, 136, 269; eschatological meaning of, 61.
Law, Jewish, attitude of Matthew towards, 186; of Christ towards, 188
Lazarus, raising of, 100, 265.
'Liberal Protestantism,' doctrines and negations of, 55, 62.
Liturgical use of Gospels, 26.
Local colour in Gospels, 97, 295.
Logia, 81, 102, 105. *See also* Q.
Logos doctrine, 37, 264, 315.
Loisy, A., on Luke, 208; on Lazarus, 267.
Lord's Supper, 61, 135, 159, 232, 246.
Luke, S., author of the third Gospel, 66, 95, 206; gained information from S. Philip, 222; visited Jerusalem with S. Paul, 240.
Luke, S, Gospel according to—
 agreement with Fourth Gospel, 241
 asceticism, 220
 attitude towards Judaism, 209
 based on Mark, 70.
 based on Q, 84.
 characteristics, 206
 date, 211.
 doublets, 88.
 geographical knowledge, 98.
 Holy Spirit in, 210.
 interpolation into Marcan order, 83.
 Josephus not used, 214
 omission of Marcan matter, 71.
 Passion of Christ in, 231
 Pauline influence on, 208.
 poverty in, 225
 prayer in, 210
 Samaritans in, 152, 242
 Septuagint influence on, 208
 special source of, 82
 the Twelve spared in, 207
 variations from Marcan order, 74.
 women in, 221, 224.
Lysanias, 214.

MACLEAN, BISHOP, on original language of Mark, 138.

Magi, 69, 171.
Magnificat, 210.
Mani, founder of heretical sect, 1.
Marcion, doctrines of, 11; his use of Luke, 12.
Marcos, the Gnostic, 21.
Margoliouth, Prof. D. S., 186.
Mark, S., Gospel according to—
 Christ in, 162.
 compared with Fourth Gospel, 161.
 date, 134.
 disciples in, 140, 145.
 eschatology of, 203.
 geography of, 146.
 last twelve verses, 139.
 original language of, 138.
 Paulinism in, 158.
 Peter in, 155.
 Roman origin of, 133.
 source of Matt. and Luke, 68, 74.
 use of Q, 82, 89, 133.
Marriage and divorce, in Matt., 190; in Luke, 222.
Matthew, S., author of Q, 105, 110, 174.
—— —— Gospel according to—
 based on Mark, 74.
 based on Q, 82.
 breaks Mark's order, 77.
 catholicism of, 182.
 church in, 183.
 date, 178.
 doublets, 87.
 eschatology of, 200.
 favourite Gospel of primitive Church, 179.
 Judaises law of marriage, 190.
 kingdom of the heavens in, 176, 202.
 method of grouping materials, 171.
 Mosaic Law in, 186, 190, 194.
 omissions of Marcan matter, 75.
 quotations in, 169.
 universalism of, 186.
Melito, relation to Quartodeciman controversy, 273.
Miracles, in the Gospels, 33, 127.
Modernism, 55.
Moffat, Dr. J., on the Church, 57 on Lysanias, 214; on S. Irenaeus, 279; on death of S John, 301.
Montanus, heresy of, 28, 277.

INDEX

Montefiore, Mr. C. G., on Synoptic Gospels, 58.
Mozarabic Calendar, on S. James and S. John, 306.
Muhammad, 1, 4.
Muhammadan belief as to Christ's death, 16.
Muratorian Canon, 9, 31, 291.
Mustard seed, parable of, 82, 119, 120, 177.

NAIN, widow's son at, 224.
Nazarene, meaning of name, 170.
Nazarenes, sect of, 194.
Nazareth, Christ's childhood at, 89, 170; sermon at, 207.

OLD TESTAMENT, the only Scripture of the Apostolic Church, 4, 102; rejection of, by Gnostics, 13; quotations from, in Gospels, 170; 250.
Omissions in Luke, 71, 234; in Matt., 75; in Mark, 77, 100, 153.
Oral theory as to origin of Gospels, 42.
—— tradition, 84.
Origen, on Matt., 169; on martyrdom of S. John, 302.
Ottley, Dr. R. L., on doctrine of Christ's Person, 265, 277.

PAPIAS, on Logia of S. Matt., 110, 112; on S. Mark, 110; on John the Presbyter, 300, 308; date of, 308.
Parables, misunderstanding of, 246.
Parousia (second coming of Christ). *See* Eschatology.
Paschal Chronicle, 273.
Passion, Christ's predictions of, 78; narrative of, whether omitted in Q, 121; how given in Luke, 231.
Paul, S., his doctrine and Christ's, 11, 198; his death, 218; testimony to date of Christ's death, 273.
Paulinism, in Mark, 158; in Luke, 208.
Paulus, H. E. G., rationalism of, 40, 266.
Peraea, 147, 151, 257.

Peraean section of Luke, sometimes so-called (IX. 51-XVIII. 14), 83, 153.
Peter, S.—
Apocryphal Gospel of, 8.
confession of Christ, 128, 145, 150, 262.
denial of Christ, 156, 207.
doctrine of, 11, 161, 168.
festival of S. Peter and S. Paul, 306.
S. Mark's informant, 110, 134, 155.
Pharisees, opposed in Q, 113; in Matt., 193; less in Luke, 206.
Philip, S., the Apostle, 264, 291.
—— —— the Evangelist, 222.
—— —— his daughters prophetesses, 222.
—— of Side, on S. John's death, 301
—— the Tetrarch, 214.
Philostratus, 255, 294.
Pilate, in Luke and John, 238.
Plummer, Dr. A., on Matt., 64.
Polycarp, S., Epistle of, 281; connection with S. John, 278.
Polycrates, his connection with S. John, 272, 282; on S. Philip, 291.
Portrait of our Lord, in Synoptists, 37, 163, 207; in John, 37, 261, 266.
Prayer in Luke, 210.
Protestantism, old and 'modern' contrasted, 57.
Protevangelium of James, 8.

Q, *i.e. Quelle*, source (German name for the lost document used by Matt. and Luke, and probably Mark)—
existence of, 82.
contents of, 113.
date of, 120.
Christology of, 128.
eschatology of, 201.
Quartodeciman controversy, 272.
Quintilla, Montanist prophetess, 28.
Quirinius, P. Sulpicius, governor of Syria, 215
Quotations from Old Testament, in Matt., 170; in John, 250.

322　THE GOSPELS

RAMSAY, Sir W. M., on date of Q, 120.
Rationalism, character of the older, 40; of the recent, 53, 58.
Renan, E., on our Lord, 49; on the Gospels, 50.
Resurrection, Christ's, nature of appearances, 34.
Rhossus, Gospel of Peter at, 8.
Roman Mass, described by Justin, 26; canon of, 134.
Rome, Mark written at, 133; opposed to Ephesus, 272.
Russian sectaries, on defilement, 193.

S, *i.e.* Special Source used by Luke, 82.
Sabbath, Christ's action on, 248; attitude of Matt. towards, 196.
Sadducees, 99, 172, 258.
Samaria, Christ's visits to, 147, 150, 293.
Samaritans, in Luke, 152, 242; in John, 293.
Sanday, Dr. W.—
　on Apostolic decree, 187.
　books by, 64.
　on Fourth Gospel, 283.
　on Papias, 308.
　on Q and S, 83.
　on scene of Christ's ministry, 153, 252.
　on Virgin birth, 95.
Sanhedrin, meeting at Christ's trial, 235.
Schleiermacher, F. D. E., 42.
Schmiedel, P. W., on Epistle of Barnabas, 180; on Luke and John, 258, 260.
Schurer, E., on Messianic doctrine, 254.
Schweitzer, A., on eschatology, 45, 58, 61, 201.
Septuagint (Greek) version of Old Testament, 4.
Sermon on the Mount, 81, 113.
Seventy, the, appointment of, 87.
Sheep and Goats, parable of, 177.
Shepherd of Hermas, on prophets, 29.
Simon of Cyrene, 17, 139.
Simon the Pharisee 73.

Sinaitic, or old Syriac, version of Gospels, 92.
Son of God, meaning of title, 129, 165, 264.
Son of Man, 164, 263.
Sower, parable of, 141.
Speculum perfectionis, 97.
Spirit, Holy, blasphemy against, 168; in S. Luke and S. Paul, 210.
Stanton, Dr. V. H., 64.
Strauss, D. F., 43.
Streeter, Rev B. H., references to, 133, 201.
Synoptic problem, 65.
Synoptists, relation of, to Fourth Gospel, 36, 241, 243.
Syrophoenician woman, story of, 71, 160.
Swete, Dr. H. B., 64.

TATIAN, his *Diatessaron*, 7; use of Fourth Gospel, 276.
Temptation, the, 113, 133.
Tertullian, on pope and prophets, 29.
Theodas, pretended friend of S. Paul, 22.
Theological Studies, Journal of, 20, 92, 132.
Theophilus of Antioch, attributes Fourth Gospel to John, 277, 283.
Theudas, 215.
Tosefta, on trespass-offering, 195.
Training of the disciples, 140.
Transfiguration, the, 144.
Trypho, Justin's *Dialogue with*, 23.
Tubingen school, 45, 185.
Turner, Mr. C. H., on S. Ignatius, 20; on Virgin birth, 92.
Tyrrell, Rev. G., 22, 201.

URIAH, wife of, in our Lord's genealogy, 90.

VALERIAN, Emperor, persecution under, 306.
Veil, rending of, 162.
Victor, Bishop of Rome, 272.
Vincent of Lerins, S., his rule of Catholicity, 23.
Virgin birth of Christ, 89, 221.

Von Soden, Freiherr, 54.

'WE SECTIONS' in Acts, 212.
Weiss, J., on eschatology, 58; on Lazarus, 268.
Weizsacker, C., on John, 52, 314.
Wellhausen, Prof. J., on Q, 120, 131; on the Church in Matt, 182.

Westcott, Bishop, on John, 53.
Widow's mites, 225.
Women in Luke, 221, 224.
Worship, public, influence on the canon of Gospels, 26.
Wrede, W., 58.

ZACCHAEUS, 83.
Zoroaster, 1.

www.ingramcontent.com/pod-product-compliance
Lightning Source LLC
Chambersburg PA
CBHW050837230426
43667CB00012B/2038